MAPS OF CONSCIOUSNESS

Ralph Metzner

MAPS OF CONSCIOUSNESS

I CHING · TANTRA
TAROT · ALCHEMY
ASTROLOGY · ACTUALISM

Collier Books
A Division of Macmillan Publishing Co., Inc.
NEW YORK

Collier Macmillan Publishers
LONDON

Macmillan Publishing Co., Inc.
866 Third Avenue, New York, N.Y. 10022
Collier Macmillan Canada, Ltd.

Library of Congress Catalog Card Number: 78-142346
First Collier Books Edition 1971

Fourth Printing 1976
Maps of Consciousness is also published in a hardcover
edition by Macmillan Publishing Co., Inc.

Printed in the United States of America

ACKNOWLEDGMENTS

For quotations from *The Collected Works of C. G. Jung,* ed. by G. Adler, M. Fordham, H. Read, translated by R. F. C. Hull, Bollingen Series XX, vol. 13, *Alchemical Studies* (copyright © 1967 by Princeton University Press); vol. 14, *Mysterium Coniunctionis* (copyright © 1963 by Princeton University Press); vol. 16, *The Practice of Psychotherapy* (copyright © 1954 and 1966 by Princeton University Press); passim quotes are reprinted by permission of Princeton University Press.

For quotations from the *I Ching: or Book of Changes,* translated by Richard Wilhelm, rendered into English by Cary F. Baynes, Bollingen Series XIX (copyright © 1950 and 1967 by Princeton University Press); passim quotes are reprinted by permission of Princeton University Press.

The prose and verse quotations in the Actualism chapter are reprinted by permission of the author, Russell Paul Schofield. The prose passages quoted are from an unpublished manuscript "Transmutational Mergence as Taught in the School of Actualism." All verse quotations are from *Imprint Unmistakable,* published in 1970 in Los Angeles, California. All rights reserved by Russell Paul Schofield.

Illustrations:

In the *I Ching* chapter, "Eight Trigrams in Context of Nature" is used courtesy of Rebekah Lowden.

In the *I Ching* chapter, "Eight Trigrams in Primal Arrangement" and "Eight Trigrams in Inner World Arrangement" are used courtesy of José and Miriam Arguëlles.

In the Tantra chapter, four photographs are used courtesy of Alan Atwell.

In the Tantra chapter, the illustrations of the *mudras* adapted for western sitting posture are used courtesy of George Kukar.

In the Tantra chapter, illustration of Siva Ardhanarisbara and, in the Actualism chapter, Dance of Siva are reprinted courtesy of the Archaeological Survey of India.

In the Tarot chapter, with the exception of the Empress and the Temperance cards, which are from the Waite Deck, the Tarot Cards are reproduced from the B.O.T.A. Deck, by permission of Builders of the Adytum, 5105 Figueroa Street, Los Angeles, California.

In the Tarot chapter, the cards of the New Tarot are reproduced from *T: The New Tarot,* the Tarot for the Aquarian Age, copyright © 1969 by Rosalind Sharpe Wall and John Star Cooke. By permission of Western Star Press.

In the Astrology chapters, geometric diagrams and charts are used courtesy of Wes Buist of Technical Graphics, San Francisco, California.

In the Astrology II chapter, original drawings "Three Water Signs" and "Three Fire Signs" are used courtesy of Emile Pierre.

ACKNOWLEDGMENTS

For quotations from *The Collected Works of C. G. Jung,* ed. by G. Adler, M. Fordham, H. Read, translated by R. F. C. Hull, Bollingen Series XX, vol. 13, *Alchemical Studies* (copyright © 1967 by Princeton University Press); vol. 14, *Mysterium Coniunctionis* (copyright © 1963 by Princeton University Press); vol. 16, *The Practice of Psychotherapy* (copyright © 1954 and 1966 by Princeton University Press); passim quotes are reprinted by permission of Princeton University Press.

For quotations from the *I Ching: or Book of Changes,* translated by Richard Wilhelm, rendered into English by Cary F. Baynes, Bollingen Series XIX (copyright © 1950 and 1967 by Princeton University Press); passim quotes are reprinted by permission of Princeton University Press.

The prose and verse quotations in the Actualism chapter are reprinted by permission of the author, Russell Paul Schofield. The prose passages quoted are from an unpublished manuscript "Transmutational Mergence as Taught in the School of Actualism." All verse quotations are from *Imprint Unmistakable,* published in 1970 in Los Angeles, California. All rights reserved by Russell Paul Schofield.

Illustrations:

In the *I Ching* chapter, "Eight Trigrams in Context of Nature" is used courtesy of Rebekah Lowden.

In the *I Ching* chapter, "Eight Trigrams in Primal Arrangement" and "Eight Trigrams in Inner World Arrangement" are used courtesy of José and Miriam Arguëlles.

In the Tantra chapter, four photographs are used courtesy of Alan Atwell.

In the Tantra chapter, the illustrations of the *mudras* adapted for western sitting posture are used courtesy of George Kukar.

In the Tantra chapter, illustration of Siva Ardhanarisbara and, in the Actualism chapter, Dance of Siva are reprinted courtesy of the Archaeological Survey of India.

In the Tarot chapter, with the exception of the Empress and the Temperance cards, which are from the Waite Deck, the Tarot Cards are reproduced from the B.O.T.A. Deck, by permission of Builders of the Adytum, 5105 Figueroa Street, Los Angeles, California.

In the Tarot chapter, the cards of the New Tarot are reproduced from *T: The New Tarot,* the Tarot for the Aquarian Age, copyright © 1969 by Rosalind Sharpe Wall and John Star Cooke. By permission of Western Star Press.

In the Astrology chapters, geometric diagrams and charts are used courtesy of Wes Buist of Technical Graphics, San Francisco, California.

In the Astrology II chapter, original drawings "Three Water Signs" and "Three Fire Signs" are used courtesy of Emile Pierre.

This book is dedicated to

The teacher—who provided the keys—
>	*and to*

Rebekah—most precious counterpart—
>	*and to*

You, dear reader—in the hope that you may find
in it something of what you seek—
>	*and to*

God-Children everywhere
>	with

Light and Joy

PREFACE

THIS BOOK IS AN EXPLORATION OF CONSCIOUSNESS. In such a venture we necessarily confront the limiting effects of fixed mental, emotional, perceptual, and behavioral patterns, conditioned into each level of consciousness. Maps and techniques, devised to free consciousness from these limitations, are the subject of this book. Since I cannot pretend to be completely free of bias, it is only fair to the reader to make clear some of these factors which have influenced my own thinking so that any remaining bias can be "up front."

Fifteen years ago, at Oxford, I studied the linguistic philosophy of Ludwig Wittgenstein, Gilbert Ryle, John Austin, and their followers. Wittgenstein once said, "Philosophy is the disease for which it should be the cure." This taught me respect for the perplexities of the relationship between experience and language.

Later at Harvard, I imbibed heavy doses of psychoanalysis and behaviorist learning theory, which I found a rather unpalatable and indigestible mixture at the time. Both interests came abruptly to an end, when, in March 1961, I took my first psychedelic drug. I shall always be grateful to Harvard for providing me with that extremely educational experience.

During the next six years I explored the extraordinary inner worlds opened up for me by the psychedelics. I learned a very great deal from these experiences, and from the many fellow-explorers who allowed me to share them; especially from those two remarkable individuals Timothy Leary and Richard Alpert (now Baba Ram Dass). I also investigated various other methods of changing consciousness and expanding awareness, including oriental yoga, Gurdjieff's self-observation, Reichian bioenergetics, Gestalt therapy, psychosynthesis, encounter groups, psychodrama, and others. I found most of these methods valuable in some ways, but limited.

During this time, the writings by and about Gurdjieff were a constant source of inspiration. Also very valuable and illuminating were the works of Buckminster Fuller, Teilhard de Chardin, Hermann Hesse, Wilhelm Reich, Carl Jung, Lama Govinda, Aldous Huxley, Alan Watts, Frank Herbert, Joan Grant, and of course, the incomparable *I Ching*.

About three years ago, some unusual personal experiences began to steer me in the direction of what is known as the "psychic" or the "occult"—an area academically unfashionable, but otherwise very popular. I began to see how astrology, the Tarot, and others of the esoteric systems were originally intended to be used as maps for the path of the evolutionary development of consciousness.

In 1968 I met Russell Paul Schofield and since that time I have had the privilege of being a student of *Agni Yoga* as taught in the School of Actualism, of which he is the founder. From him and Carol Ann Schofield I have learned more than I could even begin to enumerate. This book has benefited immeasurably from their wisdom, and from the perspectives which the practice of the methods they teach has opened up.

Valley Center, California
Spring Equinox, 1970

CONTENTS

MAPS OF CONSCIOUSNESS

INTRODUCTION

The New Renaissance

*Let him who seeks, not cease seeking until
he finds, and when he finds, he will be
troubled, and when he has been troubled,
he will marvel . . .*

THE GOSPEL ACCORDING TO THOMAS

IT IS BECOMING INCREASINGLY EVIDENT
that today we are living in a period of spiritual
renewal. Just as the European Renaissance of five
hundred years ago was marked by a sudden, dramatic extension of physical exploration and an
equally profound extension of perception leading
to a spectacular flowering of the arts and sciences, so now again we are witnessing the simultaneous expansion of our world in both outer and
inner directions. Emerging out of the darkness of
the machine-dominated industrial age into the
speed and brilliance of the electronic epoch, man
has, for the first time, physically left Earth's gravity field and reaches for the stars. At the same
time, enlightened with a new clarity of perception, man faces with amazement the vast, un-
explored interior spaces that open up beyond the
hitherto accepted yet artificially created boundaries of his consciousness.

The new renaissance greatly exceeds the old
in range and depth, for it is no longer a question
of simply expanding our inner and outer hori-
zons. We are completing a cycle: the era of
partial views, of divisive ideas and ideologies is
waning. The first photographs of the whole earth
returned from space signaled the beginning of
the new cycle of all-inclusiveness: there she
hung like a blue-green jewel in the velvet black
of deep space, laced with sparkling atmospheric
veils—our spaceship, our mother, our planet. The
world is one. We are all together now.

The vision of the unity of our physical world
has been repeatedly proclaimed in our time. On
the basis of his evolutionary studies, Teilhard de
Chardin, the eminent French Jesuit paleontolo-

gist, formulated the concept of the *noosphere:* the thought field of the planet, which interpenetrates and extends beyond the biosphere and atmosphere. Having developed as a natural extension of the evolutionary process, because "the consciousness of each of us is evolution looking at itself and reflecting," the noosphere is developing toward a state of concentrated yet highly differentiated unity which Teilhard called the "omega point." [1] Marshall McLuhan has pointed out how the impact of our electronic technology, which allows instant information feedback all over the planet, is placing us, whether we know it or not, in "the global village." Television, "the third parent," has brought the Vietnamese farmer into the American living room, and our social consciousness is no longer national, but tribal. [2] R. Buckminster Fuller, the Leonardo of the new renaissance, for years has been advocating and demonstrating that to consider man's environmental problems from the point of view of synergistic, comprehensive design science will enable us to overcome the rich-versus-poor differential that our obsolete, nationalist, local separatist points of view have originated and maintained. Fuller says: "Synergy (the principle that the behavior of wholes is more than the sum of its parts) is of the essence. Only under the stress of total social emergencies as thus far demonstrated by man do the effectively adequate alternative technical strategies synergetically emerge. Here we witness mind over matter and humanity's escape from the limitations of his exclusive identity only with some sovereignized circumscribed geographical locality." [3]

The vision of unity is here and is shared by many, the possibilities and the resources exist, yet the reality is that some eat and some starve; everyone wants peace, yet there is war; we proclaim freedom and equality, yet we practice oppression and separation. Our minds and perceptions may be experiencing a renaissance, but our emotions and behavior still respond to the old separative fixations. "There is not enough to go around," say our old animal fears, rationalized by Malthus and his modern successors. "Only the fittest survive," says Darwin, quoting

Nature out of context. Following this concept, one side believes we must fight to prove we are the fittest, we must have an "aggressive sales campaign" (note the military metaphors). The other half of the world, caught in the same basic fear mechanisms, follows Marx's analysis of a small segment of European industrial history and generalizes it wildly: "The workers (or rather we, their representatives) should be in control of the wealth." Power control motivated by fear; fear due to perceived scarcity: perceived scarcity due to shortsighted separateness and possessiveness; possessiveness based in part on ancient animal territorial instincts. "I have, you have not, stay away"; or: "I have not, you have, hand it over."

The conflicts and disunity in the outer world mirror the fragmentation and separative chaos within our personal nature. Here is where psychology comes in, or rather should come in, but unfortunately does not. What is man's nature that he is driven thus to fight, to kill, to blind himself to the perception of his own divinity? Is he really the killer-ape with an oversize brain, run amok, as some would have it? Or is he the victim of a sort of phylogenetic psychosis? Is *homo sapiens* an evolutionary mistake, soon to be discarded on Nature's rubbish heap, like other species that failed to adapt? Has he flubbed his role in the evolutionary drama and destroyed the scenery of the ecological theater to such an extent that the production will have to be canceled?

These are the questions the new renaissance man is asking. There must be significance in all this madness, one feels. [4] If "consciousness is evolution looking at itself and reflecting," perhaps we will still have a chance. Perhaps the visions of the prophets of unity represent the ray of hope emerging at last from Pandora's box of destructive emotions and obsessions. There is a groping and probing going on, a testing of new methods of furthering consciousness evolution. There is restless impatience with external solutions, superficial and transient because they are based on obsolete perceptions. There is growing awareness and amazement at the realization, as yet inchoate and partial, that the answers are within us, that the inner guide, the Immortal

Self, is here, within you and me, ready to teach and waiting to be heard.

One of the world's most beautiful poetic metaphors for this situation is given in the first chapter of the *Bhagavad Gītā*. Here is Arjuna, who is you and I, the human ego, in his chariot on the battlefield. The entire *Bhagavad Gītā*, or "Song of God," is sung in the midst of this battlefield of life, as a dialogue between Arjuna and his charioteer Krishna, who is an incarnation of Vishnu, the Almighty Preserver of the Universe. Arrayed against Arjuna are the legions of his enemies, among whom are his brothers, his parents, his teachers, his erstwhile friends. All the imprints and false-to-fact images that have been implanted in him, all the emotional ties with the nearest and dearest, are now obstacles that have to be dissolved if he is to follow the way (the *yoga*) to the understanding of truth. "And a man's foes shall be they of his own household" (Matt. II: 36). Throughout the ensuing battles, Krishna, the Higher Self, is the counsellor, the wise friend, who does not get involved in the struggle with externals but who holds the reins of the chariot and guides Arjuna to the goal by "inner direction." [5]

The ancient literatures of India and China are replete with formulations containing beauty, wisdom, and psychological insight. Yet often their texts are alien and inaccessible to the Western mind. Our *yoga*, our way to the truth, has been science: systematic observation and experimentation. Using this method we have gained considerable understanding of and control over the external forces of Nature. We have made no corresponding progress in our understanding of the laws of our own inner nature; and this lack of corresponding development is now making itself felt in drastic and painful ways as we awaken to the intimate ecological relationships between our own technological activity patterns and the larger macropatternings of Great Nature herself.

The notion that it is possible to approach the understanding of the psyche with the same scientific attitude that is used in the study of the physical world has been unfashionable in psychology for some time. However, this was the avowed program of many of the so-called fathers of modern psychology. Wilhelm Wundt, Gustav Fechner, and Edward Titchener all initiated projects in systematic introspection and the experimental analysis of subjective sensation and feeling states. But these projects came to an end very soon when the observers encountered material of the sort now called resistances or complexes, that is, thoughts, feelings, or sensations surrounded by something similar to a negative force field that prevents further direct awareness without outside intervention.

The inseparable interaction of the process of observation with the phenomena oberved, which is expressed in the physical sciences in Heisenberg's indeterminacy principle, is of course of paramount importance in psychology where the phenomena to be observed are the observer's own subjective states. Yet we find that the pervasive and fundamental distortions of perception caused by ego factors and personality-bound perspectives are very rarely recognized by the observer in himself, though it is frequently enough pointed out and analyzed in other, so-called sick individuals, whose distortions happen to be somewhat more crippling and idiosyncratic than most.

Ancient psychological training institutes, known as mystery schools, recognized the impossibility of overcoming the artificially created yet effectively imprinted distortions and limitations of consciousness without the help of a teacher who had already overcome these same limitations. As G. I. Gurdjieff, a modern teacher in the esoteric tradition, phrased it: "A man cannot awaken by himself. But if, let us say, twenty people make an agreement that whoever of them awakens first shall wake the rest, they already have some chance. Even this, however, is insufficient because all twenty can go to sleep at the same time and dream that they are waking up. Therefore more still is necessary. They must be looked after by a man who is not asleep or who does not fall asleep as easily as they do . . ." [6] It is of course possible that an individual will awaken accidentally or spontaneously and begin to perceive phenomena not perceived by the majority of those around him. Gustav Fechner, for example, damaged his eyes by repeatedly gazing at the sun with inadequate filters while performing his experiments on sensation. During the subsequent year, which he had to spend in total darkness, he apparently broke through to a level of consciousness which allowed him, when he returned outside, to perceive energy fields around plants and animals. He had what is usually called a mystical experience, an experience of union with the Creator, and he spent the rest of his life attempting to give quantitative expression to these newly perceived relationships; an unsuccessful effort which resulted in that uninspiring branch of modern psychology known as "psychophysics." [7]

Other individuals who have expanded perception, either as a natural development from childhood on or acquired accidently through some kind of shock experience, will, if they are able to integrate their perceptions into the image they have of themselves, use their ability in artistic expression or as professional mediums, clairvoyants, and the like. Again others may utilize their unusual gifts in regular professions such as business or medicine. Shafica Karagulla has documented numerous instances of businessmen and physicians who were clairvoyant or precognitive, some of whom did not even know their perceptions were unusual, and all of whom were understandably noncommunicative about them.[8]

There are, of course, individuals who are unable to integrate expanded perception into their self-concept, and in whom it produces dissociation of personality to such an extent that the person's relationships with external reality are either severely crippled and blocked, as in neurosis, or totally disorganized, as in psychosis. The hypersensitivity of the neurotic patient is in one way the cause of his distress and inner conflict, while at the same time it can become his greatest asset in his growth as an individual. All practicing psychologists, Freud and Jung included, derived many of their most important insights from their patients' perceptions. Equally, schizophrenics are often demonstrably telepathic and "psychic." I well recall sitting opposite a schizophrenic girl in a state hospital listening to her disconnected stream of apparently meaningless verbiage, when I began to notice that mingled in with the rest of the material were images and associations that I was silently experiencing. Indeed, the inability to distinguish their own thoughts and fantasies from the equally vividly perceived thoughts and fantasies of others is part of the reason for the schizophrenic terror.

All of the above considerations apply also to the temporary state of extended perception and awareness induced by psychedelic drugs. For someone whose ego concept is sufficiently flexible to assimilate them, the experiences can provide valuable insight into his own psychic processes and the factors obstructing his growth. For someone whose self-images are dominated by fear and defensiveness, or who is given the experience without adequate preparation or support, the drugs can produce more or less temporary disorganizing and destructive effects.

*Psychological change—
contemporary approaches*

Although there have been and are in the West numerous individuals who have opened the "doors of perception" and seen beyond—artists, mystics, saints, and sensitives—yet a truly scientific school of psychophysical transformation has not operated openly since the time of Pythagoras. The essence of the scientific method is verifiable and repeatable observation, either in natural settings or in specially arranged experimental settings. Unless an individual is able to demonstrate the observation he has made, it cannot become part of scientific data. Hence the need of a teacher, who can teach not theories but methods: methods that will reliably give results and enable others to perceive the same phenomena and relationships.

No such teacher or methods were available to the early introspectionist school of psychology, so their observations were unrepeatable and hence led to naught. From this failure, and from a mistaken analogy to physics, the Behaviorist school, which in one form or another still dominates American psychology, drew the erroneous conclusion that objective observation of subjective states is impossible, and that the only scientifically valid data are the recordable physical movements and verbal marks and utterances of *others*. In fact, as already pointed out, such observation is possible, but to be objective about one's inner states requires the difficult, lengthy, and poorly understood process of freeing oneself from inherited and acquired perceptual images and mechanisms.

This process of liberation is the central concern of schools of transformation in ancient and modern times. And once this step has been taken, once we are able to recognize accurately our own inner states, it is also possible, contrary to what Behaviorist-inspired psychology teaches, to make reliable observations about the inner states of others. Everyone knows that we can often tell, with "intuition," what another is feeling without being told. Dr. Karagulla, from her extensive interview studies of sensitives, reports that such individuals are consistently able to *see* three sets of force fields around any person: a "vital field," which reflects the state of health or disease of the organism; an "emotional field," which varies with the nature and intensity of feeling; and a "mental field," which reflects the mental activity level of the person observed.[9] All sensitives agree unanimously that their abilities are merely extensions of faculties potential within everyone, that they are not "paranormal." The techniques of the school of Actualism are resigned to actualize these potentials, to free perception from imprinted images so that awareness can expand into the many levels of consciousness that lie beyond our usual awareness.

Besides Behaviorism, the other major influence in modern psychology is of course Freud and psychoanalysis, and it is to Freud's credit that he took the bull by the horns and grappled with the problems of resistance and defense mechanisms directly. In so doing he came upon the then astounding, though now commonplace, fact that there are many things going on in our psyches of which we are not, even though they influence our thoughts, our feelings, our behavior, both voluntary and especially involuntary, and our dreams. His analysis and identification of the defense mechanisms of repression, denial, isolation, projection, displacement, conversion, and

others, was ground-breaking detective work that enabled one to trace the historical origin of many neurotic and psychotic symptoms to particular inner or outer events of childhood. His delineation of the stages of development—through oral, anal, phallic, and genital phases—was evidently valid in broad outline and confirmable by other investigators. From an Actualist viewpoint though, his work was limited to the human, the body, and the organ levels of consciousness, omitting both higher and lower levels.

Freud was the type of person who liked to build mental systems and structures, and the various syntheses of his ideas, which he continually devolped and revised during his lifetime, bear witness to the fertility of his creative imagination. But, since they were often based on data and observations that he had neither the inclination nor the ability to verify and confirm, they have not been widely accepted except by those who prefer to let others do their observing and thinking for them. His followers and disciples all developed divergent theories and points of view based on the equally unverified and unverifiable observations they made.

The weak point in Freud's entire work was of course the method, the technique of "free association," which is actually not free at all since it follows the fixed patterns of neurotic mechanisms. These mechanisms, originally programmed as defense mechanisms, have become, through associative processes linking them with false-to-fact images, destructive rather than defensive. The free association technique, which consists of a passive following of associative processes, enables one to trace the connections and relationships between instinctual impulses and defense mechanisms, and to uncover feelings and ideas which had been kept hidden, sometimes from early childhood. But unfortunately the method, even when supplemented by the analyst's interpretations, did not free one from these mechanisms. The analyzed patient could relate the whole history of his neurosis but not be one iota closer to overcoming it. The statistical studies done by Eysenck and others demonstrate unequivocally that psychoanalysis did no better than the mere passage of time in curing a patient. (In all fairness it must be added that other methods of psychotherapy have been statistically demonstrated to be equally ineffective.) Which is not to say that breakthroughs in understanding do not occur, or that patients may not often feel better, or even become better adjusted to reality. Freud himself was very much aware of the limitations of his technique. His last paper on method was entitled "Analysis Terminable and Interminable," and he speculated on the possibility of using chemicals as an adjunct to psychoanalysis, because he recognized that the "transference" relationship of doctor and patient in the office simply did not generate enough energy to effectively dislodge the highly charged cathexes (literally "holding forces") that were involved in the neurosis.[10]

I find no evidence in Freud's writings that he ever broke through to the unitive perception of the continuity and interconnectedness of all life, or to the ecstatic freedom that comes from recognizing the acquired personal relativity of one's concepts and beliefs. In fact, his formulations tended to become more deeply pessimistic as time went on. Originally he had stated that there was a basic clash between the "pleasure principle" and the "reality principle," and in *Civilization and its Discontents* he argued that the repression or suppression of pleasure was the price we had to pay for the "reality" of culture. Conversely then, the highest manifestations of human art, creativity and religion, were interpreted as sublimations of the sex instinct. Later, in *Beyond the Pleasure Principle,* attempting to explain the phenomenon of masochism, he was led to postulate an instinctual duality of life versus death forces within man. This theoretical formulation essentially represents a capitulation of the integrative tendencies within the organism; the masochistic mechanism which "perverts," literally "turns aside," the basic generative life energy, is elevated to the status of a cosmic, insurmountable principle. Many of Freud's followers refused to accept the *eros-thanatos* theory, and several modern commentators, especially Herbert Marcuse in *Eros and Civilization* and Norman O. Brown in *Life Against Death,* have attempted to salvage Freud's valuable in-

sights without getting caught in his life-negating theories.

In particular, Wilhelm Reich was able to shed light on the problem of masochism by showing that the desire for pain infliction can be seen as the individual's attempt to free the expression of the core erotic energy by forcibly cracking the protective "muscular armor" which prevents this expression, from the outside.[11] In other words, it represents the individual's attempt to free himself from defense mechanisms that have become obstructions. Intense pain can at least overcome deadness or the absence of sensation, and under certain conditions may temporarily switch to intense pleasure. The masochist's maneuver is however a misguided act of despair, since it strengthens the armor it intends to break. The only permanent "solution" is to amplify the basic core love energy so that it can "dissolve" the armor from the inside.

Reich made significant advances from Freud in both theory and method. He was not content to sit behind the patient and record and interpret his associations and repressions. Instead he turned around to face the patient to determine by direct observation what was happening to the energy that was being repressed or denied. By doing this he made the important discovery that the defense mechanisms are literally incorporated, that is, fixed into the bodily structures, a process he termed "armoring." "The armored individual is distinguished from the unarmored basically by the fact that there is a rigid wall between his biological core from which all natural impulses arise, and the world, in which he lives and works." [12] Character structure itself is functionally equivalent to muscular armor, and not only is the skeletal musculature armored, but the muscles of the internal organs, the circulatory, respiratory, reproductive, and digestive systems can also be armored, giving rise to the whole host of psychosomatic and somatopsychic disturbances and deficits. Further, Reich found that direct work with the bodily armor simultaneous with analysis of the character structure (a method he termed "bio-energetics" or "vegetotherapy") provided much more effective release from energy blocks than analysis alone.

The role of the body as the registering instrument of psychic energy and its distortions is recognized implicitly in many colloquial expressions such as "up-tight," "pain in the neck," "heavy heart," "having no guts," "stiff upper lip," or "spineless." Reich's pioneering research in this area has led to some of the most effective contemporary psychotherapeutic methods. For example, Alexander Lowen, a student of Reich's, in his book *Betrayal of the Body*, has given brilliant and detailed analyses of the body language of various types such as the hysteric, the obsessive, the masochistic, and the schizoid. Fritz Perls, the author of *Gestalt Therapy* and a student of both Freud and Reich, has developed a way of increasing the patient's total awareness of the here-and-now by highlighting the involuntary bodily gestures, postures, and sensations that normally are part of the unrecognized background of experience, and which, when brought into awareness, can cause sudden shifts in one's perception, and integrative rearrangings of fragmented elements of consciousness. The burgeoning interest in body work of all kinds, from Ida Rolf's "structural integration," Charlotte Selver's and Bernard Gunther's "sensory awareness," to various kinds of breathing, massage, and movement therapy, indicate that the paramount importance of the body in the process of evolutionary growth and development is beginning to be recognized. As *The Jewel Ornament of Liberation*, a medieval Tibetan Tantric Buddhist text noted: "The working basis is the most precious human body." [13]

In spite of Reich's pioneering genius, it is evident from the intense rage he expressed toward his wife and from the paranoid tendencies he developed in his dealings with the federal government, that there were certain aspects of his own character armor that he was unable to resolve.[14] Like Freud, Reich came from a male-dominated family in a patriarchal society, and neither recognized the need for integrating the masculine and feminine components of the personality in order to attain unitary consciousness. In fact, the notion of unification or wholeness as a state to be attained beyond the cure of neurotic or schizoid symptoms is one that is conspicuous by its absence in both Freud and Reich, and indeed in the majority of modern psychologists with the notable exception of Carl Jung. Jung, on the other hand, came from a mother-dominated family with a strong religious background (his father was a Swiss protestant minister), so he did not share Freud's distrust and fear of religion as something "occult." On the contrary, he was able to open his mind and accept the ideas and images of Christianity and many other religions and mythologies as affording valuable insights into psychological processes.

The key concept in Jung's entire psychology, to me, is "individuation": the idea that it is possible to become an "individual," not in the sense of someone who wants to be different and separate from others, but in the literal and original sense of someone who is "in-divisible," that is whole. The individuated person would indeed be different from others and stand out, but because of his rarity not his idiosyncrasies. This process of individuation was considered by Jung from several different aspects. In his theory of types he proposed that the integration of the personality would be furthered if the four functions—thinking, feeling, sensing, and intuiting—were all well developed and equally accessible as modes of relationship to the world. In his theory of "the shadow," Jung pointed at the need to integrate the "dark," unacknowledged aspects of one's nature. The shadow is the personified *alter ego* that exemplifies all the traits we reject in ourselves and project onto others. "Projections change the world into the replica of one's own unknown face." [15]

Projection of the shadow is especially rampant on a mass scale in the relations between the races, where the differential skin color provides a convenient smoke screen hiding the true nature of the process. Whites project onto Blacks the feared and hated "dark" aspects of their nature, particularly violence and sexuality; conversely the Blacks see in Whites the oppressive and exploitative attitudes with which they themselves have blocked their creative and productive activity. The fact that there is an aspect of "reality" to these perceptions only further hides the mechanism of projection.

The crucial importance of the need to withdraw and neutralize projections in the process of personality integration has often been stated. In Patanjali's *Yoga Sutras* one of the "eight limbs" of yoga is *pratyahara,* the freeing of perceptual activity from the binding forces (*samskāras*) that link it to external objects. In the "dream work" of Perls' Gestalt therapy the patient is instructed to "play" or "be" the various characters in his dream, on the assumption that the figures are unacknowledged facets of the dreamer's nature, and by owning the rejected and projected fragments he can integrate them and hence free himself from their obstructive influence in his life.

A primary role in the process of individuation, as Jung saw it, is played by the "anima" and "animus," personifications of the feminine nature of a man, and the masculine nature of a woman. "Every man carries within him the eternal image of woman, not the image of this or that particular woman, but a definitive feminine image. This image is fundamentally unconscious, an hereditary factor of primordial origin engraved in the living organic system of the man, an imprint or 'archetype' of all the ancestral experiences of the female, a deposit, as it were, of all the impressions ever made by woman." [16] According to Jung, the anima and animus archetypes manifest themselves most typically in personified form as figures in dreams and fantasies ("dream girl," "dream lover"), or in the irrationalities of a man's feeling and a woman's thinking. "In its primary 'unconscious' form the animus is a compound of spontaneous, unpremeditated opinions which exercise a powerful influence on the woman's emotional life, while the anima is similarly compounded of feelings which thereafter influence or distort the man's understanding ('she has turned his head')." [17] From this role of distorting images, the anima and animus archetypes could progress to the role of guide, or mediator with the "collective unconscious," *i.e.,* they could become constructive integrative factors if they were recognized and understood.

The primary determinants of anima and animus are of course the parents. This allows us to see Freud's theory of the Oedipus complex as a special case of Jung's theory in which the sexual aspect of the anima is the first of four stages through which this archetype can progress in psychological development. Similarly, the so-called Electra complex in women is one, though not the only, constellation of images in which the animus can manifest itself. The programs imprinted by parents in the psyche of the child, both those deliberately inculcated through education and those imposed unknowingly by unconscious emotional factors, can appear in numerous guises and forms. Jung saw that in mythology and fairy tales there exist many of the dramatic themes and variations, the comedies and tragedies which these images enact in the psyche of man, portrayed in most vivid and pertinent ways.

Jung made a significant advance in recognizing and formulating man's psychological bisexuality and man's tendency to personify images in both masculine and feminine forms. Yet Jung's concepts of polarity remained always on the purely symbolic level. Though he explored the concept of the union of opposites, the *mysterium conjunctionis,* through his four volumes on alchemy and innumerable studies of mythology, religion, and mystical philosophy, there is in Jung's writings an almost glaring *lacuna:* he never considers the body.

Jung, like Freud, was limited by his technique, or rather the absence of it. He saw the process of individuation occurring spontaneously, induced by "the Unconscious," which could produce helpful images as well as demonic ones; and he noted that the increasing centeredness of the psyche during psychotherapy was signaled by the appearance in dreams of circular *mandala* symbols. The therapist's strategy in Jungian therapy is not analytic-reductive; instead the patient's dreams and fantasies are related to mythic themes and symbols, hoping thereby to illuminate ordinary experience and show the potentially larger, integrative healing aspects. For this reason, many of Jung's works. read much like annotated anthologies of quotations and pictures from the world's limitless riches of psychological images and ideas. The technique of the "guided reverie," especially as developed by Roberto

Assagioli in his *Psychosynthesis,* is an extension of this principle: certain basic symbols that have been found to resonate to deep and transforming forces are used to initiate streams of associations leading to enlarged and healing perspectives.[18]

In this brief and sketchy survey of contemporary methods of psychological change, we may mention briefly the techniques of behavior therapy and hypnosis. These are oriented strictly toward the removal of a maladaptive cognitive, or behavioral habit and its substitution by an adaptive, that is, socially more acceptable habit. Such methods, which are of considerable value in certain situations, have little in common with the techniques of total transformation practiced in esoteric psychology schools. Here the aim is not to substitute one habit for another, but to free oneself of habits altogether, not to hypnotize oneself with a better image or imprint, but to de-hypnotize oneself from the images and imprints already there.

Even the more sophisticated psychological systems such as those of Jung or Reich have generally only perceived and formulated a one-sided, incomplete perspective of the actual situation. The contemporary seeker for self-transformation is likely to find, in the techniques of Reich and related methods of body awareness and Gestalt therapy, increased perception of and sensitivity to the flow of energy and the obstructions of that flow which operate in psychophysical systems. In Jungian methods, in psychosynthesis, and in guided imagery one works with transformation symbols and with higher perspectives; these are basically limited to the mental-imaginal processes with no linkup to the body and lower levels of consciousness.

In neither of these traditions is there any conception of levels of consciousness of a higher rate of frequency than that which we normally register in awareness. Yet the experiencing of these higher frequency levels of consciousness is becoming not uncommon, especially since the advent of psychedelics. So we find people turning to oriental and occult psychology for hints and clues to these other dimensions. The interest in the "occult," which simply means the "hidden" or the "academically unfashionable," is not, as some would have it, a fascination with obscurity and mystery; rather, it is the recognition that there is much that is obscure in the pseudoclarity of our rational world-view, and the attempt to shed light on these obscurities by taking into consideration consciousness factors generally omitted and denied.

With very few exceptions, contemporary exoteric psychology is still pretty much restricted to a point of view that sees normality or adjustment as the goal of psychological change. Even the so-called encounter group movement, which has developed powerful techniques for bringing hidden conflicts and image entrapments into awareness, has no formulations of meaning or purpose.

We are involved in evolutionary processes, and we have exquisite computer capabilities as the instruments for evolutionary growth and development. The esoteric psychological schools, as well as some of the oriental ones, have maintained the knowledge of the Higher, Immortal Self, the Krishna-consciousness, or Christ-consciousness, which is the teacher-knower within who can guide the person's evolutionary growth toward individuality. Concepts of what is "normal," or "right," or "should be," are all image-obstructions to our receptive perception of what actually is; which can only be learned by listening-looking-sensing within. "For the kingdom of heaven is within you," and the goal of the path of evolutionary growth and development, according to the most ancient and sacred teachings, is to learn to follow the inner direction of the Higher Self, so that we can externalize the divinity within, and it will "be on earth as it is in heaven."

*The way of transformation—
maps and manuals*

If we use the analogy of a journey or path to consider the process of psychological transformation to the level of individuality, we can perhaps arrive at some conclusions as to the requirements for such a process. The best way of proceeding on a long and difficult journey into unknown territory is with a guide. Claudio Naranjo has written: "The teacher-therapist-guide is the person who, by virtue of his own individual understanding of a system, may help another individual in the process of creative translation of the general into the particular, of the way into a given, unique way. Each individual is, as it were, a variation on a universal theme, and a teacher is one with enough insight into the theme to know how the idea may become flesh and deed." [19] Genuine teachers however are hard to find and there is a phase where the individual is probing, testing, and experimenting with different ways and means in order to find the one that works for him. During this stage maps are useful, and that is why in recent years there has been such an upsurge of interest in the old maps of evolutionary development.

There is an important difference between a map and a model or theory. A model or theory states that "Man is like this, he learns this way, perceives like this, and thinks and acts according to these laws." All Western psychology, insofar as it has theories at all, is of this type. A map on the other hand is pragmatic, it is designed to help us find our way. It says: "Look at it this way and observe the results"; or, "Try this procedure and the following experiences will occur." Much oriental psychology and esoteric systems such as those of Gurdjieff are of this type. They imply a model of man oriented toward this goal. Often they include instructions for the practice of certain psychological techniques. However, since the techniques are generally held to be learnable only directly from a teacher, the technical indications are usually coded in a language accessible only to those who have, through a teacher, already had practical experience of the technique. They serve therefore more as reminders. It is a characteristic of such systems that they are written on many levels, and each student will derive from them what information he can assimilate according to his level of understanding.

In addition to maps and methods it is useful to reflect on and explore the possibilities of external aids or adjuncts to the work of inner transformation. For example, so-called psychedelic substances, by temporarily enhancing perception in certain ways, can be used to give a preview of the path ahead or to amplify the effects of meditative methods. The use of these substances *per se* of course implies nothing about the goal or method, and they can and frequently are taken for purposes other than enlightenment, and with results quite other than and perhaps even opposite to inner growth.

Among other external aids and adjuncts that are beginning to be researched and explored, we might mention the possibilities of EEG feedback. In these devices certain kinds of brain waves are linked to an external signal such as a tone. If the "alpha" brain wave is registered the tone is on, if not, the tone is off. In this way, the presence of the tone becomes an index of the "one-pointedness" which is an essential aspect of all methods of meditation and concentration. As soon as concentration is lost, the tone goes off, so that the student has immediate feedback; instead of the usual situation, in which several minutes may elapse before he realizes that he has been daydreaming or thinking instead of meditating.[20]

Sensory isolation environments of the kind researched by John Lilly can also be used to heighten clear perception of inner states by reducing the "noise" of external sensory input.[21] *Yantras* and *mandalas* can be used to provide external support in the form of diagrams for certain kinds of visualization techniques, and were so used in the tantric system. Undoubtedly, the inventive ingenuity of Western technology can and will, in the years to come, contribute many more such external adjuncts to the "Great Work" from which it has for so long been divorced.

In studying and comparing the different maps described and discussed in this book it might be useful to keep in mind the distinction between two principal modes of mental functioning and communication, that is, by concrete images (visual symbols) on the one hand, and by abstract, conceptual symbols (words and sounds) on the other. Indian philosophy referred to this as *nama* (name) and *rūpa* (form). G. I. Gurdjieff described the difference as follows:

Man has in general two kinds of mentation: one

kind, mentation by thought, in which words, always possessing a relative sense, are employed; the other kind, which is proper to all animals as well as to man, which I would call "mentation by form." The second kind of mentation, that is mentation by form, by which, strictly speaking, the exact sense of all writing must also be perceived, and after conscious confrontation with information already possessed, be assimilated, is formed in people in dependence upon the conditions of geographical locality, climate, time, and in general, upon the whole environment in which the arising of the given man has proceeded and in which his existence has flowed to manhood.[22]

Since the researches of Francis Galton it has been known that people tend to be either visualizers or verbalizers, and Barbara Brown has shown that these two kinds of people show different brain wave responses to color stimuli and to LSD.[23] One simple test of the difference is to swing a pendulum in front of someone's eyes for a minute or so, then ask them to shut their eyes and remember the swing of the pendulum: visualizers' eyes will move, verbalizers' won't. It is not as generally recognized that both kinds of "mentation" can be equally developed in an individual and for complete comprehension, as Gurdieff points out, both are necessary.

There is a corresponding distinction in the design of high-speed electronic computers, which fall into two main categories, digital and analog. These two types differ in the manner in which they handle data. *Digital* computers translate the data, whether numerical or verbal, into linear sequences of digits, usually binary digits known as "bits," according to an established code. *Analog* computers, on the other hand, translate "physical variables into related electrical quantities and use electrical equivalent circuits as an analog for the physical phenomenon being investigated."[24] In other words, there is a formal, one-to-one correspondence between the data variable and the electrical analog variable used by the computer to represent the data.

To think of the human brain and nervous system as a computer is not at all degrading, as some would have us believe. On the contrary, it permits us to see brain and body in proper perspective: namely, as instruments of Higher Self,

for purposes of energy processing and transformation. In his monograph *The Human Biocomputer*, John Lilly has developed a rather sophisticated model of brain-mind-body interaction, based on neurophysiological data, as well as sensory isolation and LSD research. He sees psychedelic substances as "reprogramming" devices, means by which "higher" or "self" levels of the biocomputer can "debug" lower level programs. A hierarchical, multilevel structure of consciousness is basic to this model, as it is to all the various maps and systems considered in this book. It is a notion that is fairly rare in Western especially academic psychology, which at most, recognizes only two levels of consciousness, one of which is misleadingly labeled "unconscious." (The so-called pre-conscious and sub-conscious are not strictly different levels, but rather different areas of consciousness.)

Buckminster Fuller pointed out that "there is one outstandingly important fact regarding Spaceship Earth, and that is that no instruction book came with it." [25] An even more fundamental lack is that no instruction book came with the human biocomputer, so that we have to figure it out or learn it from others. As we work with consciousness maps we develop operating manuals for the human computer. We can learn how to consciously and deliberately program and reprogram our human computer—how to debug malfunctioning programs which lead to disease, and how to eliminate programs that are destructive and obstructive to our evolutionary growth—instead of being victimized and robotized by automatic programs not of our choosing, implanted and imprinted in us by inherited and acquired conditioning factors and images.

A friend of mine has nine TV sets up in a rack, each tuned to a different channel, and to watch this is a most extraordinary experience since it gives one a summary picture of the mass-mind programming in action. TV and the related electronic media, backed by the psychology of motivational and behavioral conditioning, program the collective consciousness, and play the role that myths, tales, and dramas have played in the past. The suburbanite glued to the TV screen is the modern symbolic equivalent of the prisoner chained to the wall in Plato's cave, hypnotized by the flickering images. His divinely created computer instrumentation is almost entirely dominated by programs imposed from without, based on fear, profit, and power motives, instead of being programmed from within to actualize its highest potentials.

The human biocomputer, like its electronic, man-made imitation, is programmed in two basic modes: the digital-verbal and the analog-formal.[26] And since we are thus programmed, we perceive the world of names (*nama*) and forms (*rūpa*), as our "reality." The fact that different people's and different cultures' "realities" are different is not surprising since the programmed names and forms are different. In order to learn to understand what is actually going on, we need desperately to understand the particular programs under which we are operating, and how to change them if we want to. "Know thyself," said Socrates, quoting the Delphic Oracle. It is only by recognizing our own programs that we can see how conflicting emotions and false information in the programs cause us to distort and misperceive the processes of energy transformation in which we are involved. It is for this purpose that the operating manuals described here were written: in the hope that man can learn to participate consciously in the evolutionary process. And, in conformance with the two types of programming, the manuals or maps were presented in both verbal-digital codes and formal-analog images. Six manuals, or maps, of evolutionary growth and development will be discussed in this work. Although there are many parallels and similarities, each system presents the path in characteristically different symbols, suggests somewhat different methods, and points to different aspects and stages of the journey.

The *I Ching*, revered by the Chinese as the oldest and wisest book in the world, permits us to step outside of the consciousness-limiting bonds of two-valued logic and sets us free from the linear, cause-effect thinking in which Western philosophy-psychology has been trapped since the time of Aristotle and Plato. It also affords a momentary glimpse, sideways, as it were, through the folds of the cloth of time into the world of constancy-in-change that interpenetrates and interweaves our regular world of events and persons.

The Hindu and Buddhist *Tantras* of medieval India rescued the body from the asceticism of the *yoga* tradition and celebrated the union of male and female energies through the exaltation of sensation–perception, transmuting ordinary sense experience into ecstatic ritual worship.

Tarot cards lead us on an upward-spiraling, ever more-inclusive, returning-renewing journey through the labyrinthine passages of the nether and upper worlds, confronting us with mythic mirrors in which we see ourselves transformed; mirrors that resonate and show us things within us of which we dare not think because they are too bright and radiant for our muddied minds.

With *astrology* we study and attend to the rhythmic cycles of those giant beings, the planets, in whose fields we live and die. Much as a cell might study the psychophysiological cycles of the man of whom it is a part and in whose larger being it lives and dies. In the microcosmos, cells shudder as one man's body moves "in opposition" to another, and tremble joyously as the man "conjuncts" with another; so in the macrocosmos we men and all living beings experience motion, commotion, and emotion in the pulsing, orbital phases of these gigantic cosmic "bodies."

Genuine *alchemy* is to chemistry what genuine astrology is to astronomy: the scientific study of molecular (or planetary-cosmic) phenomena, not as an end in itself, or for weapon-power or money-power, but for the one goal of man's evolutionary growth and development. Alchemy is psychic chemistry, the dissolving of psychomolecular binding forces and the purification of "elements" so they can be transmuted into finer and higher substances. The making of gold was only a metaphor for the alchemical adepts; repeatedly they said: "The gold we seek is not the common gold."

Actualism teaches that men are the children of God, and that through the methods of the "*yoga* of fire," men can become divine, cosmic beings. More exactly, it teaches not that they can become gods, but that they *are* gods, caught by the power of their own images into identifying with their creation, the human form, instead of realizing the God-child creator that they are. "Actualism teaches, now and here, the way to externalize the God within: to creative expression on earth. Teaches the divine strategy of gradual awakening . . ."; [27] awakening to the fact of the presence of the Creator-God within. The point is not, as has so often misleadingly been said, that we must "save our souls"; our souls are doing fine. It is the personality and the physical instrument that are asleep to the living presence that we actually are. Actualism teaches the actual design of man's being and levels of consciousness, and a method of individuation by which it can be verified, by each individual for himself.

NOTES AND REFERENCES

1. Pierre Teilhard de Chardin, *The Phenomenon of Man* (New York: Harper & Row Publishers, Harper Torchbooks, 1969), p. 420.

2. Marshall McLuhan, *War and Peace in the Global Village* (New York: Bantam Books, 1968).

3. R. Buckminster Fuller, *Operating Manual for Spaceship Earth* (Carbondale, Ill.: Southern Illinois University Press, 1969), p. 99.

4. For further discussion of this situation, see Ralph Metzner, "The Evolutionary Significance of Psychedelics," *Main Currents of Modern Thought* 25, no. 1 (1968).

5. Srī Krishna Prem, *The Yoga of the Bhagavat-Gita* (London: John M. Watkins, 1958).

6. P. D. Ouspensky, *In Search of the Miraculous* (New York: Harcourt, Brace & World, 1949), p. 143. This book is a verbatim record of Gurdjieff's teaching.

7. William James, "Concerning Fechner," *The Writings of William James* (New York: Random House, 1967), pp. 529–45.

8. Shafica Karagulla, *Breakthrough into Creativity* (Los Angeles: De Vorss & Co., 1969).

9. *Ibid.*, p. 159.

10. Sigmund Freud, *Outline of Psychoanalysis* (New York: W. W. Norton, 1949), p. 79.

11. Wilhelm Reich, *Character Analysis* (New York: Orgone Institute Press, 1949).

12. Wilhelm Reich, *Ether, God and Devil* (New York: Orgone Institute Press, 1949), p. 52.

13. Sgam. Po. Pa., *The Jewel Ornament of Liberation*, trans. H. V. Guenther (London: Rider & Co., 1959), p. 14.

14. Ilse Ollendorf, *Wilhelm Reich* (New York: St. Martin's Press, 1969).

15. Carl Jung, *Aion: Researches into the Phenomenology of the Self*, vol. 9, II, *Collected Works* (Princeton: Princeton University Press, Bollingen Series XX, 1959), p. 9.

16. Carl Jung, *The Development of Personality*, vol. 17, *Collected Works* (Princeton: Princeton University Press, Bollingen Series XX, 1954), p. 198.

17. Carl Jung, *The Practice of Psychotherapy*, vol. 16, *Collected Works* (Princeton: Princeton University Press, Bollingen Series XX, 1954), p. 301.

18. Roberto Assagioli, *Psychosynthesis* (New York: Hobbs, Dorman & Co., 1965).

19. Claudio Naranjo, "The Unfolding of Man," research memorandum EPRC-6747-3 (Menlo Park, Calif.: Stanford Research Institute, 1969), p. 39.

20. Joseph Kamiya, "Conscious Control of Brain Waves," *Psychology Today* 1, no. 11 (1968): 59–60.

21. John Lilly, *The Human Biocomputer* (Miami: Communication Research Institute, 1967). This is available from Esalen Institute, Big Sur, California.

22. G. I. Gurdjieff, *All and Everything*, First Series: *Beelzebub's Tales to his Grandson* (New York: E. P. Dutton, 1950), p. 15.

23. Barbara Brown, "Specificity of EEG Phothic Flicker Responses to Color as Related to Visual Imagery Ability," *Psychology* 2, no. 3 (1966).

24. "Analog Computer," *Van Nostrand's Scientific Encyclopedia*, 4th ed. (Princeton: Van Nostrand Co., 1968).

25. Fuller, *Operating Manual for Spaceship Earth*, p. 52.

26. This duality of data handling has been demonstrated at the neurophysiological level in research on d.c. (direct current) potentials and living organisms. See Robert O. Becker, Charles H. Bachman, and Howard Friedman, "The Direct Current Control System: A Link Between Environment and Organism," *New York State Journal of Medicine* (1962): 1169–1176. "It has been shown that the state of functional activity of cranial neurons, as measured by action potentials, is related directly to the presence of a normal D.C. potential gradient and current flow. It therefore appears that each neuron is capable of two types of activity: the first being the generation of a D.C. potential accompanied by longitudinal D.C. flow and the second being the generation of rapidly propagating action potentials as disturbances in membrane polarization. By influencing the rate of message-flow action potentials, the D.C. system qualifies as a data-transmitting control system. In addition it appears to transmit certain types of data such as pain and injury, by variations in its own state: an analog type of data transmission."

27. Russell Paul Schofield, *Imprint Unmistakable* (Privately printed, Los Angeles, 1970).

I CHING

Change—The Evolutionary Constant

The Creative and the Receptive are the real secret of the changes.

I CHING

IT IS EXTREMELY DIFFICULT FOR A WESTern mind to understand a system of thought such as that contained in the *I Ching* or Book of Changes. It is not merely a question of unfamiliar concepts, such as we might encounter in learning a new scientific discipline or in entering a new field of research, but rather it is a fundamental difference in life experience and hence in basic outlook. Since the Chinese educational tradition is very different from ours, the result is that the Chinese will take for granted certain things, which for us are quite strange, and, conversely, many of our basic assumptions will not appear to them as at all obvious. The extent of this difference and the difficulty of bridging it were brought home to me very vividly one time when I found myself seated on a plane next to a Chinese man from Hong Kong. I was on the way to India in search of a guru who would impart to me the wisdom of the East. He was on his way home after having spent eight years in England acquiring Western architectural skills and knowledge. I talked to him of my search for a teacher and the truth, of my desire and hope somewhere, sometime, to find liberation. It was out there and I had to find it, move toward it. He talked to me of the self as a circle, saying that to find liberation I must go to the center; there was no need to go anywhere; I was already there, within. I needed only to open myself to the inner self and I would be free. There was a containment and a cyclic completeness in his attitude to which by comparison my own attitude seemed intrusive, restless, and impatient. *Hunting the Guru in India* was the title of a book by an Englishwoman that had just been published and I began to feel like a hunter searching for some half-mythical animal.

Our talk turned inevitably toward the topic of the relationship between the sexes. I was in the midst of a very tempestuous relationship with a lady, from which my journey to the East was no doubt an escape, though I was not able to admit this until much later. He, on the other hand, was returning to Hong Kong to marry a girl he had never met, whom his parents had picked out for him. I was free to choose but could not accept the freedom. He accepted a constraint that seemed inconceivable to me and felt free. I talked of the pain of separation. He said, "If you miss the girl and want to write or call her, wait till you no longer miss her, and then write or call, and the relationship will be happier." Confucius, in his commentary on hexagram 42, I, INCREASE, says: "The superior man sets his person at rest before he moves; he composes his mind before he speaks; he makes his relations firm before he asks for something."

Richard Wilhelm, the German translator of the *I Ching*, probably more successfully than anyone attempted to bridge this gap of understanding.[1] Having gone to China as a Protestant missionary, he came into contact with the Book of Changes and other wisdom texts from the ancient Chinese tradition, and he had the courage to open himself up to an intrinsically alien way of thinking in order to communicate its vision of the truth to the West. To do this, an actual inner change was necessary, but ultimately his labor has enriched thousands of spirits in the West. Carl Jung, in a memorial address to Wilhelm, wrote: "The picture of the East that he has given us, free as it is of purposefulness and any trace of arbitrariness, could never have been created in such completeness if Wilhelm had not been able to let the European in himself slip into the background." [2] Apparently Wilhelm's immersion in the Chinese way of life was so complete that he had great difficulty reintegrating this vision into his basically Christian personality after he returned to Europe. Jung tells us of this crisis:

With the completion of this task [the translation], [Wilhelm's] mission reached its climax and, unfortunately, its end also. . . . there grew out of the close of the one phase the beginning of its opposite. Thus, in its culmination, *yang* goes over into *yin*, and what has been positive becomes negative.[3]

Wilhelm's physical body was not able to withstand the shock of the clashing opposites in his psyche and he died shortly afterward.

It is widely thought that the Book of Changes and the Taoist philosophy it embodies are fundamentally concerned with the complementary interplay of two polar forces *yang* and *yin*. Though this is true, it is perhaps not generally appreciated that this duality presupposes a unitive principle that is the source and support of the opposites emerging from it. "That which lets now the dark, now the light appear, is *Tao*." *Tao* is the "way," the matrix of change, that fuses the positive and negative energies. Without the *experienced* unity, the opposites conflict and diverge; by balancing them we create harmony. Thus we have a trinity of the two (*yang* and *yin*) balancing in the one (*Tao*).

The threefold unity of forces has been a central core of all wisdom teachings, both ancient and modern. In Indian mythology the three were personified as Brahma, the Creator, Siva, the Destroyer-Transformer, and Vishnu, the Sustainer-Preserver. The Catholic Church referred to the Trinity as "three in one," God the Father, God the Son, and God the Holy Ghost. G. I. Gurdjieff formulated the "Law of Three" as the interaction in all phenomena of the affirming, plus force, the denying, minus force, and the reconciling, equalizing force. Though rarely recognized as such, modern physics has also reached a tri-une formulation in Einstein's equation, $E = mc^2$, which says in effect that energy can manifest interconvertibly as matter or as radiation (light).

The experience of unity has not been common in the West until recently, when the selective use of awareness-amplifying chemicals such as lysergic-acid-diethylamide made the perception of the underlying oneness of all phenomena and life forms accessible to many persons. In searching for an intellectual understanding of this experience, not much help can be found in the usual Western philosophies. It is my belief that the extraordinary rise in the popularity of the *I Ching* is in part due to the fact that it does present a "way" in which the experienced one-ness, the *Tao,* through the dual forces and the three-fold fusion, can be related to the manifold forms of life, to the "ten thousand creatures," and to the ethical and social decisions confronted in everyday life, thus "bringing it all back home."

How the *I Ching* does this is not at all easy to understand. It seems clear in part that it simply provides a functional framework for intuition. After all, the reading has to be interpreted by the questioner. Yet one wonders how the judgments and images were finally related to the particular patterns of lines obtained by throwing the coins or sorting the stalks. Were the "holy sages" who composed the basic text clairvoyants who saw the actual patterned cycles of change and were able to code them in combinations of solid and broken lines?

The specificity and accuracy of the judgments is at times uncanny. For example, a friend once consulted the oracle to determine if he should leave the place where he was. He obtained hexagram 26, with the moving line "The axletrees are taken from the wagon"; and that very afternoon, while he was meditating on the hidden meaning of this line, a pair of youngsters driving his car succeeded in breaking its axle, thus fulfilling the oracle. I once consulted the *I Ching* about a nagging physical pain and received hexagram 18, the character for which "represents a bowl in whose contents worms are breeding"; subsequent medical examination confirmed the presence of bacterial infection in the painful area. But at times the relevance of the judgments will not become clear till much later, or the *I Ching* may answer a question that was not asked consciously but was implicit in the questioner's approach or state of mind.

It was phenomena of this kind, plus the ESP experiments of the Rhine group at Duke University, that led Carl Jung to formulate the principle of "synchronicity," which he termed "an acausal connecting principle"—that is, a lawful connection between events given not by a cause-effect relationship, but by subjective meaning. By formulating this principle Jung is in effect saying that such events as the above mentioned are not "mere coincidences," but are in fact lawful coincidences; they are simultaneous occurrences systematically related by their inner meaning. The Book of Changes is seen by Jung as being built on this principle of synchronicity. "In the West," according to Jung, "this thinking has been absent from the history of philosophy since the time of Heraclitus, and only reappears as a faint echo in Leibnitz." [4]

Heraclitus formulated a philosophy based on the notion that everything is in flux, which is a simplified version of the fundamental law of change or cyclic transformations underlying the *I Ching.* It is interesting to note that Leibnitz obtained his suggestion that all numbers could be expressed in binary form (as combinations of 0 and 1) from the *I Ching,* which is itself built on the binary principle (combinations of —— and ——). The binary number system is of course the basic alphabet of all modern high-speed digital computers, which perform their computations using on-off circuitry after translation from higher order computer languages. In this way the *I Ching* has indirectly contributed to one of the dominant influences in modern Western consciousness, besides its growing direct influence on thousands of readers. José Arguëlles has written: "The *I Ching* functions as a computer, and its functioning is only according to the truth of the programming. The truth of the programming depends on how the person who consults the Book of Changes responds to its messages." [5]

Among Western scientist-philosophers, Buckminister Fuller is one who has long advocated that we need to supplement our piecemeal, analytic approach to the facts of experience by comprehensive systems thinking and design. Having defined universe as the "aggregate of all of humanity's consciously apprehended and communicated experience," a definition which includes both the physical universe as described by scientists plus the metaphysical, Fuller states:

It is therefore possible to initiate our general systems formulation at the all-inclusive level of universe whereby no strategic variables will be omitted. There is an operational strategy of General Systems Analysis that proceeds from here. . . . It is the same procedural strategy that is used by the computer to weed out all the wrong answers until only the right answer is left. Having adequately defined the whole system we may proceed to subdivide progressively. This is accomplished through progressive division into two parts—one of which, by definition, could not contain the answer—and discarding of the sterile part. Each progressively-retained live part is called a "bit" because of its being produced by the progressive binary "yes" or "no" bi-section of the previously residual live part. The magnitude of such weeding operations is determined by the number of successive bits necessary to isolate the answer.[6]

What Fuller is describing as the systematic strategy used by a computer for generating the right answers is almost precisely the procedure used when the *I Ching* is consulted using the yarrow stalks. The procedure begins using fifty stalks; one stalk is set aside, and the others are then divided into two heaps at random; one heap is counted through by fours, and the remainder four or less is regarded as the "live" part; the same thing is done with the other heap, and the two "bits" thus generated constitute one "change." This process is repeated two more times with the two remaining heaps. The three changes give one line. This whole process, repeated six times, gives the six lines of the hexagram. This can also be done in a less complicated way by the throwing of three coins six times.

By throwing the coins or sorting the stalks we are able to gain access to a reading that tells us where we are in the current cycles of change —those cycles involved in the situation we are asking about. This is why the attitude of the questioner is so important: his state of mind determines the breadth and depth of the field of relationships the answer will embrace.

We might compare the situation to a long-distance stock-market report: we ask for the current value of a certain number of stocks, which are constantly fluctuating in value. The report could include whatever was asked for, but it will in fact only include what was requested: the present and projected future value, corresponding to the present and future hexagram. In order to be able to read the answer, we need to be aware of what cycles we are involved in; the more awareness we have, the more specific and meaningful the answer will be. This is why the use of the yarrow stalks is advisable in preference to the coin method. The counting procedure takes about twenty minutes, during which time the questioner's consciousness is focussed on the problem. If it is not, he will lose count and have to start all over. Experience has shown that a period of meditation added to the throwing of the coins will also increase the efficacy of this method of consulting, increasing the recipient's understanding of the message.

The Western scientific method of organizing experience proceeds by accumulating observations of external phenomena piece by piece, inventing hypotheses to explain the phenomena in terms of a small number of natural laws, and devising experiments that are controlled observation situations to verify the predictive efficacy of the laws formulated. In his book *The Structure of Scientific Revolutions*, Thomas Kuhn has shown how a scientific "paradigm" will be maintained until the number of observations contrary to the accepted law becomes such that a new set of paradigms can be formulated that will account for both the new and the old observations. The goal is always to arrive at single, all-inclusive formulations. Einstein's theory of relativity was a more inclusive paradigm than Newton's theory of gravitation, and included the latter as a special case. In the last years of his life, Einstein was developing an even more comprehensive formulation, which he called the "unified field theory," in which he tried to subsume both the phenomena of relativity and those of electromagnetic radiation.

The oriental way of organizing observations and experiences proceeds in the opposite way. Here the starting point is the experienced unity of the universe, the underlying, all-inclusive energy flux (*Tao*), and principles of differentiation are then introduced gradually to account for more and more detail. In the *Tao Tê Ching*, the forty-second verse reads: "The *Tao* materializes; out of one element come two; out of two come three; out of three, the thousand creatures." [7] We might compare this to the satement of the geneticist George Beadle: "Evolutionary processes are not limited to living organisms. They begin with the simplest of all elements, hydrogen. In the sun . . . hydrogen converts to helium, helium fuses to form a transitory isotope of beryllium, which can then interact with helium to yield carbon. In short, it is known how, in principle, all elements could have evolved from an assumed primordial universe of hydrogen alone." [8] Thus, working from different assumptions and with different procedures, similar formulations have been made of the basic evolutionary process.

But there is another important difference. The Western scientific method has become quite separated from any concern with human meaning or human consciousness, thus leading to the abuse of technology for power and profit. The Taoist sages related their insights into cosmic processes directly to the human psyche and social relations. A few lines later in the same verse of the *Tao Tê Ching* quoted above, we read: "What others teach I also teach. 'The violent do not die a natural death.' I shall take this as my precept." The eighty-one verses of the *Tao Tê Ching* are excursions on the physical, biological, social, and psychological implications of *Tao*, variously called "process," "energy," "way," "design," "spirit," or "that which cannot be named," or "the great." The *I Ching* takes this a step further and builds the Taoist philosophy into a structured system of practical divination or psychic programming. The third volume in this Chinese triad, *The Secret of the Golden Flower*, describes the alchemical *yoga* that is the actual method of expanding human awareness used by the Chinese, but since it is given in coded form, it is, in practice, incomprehensible to anyone not initiated in that system. [9]

Let us look in more detail at the way the *I Ching* is constructed, that is, at the programming language of this particular psychic computer. We refer here to what is called the *Ta Chuan* or Great Treatise, part of the extensive set of commentaries on the *I Ching* known as the Ten Wings. These commentaries and explanations, arranged by subject mater, are found in Book II of the Wilhelm edition (Book I contains the texts of the hexagrams with Wilhelm's summary commentaries; Book III contains the texts with detailed commentaries on each line). The commentaries explain why a particular combination of lines of trigrams has the text that it does.

The starting point of this ancient Chinese version of general systems theory is *Tao*. The undifferentiated, primal energy flux out of which everything that exists emerges, "That which lets now the dark, now the light appear, is *Tao*." *Tao* is one; one becomes two. Originally, the term *yang* and *yin* were used to designate the day-night cycle. Later, the concept was expanded to include primal polarity on many levels: light-dark, firm-yielding, movement-rest, creative-receptive, male-female. "In a state of rest the Creative is one, and in a state of motion it is straight. . . . The Receptive is closed in a state of rest, and in a state of motion it opens." The binary code of the *I Ching* is —— (*yang*) and — — (*yin*). The code in the modern theory of electromagnetic energy is + (positive charge, *yang*) and − (negative charge, *yin*).

The *yang* force goes out to its maximum, returns, softens, and changes into *yin,* just as the sun after reaching its zenith begins to sink back into darkness. The *yin* force, at its extreme, coalesces and becomes firmly *yang,* just as the longest winter's darkness contains within it the seed-beginning of new light. "As the firm and yielding lines displace one another, change and transformation arise."

In the hexagrams, a changing *yang* line is coded —Ө— and has the numerical value 9; a changing *yin* line is coded —X— and has the numerical value 6. The original hexagram obtained gives a reading for the here-now situation; the changing lines become their opposites, thus generating a second hexagram, which gives a future-probability reading. Thus, for example, the hexagram 63, Chi Chi, AFTER COMPLETION, changes into hexagram 12, P'i, STANDSTILL.

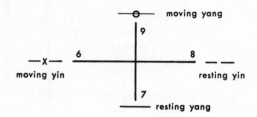

The two basic dimensions of light-dark and movement-rest may be arranged in the form of a cross or quaternity:

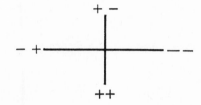

Or, more abstractly, using the electrical code:

$$+ \; -$$
$$- \; +$$
$$+ +$$

Such quaternities were believed by Jung to be symbols of structural completeness; as compared to circles representing organic or psychic completeness.

In another section of the commentaries a different starting point is given. "There is therefore in the Changes the Great Primal Beginning (*t'ai chi*). This generates the two primary forces. The two primary forces generate the four images. The four images generate the eight trigrams." *T'ai chi* literally is "the great ridgepole." The term *pole* also appears in the *yogic* text *The Secret of the Golden Flower,* where it probably refers to the central vertical axis of the human body during the work of psychic transformation. Perhaps on one level the "great ridgepole" is the vertical axis of the planet, which does in fact generate the light and dark primal energies by its rotation in the diurnal cycle. The "four images" refers to the four branches of the quaternity shown above.

Yet another way of deriving the eight trigrams is possible. Eight is the number of combinations of two types of lines in triads. Doubling the trigrams we have the sixty-four hexagrams that constitute the main body of the book. The two principles are combined in triads to indicate the mediating role of man between heaven and earth. "The Book of Changes contains the measure of heaven and earth; therefore it enables us to comprehend the *Tao* of heaven and earth and its order. Looking upward, we contemplate with its help the signs in the heavens; looking down we examine the lines of the earth. . . . Since in this way man comes to resemble heaven and earth, he is not in conflict with them. His wisdom embraces all things, and his *Tao* brings order into the whole world; therefore he does not err" (*I Ching*, pp. 315–317). Man is made up in part of creature earth-elements, and he contains also the creative power that has shaped the cosmos. Thus he is a microcosm and by understanding the laws of change in energy and matter, in heaven and earth, he is able to realize his innate capacities. This is the *I Ching*'s formulation of the law of correspondence, the idea that man is a microcosm, exemplifying within himself the laws of the universe. In the Western alchemical tradition, this law was summarized in the saying attributed to Hermes: "As above, so below."

It is necessary to understand that the terms *heaven* and *earth* have esoteric as well as exoteric significance. On one level, we contemplate the cosmic laws ("the signs in the heavens"), and the principles of mineral and biological organization ("the lines of the earth"), and we recognize how we as human beings are part of this ever-changing network of relationships. On a deeper level, the "*tao* of heaven" refers to the design of the higher frequency energy systems within, while the "*tao* of earth" refers to the corresponding lower frequency systems, which are dark because they are obstructed and beclouded by false perceptions and beliefs conditioned by personality factors. Man's role as a mediator then is to remove these obstructions, so that he "comes to resemble heaven *and* earth," so that it will be "on earth as it is in heaven," and in this way his *Tao*, or his way, "brings order into the whole world." For this reason the Hermetic saying could be, and was, also expressed: "As within, so without"; or as the Indian tantric masters later phrased it, "What is here is elsewhere; what is not here is nowhere."

In the hexagrams, this principle is given a spatial symbolism: the two lowest places represent earth, the two top places heaven, the middle pair man. In addition the places are alternately light (odd numbered) and dark (even numbered). Since we might obtain changing or resting lines in light or dark places, in the places of heaven, earth, or man, a great multiplicity of situations and changes can be symbolized and

expressed this way. In the interpretation of a hexagram we begin with the interrelationship of the two trigrams, which gives us the image, usually expressed in terms of the nature symbols (for example, "water over fire"). The so-called judgment, or decision, attributed to King Wên, describes the course of action appropriate to the situation shown in the image. The judgments appended by the Duke of Chou to the individual lines, are used only for moving lines (nines or sixes), which are the ones having the greatest potential for change.

The trigrams, the eight basic change vectors, are given in two arrangements in the *I Ching*. In the Primal Arrangement, or Sequence of

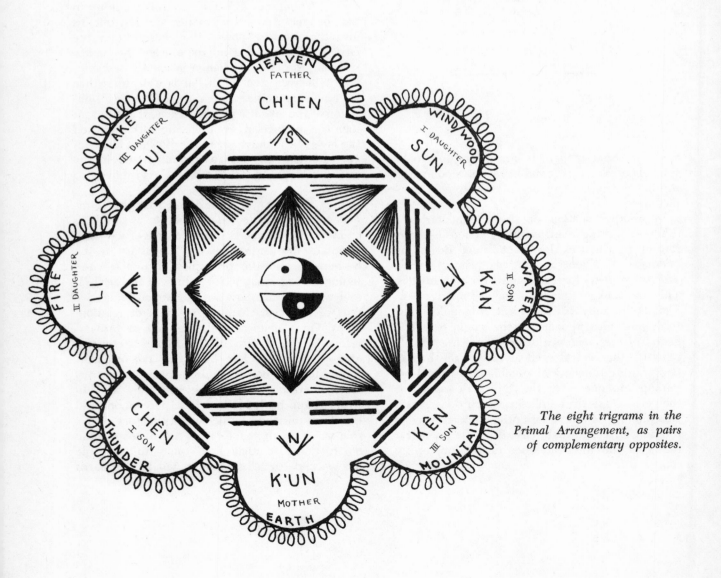

The eight trigrams in the Primal Arrangement, as pairs of complementary opposites.

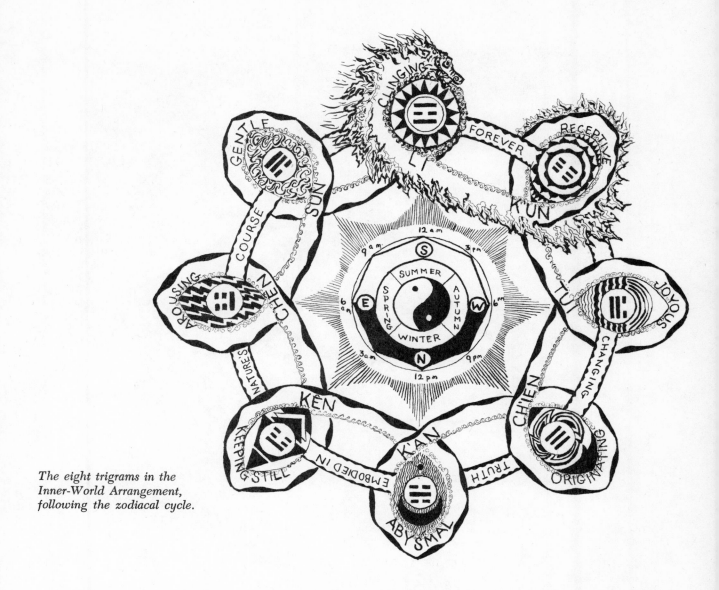

*The eight trigrams in the
Inner-World Arrangement,
following the zodiacal cycle.*

Earlier Heaven, they are shown as pairs of op-posite-complementary forces. "Heaven and earth determine the direction. The forces of mountain and lake are united. Thunder and wind arouse each other. Water and fire do not combat each other. Thus are the eight trigrams intermingled." This, then, is the first layer of symbolism: two superimposed quaternities showing the basic interplay of pre-life, inorganic energies in terms of nature symbols.

In the Inner-World Arrangement, or Sequence of Later Heaven, the trigrams are set in a circle corresponding to the changing seasons, the sun's yearly path. This is similar to the astrologer's ecliptic, though Chinese astrologers did not use

the ecliptic, at least originally, relying instead on the circumpolar stars.[10] This second layer of symbolism, the Inner-World Arrangement, indi-cates how the eight basic forces produce the ever changing phenomena of organic life. "God comes forth in the sign of the Arousing; he brings all things to completion in the sign of the Gentle; he causes creatures to perceive one another in the sign of the Clinging (light); he causes them to serve one another in the sign of the Receptive. He gives them joy in the sign of the Joyous; he battles in the sign of the Creative; he toils in the sign of the Abysmal; he brings them to perfection in the sign of Keeping Still" (*I Ching*, p. 287).

The eight trigrams as symbols of natural changes.

The idea of symbolizing the beginning of life, the first point of Aries at the spring equinox by the trigram for thunder (THE AROUSING), is in perfect accord with modern theories of the origin of life. Biologists believe, and have demonstrated experimentally, that lightninglike electric discharge in a medium of methane, ammonia, and water, the presumed elements of the earth's early environment, can cause the synthesis of porphyrins, the basic ingredients in chlorophyll; this in turn permits photosynthesis, the process by which plants transform radiant sunlight into carbohydrates and thus make food for all animals and men.

The eight trigrams have many levels of symbolism, each and any of which may enter into the interpretation of the hexagram obtained in a reading. We have already mentioned the inorganic polarized energy symbolism and the solar cycle of organic life. According to Wilhelm, "To understand fully, one must always visualize the Inner-World Arrangement as transparent, with the Primal Arrangement shining through it." In addition, each of the trigrams has a certain psychological quality or attribute; each is related to a certain animal and to a part of the body, also to plants, tools, and substances. All these associations may enter into the meanings of the judgments and images.

The trigrams also form a family of heaven-father and earth-mother and three sons and three daughters. "In the trigram of THE AROUSING she [the mother] seeks for the first time the power of the male and receives a son. Therefore THE AROUSING is called the eldest son. In the trigram of THE GENTLE the male seeks for the first time the power of the female and receives a daughter. Therefore THE GENTLE is called the eldest daughter." These family relationships are extremely important in interpreting the hexagrams.

At the innermost level the eight trigrams are also related to the *yogic* process of psychic transformation, although this set of meanings is brought out more clearly in *The Secret of the Golden Flower* than in the *I Ching* itself, where it is alluded to but rarely made explicit. Here is Wilhelm's summary of the role of the trigrams in working with the inner light:

The trigram *Chen* ☳ , thunder, the Arousing,

is life which breaks out of the depths of the earth; it is the beginning of all movement. The trigram *Sun* ☴ , wind, wood, the Gentle, characterizes the streaming of the reality-energies into the form of the idea. Just as wind pervades all places, so the principle for which *Sun* stands is all-penetrating, and creates "realization." The trigram *Li* ☲ , the sun, fire, the lucid, the Clinging, plays a great role in this religion of light. It dwells in the eyes, forms the protecting circle, and brings about rebirth. The trigram *K'un* ☷ , earth, the Receptive, is one of the two primal principles, namely the *yin* principle which is embodied in the energies of the earth. It is earth which as a tilled field, takes up the seed of heaven and gives it form. The trigram *Tui* ☱ , lake, mist, the Joyous, is a final condition on the *yin* side, and therefore belongs to autumn. The trigram *Ch'ien* ☰ , heaven, the Creative, the strong, is the embodiment of the *yang* principle which fertilizes *K'un*, the Receptive. The trigram *K'an* ☵ , water, the Abysmal, is the opposite of *Li* ☲ , as is already shown in its outer structure. It represents the region of Eros, while *Li* stands for Logos. *Li* is the sun, *K'an* the moon. The marriage of *K'an* and *Li* is the secret magical process which produces the child, the new man. The trigram *Kên* ☶ , mountain, Keeping Still, is the symbol of meditation, which by keeping external things quiescent, gives life to the inner world. Therefore *Kên* is the place where death and life meet.[11]

In addition to the two primary trigrams, upper and lower, use is also made in interpreting the hexagrams of the *hu kua* or nuclear trigrams. They are, so to speak, the trigrams contained completely *within* the structure of the hexagram.

Although Wilhelm does not say so, it may be supposed that the nuclear trigrams would be particularly appropriate for determining the inner, psychic essence of a situation, along the lines of the *yogic* interpretations given above. In fact, the relationships between primary (or outer) and nuclear (or inner) trigrams is important in evaluating the lines in the appended judgments. Thus, the top and bottom line, which are each part of one trigram only (the upper and lower primary), tend not to be part of the situation; they represent either residue from the previous phase or seed of the coming phase. The second and fifth line each belong to two trigrams, one primary and one nuclear; thus there is usually a favorable state of equilibrium for these lines. The third and fourth line each belong to three trigrams, to the upper and lower primary respectively and to both nuclear. This tends to a state of disturbed balance, as reflected in the judgments of the lines.

It may be helpful at this point to give an example of the operation of the *I Ching* as a psychic computer, showing how its symbolically coded answers can be helpful guides both to outer conduct and to inner meditation. In ancient China, the Book of Changes was widely used as a guide to statecraft, which accounts for the many interpretations couched in terms of what the ruler, or prince, should or should not do for the people. It is unlikely that modern politicians or rulers will permit themselves to take the *I Ching* seriously, though its consistent advocacy of patience, caution, humility, and perseverance suggests that were they to do so the results could only be beneficial. That its use in statecraft and strategy may not entirely be a thing of the past has been suggested by John Blofeld, who writes: "Many Japanese believe that the naval victories they won in the earlier part of the Pacific War owed much to the fact that books of strategy based upon the Book of Changes were required reading for the higher ranks of Japanese officers. . . . the movements of the Chinese army along the Indian frontier in 1962–1963 possessed characteristics reminiscent of the lessons traditionally drawn from the Book of Change by strategists." [12]

Its use in modern times is more likely to be by individuals or by pairs, partners, or small groups.

I know of several communities of like-minded persons where it is regularly used to help resolve some of the interpersonal conflicts that inevitably arise and which could not be solved from the fixed perspective of any one member of the group, no matter how experienced. A highly successful corporation in New York used the *I Ching* on a daily basis to regulate the interrelations of the office staff. I myself have used it as an aid to the practice of psychotherapy, particularly in situations where neither patient nor therapist knew what was going on. Invariably the *I Ching* is like a ray of light from a higher source, pointing out the obvious facts and the nature of the obstacle. Although it is customary for the inquiry and hence the consultation to be made by an individual, I have seen it used successfully by couples conjointly, with both partners actually throwing the coins or sorting the stalks. However, this tends to be less clear than an individual's approach because of the different interpretations that can be put on a given passage.

The following example given here actually occurred. A couple was having a lively and bitter argument, but somehow in the midst of it collected themselves sufficiently to agree to try the *I Ching*. They decided to each compute one trigram using the yarrow stalks. A coin was tossed to see who should go first. The woman began and obtained three *yang* lines for the lower trigram. The man then obtained three *yin* lines for the upper, primary trigram. This yields hexagram 11, ䷊ T'ai, PEACE, in which the receptive, earth energy moves down from above, and the creative, higher energy moves upward from below. If the trigrams had been reversed, the two forces would be moving in opposite directions, giving rise to hexagram 12, ䷋ STANDSTILL (STAGNATION). The hexagram thus describes a situation of deep and natural harmony, modeled on the uniting of forces that takes place in Spring (the consultation took place in March, which is the month of this hexagram). Although the personalities of the couple certainly did not experience this harmony at the time, the answer from the *I Ching* put an end to the conflict they were then engaged in. The judgment for this hexagram reads: "Peace. The small departs, the great approaches. Good fortune. Success." This judgment could be interpreted to mean that the "small" or petty aspects of their relationship were diminishing in favor of "great" or magnanimous aspects.

As exemplified in this situation, a major value of the use of the *I Ching* in everyday life lies in its ability to shift the questioner's point of view and to lift him out of personality-bound perception and enable him to look at the events from the point of view of ever transforming cycles of change. Conflicts, after all, can arise only where interpretations clash with the actual movement of events in space-time. The "superior" man, according to the Chinese wisdom, is able to determine where he stands in the ebb and flow and thus regulate his activities accordingly. He knows that every trough is followed by a crest, as inevitably as every crest is followed by a trough. It is delusion to attribute successes and failures to the ego-personality. As Lao-tse says in verse nine of the *Tao Tê Ching:* "To be proud with wealth and honor is to sow the seeds of one's downfall. To retire when your work is done is the *Tao* of heaven." Humility is simply not taking credit for one's positive experiencings; serenity is the complementary refusal to take blame for one's negative experiencings.

The unity spoken of in the hexagram PEACE is that between higher and lower forces within. At the highest level, the couple were in unity, as father-sky and mother-earth are in unity; at the lower, small level, there was conflict, but this was departing. The two nuclear trigrams are ☳ Chên, THUNDER, THE AROUSING, the eldest son, and ☱ Tui, LAKE, THE JOYOUS, the youngest daughter. We take this to mean that the son and the daughter, the offspring of the highest forces, the personalities of the couple, are moving toward the same unity as prevails in the cosmos at higher levels. Hence the text for the moving *yin* line in the fifth place reads: "The sovereign I gives his daughter in marriage. This brings blessing and supreme good fortune."

Finally, when the two nuclear trigrams (lines 5, 4, 3, and lines 2, 3, 4) are combined into a hexagram, we get hexagram 54, Kuei Mei, THE MARRYING MAIDEN. The question of marriage was a major factor in the conflict the couple was experiencing, though it was rarely explicit. The image text for hexagram 54 reads: "Thunder over lake; the image of THE MARRYING MAIDEN. Thus the superior man understands the transitory in the light of the eternity of the end."

The couple in question did not get married; indeed, they separated shortly afterward. About a month later, the man consulted the oracle again about the situation and obtained hexagram 41, ☶ Sun, DECREASE. This hexagram is formed through a change in hexagram 11, PEACE: the strong line in the third place of 11 has moved to the top in 41, causing a decrease of the lower trigram in relation to the upper. Thus, apparently, the outer course of events was following an inner ebb and flow, and indeed the text of hexagram 41 shows how decrease is to be understood: "DECREASE combined with sincerity brings about supreme good fortune without blame." The image reads: "At the foot of the mountain, the lake; the image of DECREASE. Thus the superior man controls his anger and restrains his instincts." He obtained a six, a changing line, in the third place, "When three people journey together, their number decreases by one." This pinpointed another aspect of the situation most accurately in that part of their difficulties stemmed from the role of the man's child from a previous marriage. This line continues: "When one man journeys alone, he finds a companion." This could be interpreted to mean he would find another companion, or he would finally really find the companion he had lost, or he would attain inner unity. The commentary on this line reads: "Through this separation, three become two; further, through the union one becomes two. Thus what is excessive is decreased, and what is insufficient is increased." Further advice was given by another changing line, six in the fourth place, which stated: "If a man decreases his faults, it makes the other hasten to come and rejoice. No blame." The future probability reading was hexagram 14, Ta Yu, POSSESSION IN GREAT MEASURE, fire in heaven; the two nuclear trigrams combined indicated thunder within the earth, hexagram 24, Fu, RETURN. Both of these indications were accurate.

A key notion in the Taoist philosophy of action is timing. There are no external criteria by which a given action can be judged good or bad. Indeed Lao-tse and his school tended to regard such judgments as a kind of mental illness. Rather, they say, "good fortune" results when an action is in harmony with the current phase of the cycles of change; actions are good if they further evolutionary growth and development, and "misfortune" results when an action is contrary to the direction of change. Such an action will necessarily fail. The terms *remorse* and *humiliation,* which recur frequently in the Book of Changes, refer to the appropriate timing of trends and activities. "Remorse" indicates not guilt or blame, but afterthought, literally "biting through again" (*remordere*) experiences or events not yet fully assimilated. "Humiliation," conversely, is not a counsel of shame or self-denial, but rather a counsel of forethought meant to check impulses to reckless, arrogant action. "Remorse" and "humiliation," therefore, refer to trends of action that are deviating somewhat from the *Tao;* "good fortune," and "misfortune" refer to actions that definitely further or counteract evolutionary change.

Many readers of the Book of Changes are likely to be put off by what seems at times a rather moralistic tone, not unlike a Christian sermon. The *I Ching* contains many layers of meaning, and the ethical teachings of the Confucians are certainly a major factor, constituting perhaps as much as half the bulk of the present version. I am inclind to agree with John Blofeld, who on the basis of his extensive study of oriental philosophy and language, expressed the opinion that "Confucius quite possibly did not fully understand the *I Ching.*" It seems certain that the men who originally composed the *I Ching* were beings of superior insight who had direct experience of levels of reality that very few others have. They expressed their insights into the workings of cosmic laws in terms of the nature

metaphors preferred by the Taoists. The qualities of water, for example, were especially admired and extolled by Lao-tse: "In the world there is nothing more submissive and weak than water. Yet for overcoming that which is hard and strong nothing can surpass it" (*Tao Tê Ching,* verse fifty-eight). For the Taoists supreme wisdom consists in adapting to the natural laws, and as far as human conduct is concerned, this means the natural inner laws of one's true being. Confucius no doubt accepted and practiced this philosophy, but in addition he was very much an upholder of authority and believed in the importance of following the traditional rules governing the relationships between members of a family and maintaining the proper patterns of rulership within a community or state. Thus in many instances the commentaries of Confucius and his school give exoteric interpretations, in terms of statecraft, military strategy, and public administration, to texts that may very well originally have had esoteric or psychic meanings.

The modern reader, who is more likely to be interested in the *I Ching* as a guide to inner growth, will have to do a considerable amount of sifting the grain of psychological wisdom from the chaff of moralistic and monarchistic interpretations. For this purpose it is advisable to pay more attention to the text than the commentaries, and particularly to work with the eight trigrams and their interrelations which are of great antiquity, antedating by many centuries the Book of Changes itself. They are said to have been first observed on the shells of tortoises by the legendary ·Fu Hsi, a kind of Chinese Prometheus.

The *I Ching* is in many ways like one of those fascinating Chinese puzzle boxes, in which each apparently self-contained receptacle includes yet another container hidden within it. How much essence of truth may be extracted from the meanings within meanings depends very much on the spirit with which the text and the consultation are approached, and on whether or not the questioner has had the relevant experiences and perceptions to which the symbols point. It is hoped that the psychological exercises described in the following section may help the genuine seeker unlock some of the mysteries of this baffling, ancient, and subtle book, and through it to find clues that will guide him to his true inner light-nature.

EXPERIENTIAL EXPERIMENTS

The best way to gain understanding of the *I Ching* is of course to use it: to use it in a concentrated and systematic fashion. Some have experimented with consulting it every day—in the morning, with a period of meditation, asking not a specific question, but simply requesting a reading for that day—and attempting to actually practice the advice of the hexagram during the day. This latter is important since it heightens awareness of some of the obstacles and resistances to the practice, and this can provide valuable insights.

Keeping a record of the readings obtained, together with the questions asked, is valuable in that somethimes, months later, patterns of change in inner development are discernible, which at the time of the reading were quite obscure. For instance the man in the example of the couple given above discovered certain aspects of the significance of the readings only on writing this chapter, over a year after the events described occurred.

For me, the important breakthrough in my appreciation of the *I Ching* came when I was willing to approach the oracle with a question that really mattered. At first I felt silly, asking an old Chinese book about major life decisions; our so-called scientific education and false notions of who we really are prevent us from recognizing that maybe our mind isn't the best instrument in the world for arriving at truth. But if we are willing to make the experiment and ask, in all humility, a genuine question, the most surprising responses will be forthcoming. It helps to approach the *I Ching* not as a book, but as a being of superior wisdom. I actually say, inwardly, "Dear *I Ching*, please shed light on the following situation or question." After all, we are *not* consulting a book, but rather using a specially constructed verbal computer to gain access to our higher selves. And the higher self *is* a being of superior insight into our situation or question. Approached in this way, with reverence and receptive contemplation, it sometimes provides guidelines for persons embarking on psychedelic explorations. The images and texts obtained can be written down or tape recorded and reread or listened to during the trip. This will assuredly provide insight into the multileveled meanings of the images and perhaps trigger off an experience of the essence.

Specific meditation on the eight trigrams is very helpful. Using both the polarized Sequence of Earlier Heaven and the cyclical Sequence of Later Heaven, as *yantras* or meditation maps, one inwardly becomes each of the trigrams. In other words, we treat them as symbols for states of consciousness and feel what it is like to be Ch'ien, the creative, male, dynamic force; and K'un, the receptive, female, magnetic force; and the balance of Ch'ien and K'un, the great axis (*t'ai chi*) of polar energies. We become Li, the lucid, fiery, light of the sun; and K'an, the watery, enveloping, lunar energy; and the balance of Li and K'an. Then we become Chên, the arousing, electric thunder that incites movement within and shakes loose psychic rigidities; and Sun, the gently penetrating energy that moves like wind through trees; and we experience the harmonious interplay of Chên, the firm, and Sun, the yielding. Finally, we enter into Tui, which reflects pure joy, like a mountain lake in autumn; and Kên, the principle of stillness; and we feel the mutual attraction of the feminine Tui and the masculine Kên. A similar meditation sequence can be constructed for the seasonal progression, from Chên (Spring), the sign in which "God comes forth," through Li (Summer), Tui (Autumn), and K'an (Winter), to Kên, the sign in which "God brings all things to completion."

Having gone through meditations of this sort, we gain an experiential *sense* for these symbols, which mere verbal reading and intellectual grasp cannot produce. A similar approach can be used when a hexagram is obtained in a reading: that is, one internalizes the sense of the component primary and nuclear trigrams and then looks at the original question from a perspective attuned to the cosmic, inner cycles of transformation.

Having reached this point in the writing of this chapter, I decided to leave the final word to the *I Ching* itself. I therefore consulted it with due reverence and ceremony, using the coin method, and asked it to help me make a final suggestion or comment to the reader of this book. I obtained hexagram 46, ䷭ , Shêng, PUSHING UPWARD, with a 9 in the third place and a 6 at the top; the future-probable development therefore is hexagram 4, ䷃ , Mêng, YOUTHFUL FOLLY. The text of hexagram 46 reads: "Pushing upward has supreme success. One must see the great man. Fear not. Departure toward the south brings good fortune." "PUSHING UPWARD" is translated "ascending" in John Blofeld's version, which better suggests what I take to be the import of this message from the Book of Changes: ascend in consciousness, grow.

The component trigrams are Sun, ☴ , the gentle, wind, wood, below; and K'un, ☷ , the pure receptive, earth, above. Thus we have the image of a tree growing up out of the earth. "Adapting itself to obstacles and bending around them, wood in the earth grows upward without haste and without rest," says the commentator. The tree has always played a major role in systems of evolutionary growth of consciousness, symbolizing upward growth with inner direction. The Higher Self is receptive to this upward motion. "One must see the great man. Fear not," indicates that it is advisable to look for a teacher, someone who can help us overcome our fears. "Departure toward the south brings good fortune," says to me that to actually take the step of moving upward with inner direction and to look for the wise teacher will meet with fulfillment. The two moving lines reinforce this message: "One pushes upward into an empty city," *i.e.*, apparent obstructions fall away. And "Pushing upward in darkness, it furthers one to be unremittingly persevering," *i.e.*, even though the

way is obscure, perseverance still furthers growth.

The future-probability reading, hexagram 4, YOUTHFUL FOLLY, at first sight suggests I might be making a mistake. But even though it may be a sign of youthful folly on my part to try to interest readers in the *I Ching*, yet, "YOUTHFUL FOLLY has success. It is not I who seek the young fool; the young fool seeks me. At the first oracle I inform him. If he asks two or three times, it is importunity. If he importunes, I give him no information. Perseverance furthers." The message here is that I have already been answered in the first hexagram. The answer is clear and further questioning is unnecessary and will lead to no further insight. I will therefore drop the matter here. If the reader wishes to pursue it further, I leave it to him to ponder the meaning of the nuclear trigrams thunder (Chên) and lake (Tui).

The counsel, which, in the *I Ching*, runs like Ariadne's guiding thread through the mazelike intricacies of the fabric of life's changes, may justly be quoted here: "Perseverance furthers. No blame." Change is the one constant in both constructive and destructive processes; there is change for growth and development and change for decay and degeneration. The choice is ours.

NOTES AND REFERENCES

1. Richard Wilhelm and Cary F. Baynes, trans., *The I Ching or Book of Changes*, 3rd. ed. (Princeton: Princeton University Press, Bollingen Series XIX, 1967). Of the existing English-language versions of the *I Ching*, the Richard Wilhelm translation is the one most widely used and will be most often referred to here. It is recognized as an outstanding translation. The more recent version translated directly from the Chinese by John Blofeld, *The Book of Change* (London: Allen & Unwin; New York: E. P. Dutton, 1965), is much briefer because it omits the philosophical commentaries entirely and restricts itself to elucidating the practical use of the *I Ching* in divination. Blofeld is a distinguished orientalist with both experiential and scholarly knowledge of Zen, Tantras, and Taoism. His version has much to recommend it and his introduction and explanatory chapters are especially admirable. There is also a much older

English version by James Legge, *The Yi King.* vol. 16, *Sacred Books of the East* (Oxford: Clarendon Press, 1899), and a very recent version by Gia-fu Feng, published by Macmillan in 1969.

2. Carl Jung, "In Memory of Richard Wilhelm," appendix to *The Secret of the Golden Flower: A Chinese Book of Life,* trans. Richard Wilhelm, trans. from the German by Cary F. Baynes, rev. ed. (New York: Harcourt, Brace & World, 1962), p. 148.

3. *Ibid.,* p. 148.

4. *Ibid.,* p. 143.

5. José Arguëlles, "Compute and Evolve," *Main Currents in Modern Thought* 25, no. 3 (1969): 4.

6. R. Buckminster Fuller, *Operating Manual for Spaceship Earth* (Carbondale, Ill.: Southern Illinois University Press, 1969), p. 63.

7. Many versions of the *Tao Tê Ching* exist. The quotations used here represent an amalgam of several translations.

8. George W. Beadle, "The New Genetics: The Threads of Life," *Encyclopedia Britannica Yearbook 1964,* pp. 44–72.

9. Wilhelm, trans., *Secret of the Golden Flower.*

10. The astrology and numerology of the *I Ching* is intricate and probably much distorted in the versions that have come down to us. Suffice it to say that the numbers used in designating the lines (6, 7, 8, and 9), as well as the details of the yarrow stalk oracle are intimately related to ancient Chinese astronomy-astrology, which used a month reckoned from the phases of the moon, and a circle of twenty-eight *hsiu* (asterisms). See Rupert Gleadow, *The Origin of the Zodiac* (New York: Atheneum, 1969), especially the chapter on "The Zodiac in China." Chinese astronomy also had a division of the sky into four palaces, corresponding to the four seasons and elements: the Green Dragon (Spring, wood); the Red Bird (Summer, fire); the White Tiger (Autumn, metal); and the Black Tortoise (Winter, earth). Lāma Anagarika Govinda, the eminent Buddhist scholar and commentator on Tibetan philosophy, has told me that it is possible to obtain from the *I Ching* a hexagram that corresponds to the date and year of one's birth; a kind of life-reading. He did not however disclose the method of doing this, indicating only that it involves analyzing the geometric pattern made by the sequences of hexagrams; and that this geometric problem can be solved only when it is recognized that two of the hexagrams are in the wrong place as presently arranged.

11. Wilhelm, in *The Secret of the Golden Flower,* pp. 17–18.

12. John Blofeld, *The Book of Change,* p. 15.

TANTRA

The Exaltation of Experience

*He who realizes the truth of the body
can then come to know
the truth of the universe.*

RATNASARA TANTRA

THE SANSKRIT WORD TANTRA, LIKE THE Chinese word *ching*, is related to the concepts of weaving, thread or fabric, hinting at the ecological interrelatedness of phenomena, at an extended, all-inclusive point of view. For millennia it was (and is) the concern of Indian philosophy and *yoga* methods to extract oneself from the subtle web of illusion (*māyā*) spun by sense experience. With the psychoreligious movement known as *tantra*, which began in the third and fourth centuries A.D. and spread through all the various Indian subcultures and religions over a period of a thousand years, there is a distinct shift of emphasis. The earliest tantric writers are outspokenly antiacademic and antiascetic. To obtain "self-realization" they advocate a practical, experimental approach, rather than a philosophical one, and they ridicule the practitioners who concern themselves with clothes, diet, and the like. "If only the naked attain liberation, the dog and the fox would also attain it; . . . if the eating of grass ensures liberation, why should not elephants and horses be liberated?" [1] asks one author; and another enjoins: "Do not cast away the five objects of desire and do not inflict strain on the body through penance; try to attain *bodhi* ["perfect knowledge"] in a pleasant way by following the injunction of the science of esoteric yoga." [2]

The Upanishadic strategy of realizing the immanent self by successively stripping away the various false conceptions and perceptions of self that arise in meditation (*neti, neti*, "not this," "not that"), had become distorted and perverted into practices that denied the body, rejected sense experience, and idealized penance and suffering. The *tantras* set up a powerful counter-current to this ascetic tradition by affirming and glorifying the role of the body and of sense experience, and by teaching that although ordinarily they were obstacles to realization, when transformed through the esoteric practices of tantric *yoga* they become the very vehicles of liberation.

Thus, "In the *Hevajra-tantra* we find that the Lord [Bhagavan] was asked by a Bodhisattva whether there was any necessity at all of this physical world and the physical body, everything being in reality nothing but pure void. To this the reply of the Lord was that without the body there was no possibility of the realization of the great bliss and here lies the importance of the body." [3] Indeed one can observe in the philosophical formulations of the Buddhists subtle but profound changes as they experienced the influence of the tantric way. The concept of *nirvāna* was used to designate the supreme goal in the earlier schools of Buddhism: it encompasses the ideas of cessation (of the cycles of death and birth), extinction (of the flames of desire and impulses), release, tranquillity, and peace. The Buddha himself however refused to discuss its attributes. In the *tantras* we find the supreme goal referred to more usually as "great bliss" (*mahāsukha*), a very different notion indeed, and there are extensive passages in tantric literature describing various stages and levels of bliss.

Similarly, the concept of "voidness" (*sunyata*), regarded as the supreme reality underlying all phenomena whatsoever, is much less emphasized in the tantric forms of Buddhism; instead we find more emphasis placed on the notion of *vajra*, which means both "thunderbolt," suggesting creative energy, and "diamond," suggesting indestructibility. It has also been translated as "adamantine essence." "*Sunyata*, which is firm, substantial, indivisible, impenetrable, incapable of being burnt and imperishable, is called the *Vajra*," says one tantric text.[4] The term *vajra* led to the designation *Vajra-yāna*, "diamond (or thunderbolt) path," for the tantric, experiential branch of Buddhism. While the *Hīna-yāna*,

"lesser path," monastic schools of Southern Buddhism taught that one should merely try to reach *nirvāna* and then leave the body, the *Mahā-yāna*, "greater path" school of Northern Buddhism, which inspired Zen in China and Japan, introduced the procedure in which the *Bodhisattva* (candidate for Buddhahood) takes a vow to return to earth and postpones his final "release" until all beings have been enlightened.

The *Vajrayāna* then is the tantric adaptation of *Mahāyāna* Buddhism, also known, especially in Tibet, as the "direct path," or "the path of seeing," or "the path of attaining liberation in one lifetime." There is also a Hindu *tantra*, and there are interesting differences between the two systems, as well as many similarities; and much argument among scholars, which need not concern us here, as to which came first.

Mircea Eliade has pointed out that "Tantrism served as the vehicle by which a large number of foreign and exotic elements made their way into Hinduism [and Buddhism] . . . exotic rites and beliefs are clearly discernible in it." [5] In addition, he argues that Gnostic influences from the West cannot be ruled out since "more than one curious parallel can be noted between Tantrism and the great Western mysterio-sophic current that, at the beginning of the Christian era, arose from the confluence of Gnosticism, Hermetism, Greco-Egyptian alchemy, and the traditions of the Mysteries." [6] It must be remembered though, that insofar as *tantra* represented a genuine experimental method for the attainment of higher consciousness, the results it obtained would be similar to those obtained by other genuine systems, and this could explain the curious parallel.

Since the essence of *tantra* is verifiable experience of definite states of consciousness, the methods are not and could not be written down, except again in the form of codes serving as reminders to those initiated in the system. The genuine teachings were secret, that is, transmitted orally from teacher to student, both because they would be incomprehensible to uninitiated people, and because if practiced without the guidance of a teacher they could be dangerous. The existing tantric texts concern themselves principally with the general philosophy behind the methods, and with what we have earlier called external aids. Thus there are lengthy and elaborate descriptions of meditation rituals and rites of various kinds. In particular, the external aids developed by the tantric yoga-psychologists were *yantras*, geometrical designs used for the transformation of visual sense experience through visualization exercises; *mantras*, for the transformation of auditory sense experience through exercises with the power of sound; and *mudras*, for the transformation of bodily experience through the channeling of energies by means of special postures and gestures. In addition, *maithuna*, or ritualized sexual union, played an important part in certain branches of the Hindu *tantras*, leading to endless misunderstanding and disapproval on the part of both Eastern and Western commentators under the influence of taboo conditioning factors.

Tantric psychology

Tantric psychology begins where modern Western psychologies such as those of Whilhelm Reich and Carl Jung leave off. Recognizing the importance of the body and understanding the principle of the union of opposites (*yuganaddha*), the avowed purpose of tantric *sādhanā* (practice) became "the reunion of the two polar principles within the disciple's own body." [7] We find, with the rise of *tantra* in India, along with other antiascetic tendencies already noted, increasing attention again being given to the feminine, a "sort of religious rediscovery of the mystery of woman." [8] On one level this was expressed in the notion of the union of male and female—*Siva* and *Sakti* among the Hindus, *Prajñā* and *Upāya* among the Buddhists—within the consciousness and within the body. For the body is the microcosm of the macrocosm, and just as the great universe itself is the manifestation of polar opposites, so by uniting the opposites within ourselves we attain to a state of union and at the same time to supreme illumination and knowledge of the universe.

On another level, among certain sects of the Hindu *tantra*, known as "followers of the left-hand path" (*vamacari*), the acceptance of the female took the form of yogic *sādhanā* by couples rather than individuals, and the union of male with female was practiced on both the inner and the outer planes, preferably of course by the woman as well as the man. The left side of the body in *tantra* is the female side, and so *vamacari* has become for some, either in reality or in fantasy, the designation of those who indulge in practices that are perhaps "not right," particularly the use of meat, wine, and sex in a ritual worship context. A deeper interpretation of this term was given to me in conversation with the late Srī Krishna Prem, an Englishman who had made a profound, lifelong study of the Hindu yogas and *tantras*. The left hand is our undeveloped hand, our more unconscious aspect; and so the *vamacari* represents the strategy of developing one's weakest function in order to bring about integration; a strategy we find especially emphasized by the Sūfis and by Gurdjieff.

In the highly stratified social system of India, philosophic and religious ideas and movements always appeared in many different forms and on different levels of abstractness, according to the level of education and understanding. What was conceived of as highly recondite philosophy by learned scholars and brahmins, or as psycho-physiological energy systems by practicioners of tantric *yoga*, was symbolized for the popular understanding in terms of the innumerable deities of the Hindu pantheon. Thus we have the mythic trinity of Brahma, (the Creator), Siva (the Transformer), and Vishnu (the Preserver) each with their female counterparts, represented as the personified supreme forces. Yet for some groups, Vishnu is the supreme deity (as in the *Bhagavad Gītā*); or Siva is regarded as the highest, manifesting both creative and destructive energy; or, as in Bengal to the present day, the supreme deity is Kali, the Black Mother, She who has given birth to all three deities, the creative-destructive womb of the worlds, nourishing with one hand, destroying with the other.

Siva, as Lord of Yogis, as He who dances uni-

Siva Ardhanarisvara.

Siva Trimurti, *from cave temple at Elephanta.*

verses in a ring of fire, is the preferred personification of the Hindu tantrics. Universally, when shown with his *Sakti*, his female counterpart, she is on the left, he on the right, and very often, their hands are, through *mudrās*, expressing higher feeling states or aspects of the relationship between male and female polarities. In one iconographic version of the *Siva-Sakti* principle, the so-called *Siva Ardhanarisvara*, the psychophysiologic bisexuality of the *tantras* is made explicit in that the body of the statue is hermaphroditic: male on the right and female on the left. The bisexuality referred to here has

nothing to do with the sexual behavior preferences sometimes denoted by that term since the physical body is not literally hermaphroditic and natural sexual consciousness is polarized according to the male or female structure of the body. The sculptured *Siva-Sakti* and *Siva Ardhanarisvara* represent in three-dimensional form a multidimensional polarity aspect of the human being. It is the organizing force field of the body, which is polarized male-right and female-left, and this is what the dual or single statues are indicating.

An even more basic symbolism, prevalent

throughout India, is the upright *lingam* encircled by the *yoni* at its base. *Lingam* and *yoni* are the Indian Sivaite equivalent to *yang* and *yin,* male-female creative tension. Ananda K. Coomaraswamy has written: "The fiery *lingam* is a form of the Axis Mundi, and can be equated with the shaft of light or lightning (*vajra, keraunos*) that penetrates and fertilizes the *yoni,* the altar, the Earth, the mother of Fire—for 'light is the progenitive power': in the older Christian nativities it is represented by the Ray that extends from the Sun above to the interior of the cave in which the Earth-goddess bears her Son." [9] Using an analogy from the language of physics we could say here that the vertical flow of electric force represented by the *lingam* is associated with a circular magnetic force field perpendicular to the line of flow, represented by the *yoni.*

In the gigantic cave temple at Elephanta, hewn out of the solid rock on an island in the Bay of Bombay, the *Siva-Lingam,* in a monumental square shrine with entrances on the four sides guarded by huge divine doorkeepers, is the central sanctuary of the temple, "emanating to the four quarters its all-productive energy." Around the sides of the rock-hewn cave are sculpted reliefs of the several aspects of *Siva,* but one in particular stands out, consisting only of three overpoweringly huge faces. One, facing right, is masculine, virile, dynamic, with twirling mustache; the second, facing left, is feminine, softly rounded, with full lips; the third and central head faces out, yet it is oriented inwardly—the eyes closed, it is absorbed in the meditative process of fusing and merging the two opposing aspects—still, yet charged with tremendous power, immovable, yet all-encompassing. It is the neutral, transcendent consciousness, which enters into the male or female polar aspect, but does not become involved; it is their source and support, but it does not act in the drama. This carving is a matchless symbol of the threefold unity.

In the Tibetan Buddhist iconography, the union of opposites is presented in painting and sculpture as father-mother (*Yab-Yum*) deities locked in such close embrace that it is virtually impossible to tell which of the many arms belongs to whom. When I first encountered this form of art, I was irritated at the apparent lack of clarity until I realized that this fusion to the point of indistinguishable form is precisely the experience the Tibetan tantric artists were trying to convey. "When through the *yogic* process one enters into the state of supreme bliss (*mahā-sukha*), the whole world becomes of the form of unique emotion in the nature of *Mahā-sukha,* and through this unique emotion of bliss the whole world as static and dynamic becomes one." [10]

It is helpful in understanding the extraordinary art of the *tantras* to remember that this is not merely symbolic art, but that it also represents actual psychophysiological experiences. Thus, the *Yab-Yum* statues are not merely a symbol for the union of *Prajñā,* "knowledge," the female principle, and *Upāya,* "compassion," the active male principle, but they also depict actual inner experiences of the uniting dynamic and magnetic forces within the microcosmic body. The presence of many arms on the deities is not just a symbol for the many powers of the enlightened beings, it is a literal representation of the arms of the many bodies of the human being.

The notion that man actually has several bodies or sheaths of different density or vibratory rate which interpenetrate one another was well known to yogis and tantrics. "These 'sheaths,' therefore, are not separate layers, . . . but rather in the nature of mutually penetrating forms of energy, from the finest 'all-radiating,' all-pervading, luminous consciousness down to the densest form . . . which appears before us as our visible, physical body. The correspondingly finer or subtler sheaths penetrate, and thus contain, the grosser ones." [11]

We have noted in the Introduction how many of the sensitives interviewed by Dr. Karagulla are able to see one or several of these sheaths, as fine networks of lines of light extending through and around the physical body. This idea of man having inner bodies of successively

Tibetan Yab-Yum *(father-mother) figure, representing multidimensional ecstatic inner union.*

finer and finer substances within the physical body is found in esoteric Christianity, in occult philosophy and theosophy, in Gurdjieff, and in Actualism, where it is explained on the basis of different frequency rates. These bodies can be experienced consciously when they are awakened, which is possible with certain yogic methods. The many armed deities of the Hindus and Buddhists can, I think, best be understood from this point of view.

The concept of the microcosmic nature of man is basic to the *tantras,* as it is to all so-called occult psychologies and philosophies. It is precisely because man is a cosmos on a small scale that it is possible to attain to knowledge of the large-scale cosmos by methods of internal observation. Modern science is beginning to recognize something of this in the idea of "scales of nature": there are, after all, no departments of chemistry and physics in Nature, and we, as human beings, conform to and exemplify, within our own nature, all the laws and principles that science studies by external means. We are collections of atoms, molecular aggregates, groups of cells organized into organs to perform specialized functions. We recapitulate in the uterus the evolutionary history of man from the single cell to the completed body. And recent research on the molecular basis of memory, on information transfer by RNA molecules, certainly makes the possibility of evolutionary consciousness not wildly remote.[12]

In Gurdjieff the concept of scales of nature is further developed when he compares the relationship between levels or scales to the relationship between octaves of different pitch: though the frequency (pitch) is different, the ratios of frequencies (intervals) are the same; though the absolute magnitudes of atomic phenomena and cosmic phenomena are vastly different, the patterns of relationships are similar. The atom with its concentric rings of electrons orbiting the nucleus is a miniature sun with its orbiting planets and satellites. "As above, so below" were the words of the great initiate Hermes Trismegistos. And man, standing midway between the microscopic and the telescopic worlds, is the mediator of heaven and earth. This is why ancient Indian sages were able to determine the lengths of various cosmic cycles with such accuracy that their figures correspond with the best modern calculations. "What is here is elsewhere. What is not here, is nowhere" (*Vishvasara Tantra*).

Although in the later tantric theories the identification of man's physiology with different aspects of the cosmos was carried to fantastic lengths, let us consider here merely some of the basic concepts. The body, or bodies, has a central axis, just as the planet has an axis. "Imagine the central part (or spinal-column) of thy body to be Mt. Meru [the world axis]," begins one Tibetan visualization exercise.[13] Along this axis are arranged various centers of force, known as *cakras,* literally "wheels" or "discs." The *cakras* are not physiologic organs, rather they are "the points in which psychic forces and bodily functions merge into each other or penetrate each other. They are the focal points in which cosmic and psychic energies crystallize into bodily qualities, and in which bodily qualities are dissolved or transmuted again into psychic forces." [14] The sensitives interviewed by Shafica Karagulla recorded observations of centers along the vertical axis of the vital field, these centers being in the form of vortices of energy. The vortices had smaller cone-shaped vortices ranged around them, the point of the cone oriented inward.[15] This yields a picture not unlike the tantric yogi's image of the *cakra* as a lotus blossom with different numbers of petals ranged around it.

The notion of energy centers in the organism is not fashionable in current academic physiology, though individual scientists have here and there made observations leading to related concepts. Thus Robert O. Becker and associates at the State University of New York Medical Center, in their studies of d. c. (direct current) potentials in amphibians and man, observed that "a complex electrical field was found, . . . and its spatial configuration was noted to bear a close relationship to the gross anatomic arrangement of the central nervous system. Positive areas were located over the cellular aggregates of the neuraxis (cranial, brachial, and lumbar) with increasing negative potentials along the peripheral nerve outflows from each." [16] In his studies of the distribution and damming up of energy flow in man and in single cells, Wilhelm Reich was led to postulate a "functional antithesis between center and periphery" in biological organisms. Growth processes were found to be associated with energy radiating from the center to the periphery, so that in a longitudinal body such as the human, the flow of energy proceeds through a number of different "segments," *i.e.*, ocular, oral, thoracic, lumbar, sacral, and can be dammed up or blocked at one or more of these segments.[17]

Both of these researchers thus made observations of energy polarity phenomena occurring between the center and the periphery of the body. In the *tantras,* the centers and axis refer not only to the physiological organism but also to the total ensemble of man's bodies and fields. What we would call the "field-force lines" were referred to by the tantrics as *nādīs,* a vastly intricate network of current carriers extending throughout and around the physical body, paralleling the nervous system but not identical with it. The three principal *nādīs* were *sushumnā,* the central vertical axis; *idā,* the negatively charged, lunar current; and *pingalā,* the positively charged, solar current. "According to the tradition, *idā* and *pingalā* are represented as two spirals, starting from the left and right nostril respectively, and moving in opposite directions around *sushumnā-nādī,* . . . meeting in the perineum at the base of the spine." [18]

Again, it is interesting to note that although Western physiology does not recognize these subtle bodies, a similar threefold functional division exists on the biological-anatomic level: the nerves mediating voluntary movements and external perception are channeled through the spinal cord; those mediating the involuntary, instinctual-emotional processes and internal perceptions, are channeled through the autonomic or vegetative nervous system; the two branches of this system, known as parasympathetic and sympathetic, or more simply, the negative and positive systems, are involved in mutually antagonistic yet functionally complementary processes of excitation and inhibition.

The association of *idā* and *pingalā* with moon and sun is not as fanciful as it might at first seem when we consider that our relationship to those two cosmic bodies is in fact polarized in an analogous way. The sun radiates positive energy in the form of heat and light, which stimulate, nourish, and sustain life processes on earth. The moon, by contrast, acts like a magnet; it has no radiation of its own, but it draws the huge masses of earth's liquids toward it in daily tides. Since we are 70 percent liquid it has an understandably profound effect on our consciousness, on our cells, organs, bodies, feelings, and thoughts. Experientially, in looking at the moon, we often feel a magnetic attraction, a female-related force which renders animals and poets "moonstruck"; by contrast, the radiating force of the sun is such that we cannot look at it at all.

Part of the esoteric practice of the tantric psychologists undoubtedly consisted of increasing one's awareness of the psychophysical field by amplifying energy flow through the *nādīs.* Eliade states that "the texts insistently repeat that, in the uninitiate, the *nādīs* have become 'impure,' that they are 'obstructed' and must be 'purified.'" [19] When purified and awakened, they become exquisitely tuned conductors of ecstatic energy. "She (one of the *nadis*) is beautiful like a chain of lightning and fine like a (lotus) fibre, and shines in the minds of the sages. She is extremely subtle; the awakener of pure knowledge, the embodiment of all Bliss, whose true nature is pure Consciousness." [20]

In all Indian *yoga* systems, both classical and tantric, the importance of the physical and breathing exercises of *Hatha Yoga* [literally: sun-moon union, from *ha* (sun), *tha* (moon), and *yog* (union)] is emphasized since they provide the necessary strengthening of the body without which it cannot tolerate the experiences produced by the *sādhanā.* "Unless the body is made ripe through the practice of *hatha yoga,* the supreme realization . . . becomes a lulling sleep of the senses or something like a swoon." [21]

It is my impression, from personal observation, that many users of large doses of psychedelic substances are having experiences of this sort, since their bodies are not prepared for the magnification of higher frequency energies; so that apart from certain optic phenomena and conceptual insights, the person actually becomes, for longer or shorter periods of time, unconscious. Often he will not be able to give any account at all of long stretches of the experience, or he will use expressions such as "wiped out," or "stoned," suggestive of a quasihypnotic sleep state.

The union of male and female polar energies within the adepts' own bodies—such is the goal of tantric *yoga*, through which great bliss (*mahāsukha*) is realized and supreme illumination attained. But how is this to be done? On the details of the method, the texts are either silent, or deliberately obscure, employing a language of paradox and flowery metaphor. The reason for this is not only to protect the uninitiated from the dangers that might arise through the practice of these techniques without a teacher, but also to protect the method from the misunderstanding that would and does arise when it is described without being shown. I know from my own personal experience that when I was told of certain techniques of *Agni Yoga* by someone who was not a teacher and attempted to practice them, no result ensued; I was consequently disappointed and lost interest. When I was later shown the technique by the teacher who was able to amplify its effects for initial perception, very definite results occurred.

In general, it may be said that one aspect of the union of plus and minus energies is the centralizing of the currents flowing through *idā* and *pingalā*, the left and right *nādīs;* and another aspect is the harmonizing of "higher" and "lower" centers. "We are dealing here, in other words, with the integration of a double polarity, which presents itself on the one hand as 'right' and 'left,' *i.e.*, as solar and lunar forms of *prāna* on the human or mundane plane—and on the other hand as 'above' and 'below,' *i.e.*, as immaterial and material forms of *akasa* (ether) on the 'vertical axis' of cosmic-spiritual realm. This integration is experienced in successive stages,

namely in successive *cakras,* of which each represents a different dimension of consciousness, and in which each higher dimension includes the lower one without annihilating its qualities." [22]

There is no space here to enter into a discussion or description of the different *cakras,* especially as there is much disagreement in the literature on the number and significance of *cakras.* It is a widely popularized notion that the key process in tantric *yoga* is the raising of the *kundalinī* ("serpent fire") from its latent position at the base of the spine, upward through the *cakras* to the top of the brain. Careful reading of the published texts, however, indicates to me that this is both oversimplified and probably misleading. The techniques described, in works such as Lāma Govinda's *Foundations of Tibetan Mysticism,* and W. Y. Evans-Wentz's *Tibetan Yoga and Secret Doctrines,* indicate careful work principally with the vibratory power of certain sounds and with *tūmmō* ("inner fire"), on establishing correct relationships between the various centers. This is done, with the help of a guru, in the context of a definite manner of working so that the body becomes the instrument and means through which Higher Self can accomplish the purposes for which it entered into incarnation. Simply to try to raise the *kundalinī,* or open the *cakras,* divorced from the purposeful context of evolutionary growth, and rather as a way of attaining power or higher perception without the necessary purification of the bodies and *nādīs,* can be both pointless and hazardous. Persons with prematurely opened *cakras* can be found in mental hospitals. I know personally at least one individual who succeeded, with LSD, in raising *kundalinī* to the brain, and was quite the opposite of pleased with the outcome.

According to Gurdjieff,

none of the known theories gives the right explanation of the force of Kundalini. Sometimes it is connected with sex, with sex energy, that is with the idea of the possibility of using sex energy for other purposes. This latter is entirely wrong because Kundalini can be in anything. And above all, Kundalini is not anything desirable or useful for man's

Yantras *from the Hindu tantric tradition.*

Tibetan mandala *showing twelve zodiac animals and the eight trigrams of the* I Ching, *surrounded by the fiery Wheel of Time* (Kalacakra).

development. . . . In reality Kundalini is the power of imagination, the power of fantasy, *which takes the place of a real function.* When a man dreams instead of acting, when his dreams take the place of reality, when a man imagines himself to be an eagle, a lion, or a magician, it is the force of Kundalini acting in him. Kundalini can act in all centers and with its help all the centers can be satisfied with the imaginary instead of the real.[23]

The confusion surrounding the functions of the *cakras* and the role of *kundalini* afford a good illustration of a process that has happened to all genuine teachings of evolutionary growth: concepts and symbols that are originally related to certain definite experiences encountered in the process of inner work with a teacher, become, in the hands of persons who do not have those experiences because they are not engaged in the inner work, distorted and fantastically deviated from their original sense. Subsequent academic commentators and translators who know only the language and not the methods or the work, only compound the distortion. The situation is not unlike what would happen if we didn't know anything about flying, nor even that flying was possible, and we found an aircraft operating manual and tried to interpret it. Not having either the equivalent terms in our own language, nor the structures and functions of the aircraft to which the terms refer, the results could only be hopeless confusion. And it would be harmless confusion, if it weren't for the fact that the aircraft in this instance is the human organism, and misinterpretations can be made which are hazardous to health and obstructive to growth.

Tools of transformation

The union of solar and lunar energies, the integration of higher and lower functions, the harmonizing and balancing of the *cakras*, the purification of *nādīs,* are expressions referring to processes of inner work. In addition, the tantric researchers devoted much attention to the integration of inner and outer, and particularly to the transmutation of sensory experience from a binding to a liberating role, through visual (*yantra*), auditory (*mantra*), and postural-gestural (*mudra*) means.

A *yantra* literally means "a tool or instrument serving to hold," that is, a diagram designed to hold the attention during meditation and support the practitioner's effort to maintain concentration, or one-pointedness, while practicing a particular technique. Some *yantras* are in the form of geometric designs, often interlaced triangles superimposed on flower-type designs with varying number of petals, usually framed by a square with "doors" at the four sides. The colors and forms would be understood by the meditator as referring to definite aspects of the method; just as the colors and shapes on a road map are understood to refer to definite features of the landscape such as rivers and towns.

Mandalas are circular *yantras* developed to a particularly high art form by the Tibetan Buddhists. They may be regarded as externalizations of the state of wholeness, the center point of creative energy, and the series of stages through which the center is reached and integration attained. Carl Jung observed that patients who were beginning to integrate fragmented psychic components into a totality, would spontaneously, without having any knowledge of Tantric Buddhism, begin to see simple *mandala*-type forms in their dreams. This led Jung to formulate the notion that the *mandala* is an "archetype of psychic integration."

Tibetan Buddhists made the process, which in Jung's patients operated unconsciously, into a conscious deliberate method. The *mandala* becomes a chart for a gradually unfolding series of visualization exercises. To the initiate, the *mandala* is a map of a series of stages by which an experience of wholeness-unity is reached. Thus, for example, the outer border of the *mandala* usually consists of three concentric rings: the outermost ring of fire, to purify by burning away false concepts; a ring of *vajra*, "diamond-thunderbolts," to indicate indestructible essence-consciousness; and a ring of lotus petals, to indicate opening of the psyche to the light of wisdom. Then there are frequently areas, called "cemeteries," in which the sloughed-off aspects and fragments of ego-consciousness are depicted

Tibetan painting showing fierce Buddha in Yab-Yum embrace with female consort, expressing consuming fire aspect of tantric yoga.

dead and dying; and there is usually a massive square with four entrances on the sides, each often guarded by fierce images of divinities.

The role of the demonic and ferocious Buddha images in Tibetan Lāmaism can be understood as externalizations of the consuming fire power necessary for the destruction (de-structuring) of the false, personality-bound concepts and emotional factors obstructing the path to enlightenment. In order to combat the terrifying images produced by his own "unconscious," the initiate must himself become equally ferocious, like one of the flame-surrounded, blood-drinking, weapon-wielding, eyes-bulging, demon-crushing, multi-headed, many-armed images of the *mandala*. Paradoxically, there are often fierce figures who are also in *yab-yum* embrace with their female consort, indicating clearly that they represent breaking-through forces on the way to integration. At the outer edges of the flame-filled aura (or field) of these warrior Buddhas one will often find small grotesque puppet-like figures falling off and away: these represent the false-to-fact images that are eliminated in the consuming fires and are sloughed off like worn-out masks.

The meditator thus identifies himself with the figures on the *mandala* to induce a certain state of consciousness by a kind of resonance process. Having entered the square sanctuary, there are often more Buddha figures, sometimes four or eight emanating out from a central one, again representing different aspects of the nature of the immanent Higher Self on emotional or mental planes of consciousness. The *mudras* made by the figures, their colors, and the symbols they hold would carry definite experiential meanings to the initiate. "By mentally entering the *mandala*, the yogin approaches his own 'center' . . . to reach the center the yogin re-enacts and masters the cosmic process, for the *mandala* is an image of the world . . . and starting from this iconographic 'support' he can find the *mandala* in his own body." [24]

Through the *mandala*, by the creation and dissolution of a visual microcosm, the adept learns to know and understand the processes of the creation and dissolution of forms and images in his own consciousness. [25]

The basic symbolism of the *mandala* is universal, and analogous forms can be found in every religious system, from the stained-glass rosetta windows of the Gothic cathedrals, to the sand paintings of the North American Indians. Among the latter, the circular paintings with multicolored sands (which were always dissolved within twelve hours after use) are oriented specifically toward healing; the patient is placed in the center and the particular symbols and images used are chosen by the initiate medicine man to guide all the senses and forces of the patient's body and soul toward wholeness. "During the ceremony the patient becomes the apex of the whole cosmos, and, amidst the outpouring of living attention, he becomes the center of a circle of prayer." [26]

The symbolism of the Tibetan *mandalas* (particularly those with a fierce image at the center) is also related to the labyrinth, the mazelike city of the interior, which holds at its core the greatest dread, and which the initiate must enter in order to slay and overcome that fear-generating image in his own psyche. Other types of *mandalas* again are more paradisal in character, full of light, joyous beings, harmonious landscapes, sweet colors and forms. Paradise, or as it is sometimes called by the Buddhists, the "Four States of Formless Existence," was regarded as a level of consciousness attainable in meditative practice, but not the highest state (*nirvāna*). "These four states of consciousness, which are among the highest attainable, . . . are reached in *yogic* trance induced by deep meditation. So transcendent are they that the unwisely directed *yogin* is apt to mistake the realization of them for the realization of *Nirvāna*." [27]

Although on one level the *yantras* are technical devices for channeling psychic energy during meditation, they can, and are, of course, also seen on the symbolic or philosophic level. The famous *Srī Yantra*, which consists simply of a set of nine interlaced triangles of different size, five downward pointing and four upward, is probably technically a chart showing a way of balancing the *cakras*. Looking at it philosophically, Heinrich Zimmer wrote:

The nine signify the primitive revelation of the Absolute as it differentiates into graduated polarities, the creative activity of the cosmic male and female energies on successive stages of evolution. . . . The Absolute is to be visualized by the concentrating devotee as a vanishing point or dot, 'the drop' (*bindu*), amidst the interplay of all the triangles. This *bindu* is the power-point, the invisible, elusive center from which the entire diagram expands. And now, whereas four of the triangles link with their . . . counterparts, the fifth, or innermost, remains over, to unite with the invisible point.[28]

One might wonder at the extensive use of visualization techniques in Tantric Hinduism and Buddhism. How does the yogi distinguish between, on the one hand, illusory images (*māyā*) that keep him in bondage through desires and fears to the objects of external perception and that he attempts to destroy or transcend; and, on the other hand, the images of the peaceful and wrathful deities and Buddhas that he visualizes and identifies with, and that guide him in the process of meditation? It is precisely because the deceptive power of *māyā* is so great that it must be confronted again and again in the work of psychic integration; and because it is so easy to confuse images with reality, and constructive with destructive images, the help of the already awakened man is necessary, for otherwise we have fantasy "taking the place of a real function," as Gurdjieff pointed out. But if the transmutation of these image-producing, enslaving perceptual processes is successful, then, as the tantric texts say: "By the same acts that cause some men to burn in hell for thousands of years, the yogin gains his eternal salvation."[29] Among other aspects, the term *illumination* or *enlightenment*, refers precisely to the ability to see beyond the illusive play of images with the Wisdom of Discrimination associated with the radiant Buddha Amitābha, which discriminates between the "clear light" of unconditioned consciousness and the "dull light" of the six worlds of illusion.

Mantras are devices for tuning and centering auditory perception in such a way that the precise intoning of selected sounds can induce a definite state of consciousness. *Mantra* is the essence of prayer: in prayer, as usually understood in Western and other religions, the symbolic meaning of the words only is considered, whereas in *mantra* the meaning is often irrelevant, or even absent, and the focus for the yogi is on the evocative ("calling-forth") power of the vibratory sound patterns. Thus the classic Indian *mantra OM* has no meaning in the usual sense, yet it contains in a way the whole "ground" and power of the universe. In Indian music the tonic *OM* produced by the tamboura provides continuous undercurrent and support, the source and the returning point, the home base as it were, for the dialogue and interplay between the melodic weavings of the female-magnetic string instrument and the dynamic-male rhythmic activity of the drums. *OM* is like the "carrier wave" of the universe, the all-containing sound, which, when modulated in frequency or amplitude gives us the audible array of localized sources of waves.[30] These we then distinguish into sounds and noises, in the same way we discriminate figure and background in the array of visible sources of light.

The efficacy of sound in evoking feelings and states of consciousness in us is well known to every performer of and listener to music. Almost all music uses this efficacy in an intuitive way. There is no systematic, scientific understanding of the precise relationship between sound and consciousness. The tantrics and other schools of *yoga,* and especially the Islamic Sūfis, attempted to develop such a scientific understanding of the power of sound. The use of the *mantra*, to this day in India the most widely used technique, is based on the idea that the guru knows what particular vibratory pattern is needed by the student for his further growth, and so the *mantra* is handed down in this personal way.

Among the Tantrics, a certain class of *mantras*, known as *bīja,* or "seed," *mantras* assumed special importance. These were not words, but single phonemes such as *HUM, TRAM, PHAT, HRĪH*, which were associated with *cakras* and parts of the subtle bodies, much as the colors and forms of the *yantra*. Considerable use is also made of the Sanskrit or Tibetan letters representing the *mantra* in highly specific processes of inner work.

Here for example is part of an exercise from the *yoga of psychic heat,* one of the *Six Yogas of Naropa:*

Now visualize, clearly as before, thyself as being Sambhāra-chakra, hollow like a blue filmy silk tent, and at the centre of the vacuity the three chief psychic-nerves (*nādīs*), the four chief psychic-nerve centres (or *chakras*), the half-*A,* and the letter *HAM* as vividly defined. The vital-force setteth the half-*A* aflame; and, by the heat thus engendered, the letter *HAM* is melted and the drops of it fall on the half-*A*. With a crackling sound, the flame quickly moveth downward; and then, with increased burning force, it reacheth the navel nerve-centre. The letter *HAM* being very much melted, the drops of it falling downward, cause the flame to increase in intensity till it reacheth the heart nerve-centre, then the throat nerve-centre, then the brain nerve-centre. Finally, the flow of the completely melted letter *HAM* descends to the nerve-centre of the throat and completely permeateth it; and thereby is experienced 'Bliss of Delight,' or physical blissfulness.[31]

In other words, the sounds and the physical shape of the letters representing the sounds are here being used as anchoring devices for the movements of consciousness during meditative practice.

Srī Yantra.

During the course of training, the *mantras* become associated in the student's mind with particular centers, *nādīs*, or energies, as well as with the Buddhas or divinities personifying various aspects of higher consciousness planes. They thus come to play a role in the mapping of consciousness analogous to the role played by mathematical formulae in the mapping of the physical world.[32] If the meditator then is able to concentrate his awareness, all the factors associated with the *mantra* will cause his consciousness to modulate and extend in the desired ways.

The *bīja mantra* is not a summary, intellectually, rather, it relates to the unfolding state of consciousness the way a seed relates to an unfolding plant: all the potentialities are contained within, needing only to be awakened. Or, to be more exact: the seed syllable causes the corresponding seed state of consciousness to resonate, which then awakens and unfolds that level of consciousness. And the awakening comes through awareness.

An example of the efficacy of *mantra* may be pertinent. During a period when I was doing considerable experimentation with a short-acting psychedelic called DMT, I used to be frustrated and annoyed by my inability to prevent a kind of hyper-reactivity of the eyes in which I would see repetitive geometric designs with a kind of unpleasant metallic equality to them. An Indian friend taught me the use of the *mantra RAM*, and immediately when I began to use it, the visual phenomena abated and instead a region of light began to form in the area of the throat and heart. It seems the effect of the *mantra* was to center the amplified nervous energy, which had been pointlessly irritating the peripheral visual system, and turn the energy instead to opening up the inner spaces.

The third branch of the method of transforming sense experience is *mudra*, special gestures of the hands which evolved out of the postures (*āsanas*) of *Hatha Yoga*. *Āsanas*, as pointed out before, were designed to strengthen the body and particularly the nervous system so it could tolerate the higher frequency energies which would be received during meditation. From the *āsanas*, which principally involve loosening and realigning the spine and hence the central axis, evolved, particularly among the Tibetan and Japanese Buddhists, a series of ritual gestures that channel energy flow through the body. To the observer they *symbolize* different attitudes and states of feeling; to the practitioner they *express* these attitudes and feeling states.

The classic oriental meditation posture, the cross-legged lotus *āsana*, represents the smallest circle that can be made with the human body and an upright spine; hence the most intense potential energy focussing power. By contrast, in *Agni Yoga*, and, to judge by their art, in the Egyption Mystery Schools, the free flowing of energy through the entire body, including the pelvis and legs, is valued; and so a sitting posture with uncrossed legs is used. This is not to say one posture is better than the other—rather, the purposes are somewhat different.

To illustrate *mudras* let us consider the gestures and attributes of the five so-called Dhyānī Buddhas, who are probably the Tibetan equivalent of the Judaeo-Christian archangels: guardians of paradise or representatives of the paradise states of consciousness. They are arranged

Mudrā *of teaching.*

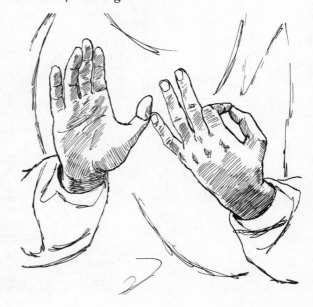

on a four-petalled lotus, each in *Yab-Yum* (father-mother) embrace with his consort. In the *Tibetan Book of the Dead*, the *Bardo Thödol*, they appear as the "peaceful deities" in the second phase of the experience, after the highest, pure white-light phase, has passed. The Dhyāni Buddha of the Center is called "Vairochana": his body is white and he represents the *Dharma-Dhātū*, wisdom of pure, primordial consciousness, also known as the Wisdom of the Universal Law. His *mudra* is one related to his function as teacher of the Law: his two hands are raised to the level of the heart, the right is palm outward, the left makes a circle with thumb and first finger. Thus, the receptive left appropriately holds the Wheel of the Law, while the expressive right allows its energy to stream outward.

Earth-touching mudrā
(adapted for Western sitting).

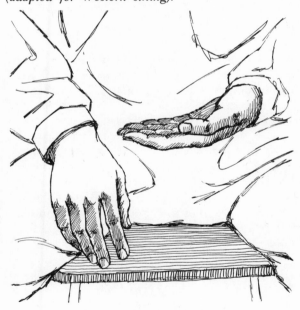

The Dhyāni Buddha of the East is called "Aksobhya"; his body is blue and he represents the Mirrorlike Wisdom of Equality, in which "things are freed from their 'thingness,' their isolation,

without being deprived of their form." [33] His *mudra* is the earth-touching *mudra,* in which the right hand is over the right knee, touching earth with the finger tips, while the left is lying, palm upward, in the lap. The dynamic right-side energy is here grounded: this is the *mudra* allegedly made by Gautama, the historical Buddha, when just before his enlightenment he was challenged to his severest test by Māra, the Lord of Death. "Who are *you,* to seek enlightenment?" asks the Dark Lord; and Gautama's reply was to call the earth to witness, with this *mudra,* that it was not he, the personality, who was seeking the final goal, but rather his Immortal Self, which had devoted many lifetimes preparing for this moment of realization. With that, he was able to maintain the mirrorlike wisdom of impartial perception and be freed from Māra's illusory threats. Experimentally it has been found that this is an excellent *mudra* to use on a bad trip, in moments of fear or turmoil: if the earth-touching gesture of the mirrorlike wisdom is remembered, it will surely help to reestablish contact with the ground.

Mudrā *of giving (adapted).*

The Dhyānī Buddha of the South is called "Ratna-Sambhava," the "jewel-born," whose body is golden yellow like the sun at noon and who exemplifies the Wisdom of Equality, love and compassion for all beings. In his *mudra*, the gesture of giving, the left hand is again resting in the center of the body, while the right is in the same position as before, over the right knee, but the palm is turned out, thumb and forefinger touching. Pure positive feeling radiates forth from the open hand on the right.

Mudrā *of meditation (adapted).*

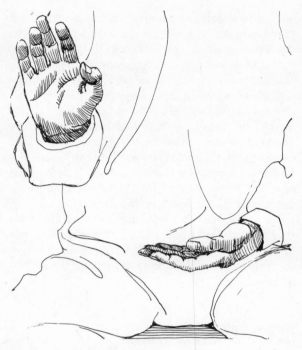

Mudrā *signifying "Fear not."*

The Dhyānī Buddha of the West is called "Amitābha"; his color is red and he is the personification of the Discriminative Wisdom of Inner Vision. His hands rest in his lap, right hand in left, holding a lotus, the *mudra* of pure centering and creative meditation.

The Dhyānī Buddha of the North is "Amogha-Siddhi," whose color is green and who represents the All-Accomplishing Wisdom, the power to act wisely; his double *vajra* symbolizes inward *and* outward oriented spiritual activity. His *mudra* is: left hand receptively centered, and right raised up to the level of the heart, palm

facing out, in a gesture which signifies "Fear not." This again is excellent for nonverbal communication in states where words are inadequate or unacceptable.

Although the specific *mantras* of the Indian tantrics might prove difficult to adapt to the Western mind, one can see that abstract *yantras* and *mudras* are universal enough to allow for use by anyone. And since they are formed, especially the *mudras*, according to the intrinsic, verifiable design of the human organism, and are not arbitrary codes, they could be part of a truly universal, nonverbal language.

The ritual exaltation and transmutation of sense experience in *tantra* is a kind of sacrifice in the original meaning of that term: a "making sacred," *sacer facere*, of that which was not sacred. An activity or process is made sacred when it is done, not for ego-personality, but for Higher Self, for the God within, and for the furthering of the evolutionary process whose goal it is to let the Higher Self be realized more and more through the ego-personality and body. Thus only from the personality's point of view is sacrifice a kind of deprivation, whence it has acquired a negative connotation.

Nowhere is the procedure of making sacred, or performing a sacred ceremony, more charged with both positive and negative emotion than in the area of ritual sexual union, or *maithuna*. This is the attempt to externalize the union of male and female which has first to take place within. Then, from the inner union of the couple, within each one and with each other, they proceed to the outer expression of this union, in a slow, deliberate, ceremonial manner; instead of, as is the usual situation, two separated persons attempting, inevitably vainly or at best very momentarily, to attain union by external physical means. The rite was practiced in stages, only after lengthy preparations to ensure that inner union preceded outer. "The neophyte . . . must approach the 'devout woman' by stages and transform her into a goddess. . . . Thus for the first four months, he should wait upon her like a servant, sleep in the same room with her, then at her feet. During the next four months, while continuing to wait upon her as before, he sleeps in the same bed, on the left side. During a third four months, he will sleep on the right side, then they will sleep embracing, . . . " [34]

The sense and essence of *maithuna* has probably never been more lucidly described than in John Donne's poem *The Ecstasy:*

Where, like a pillow on a bed,
A pregnant bank swelled up, to rest
The violets reclining head,
Sat we two, one anothers best;

Our hands were firmly cemented
With a fast balme, which thence did spring,
Our eye-beams twisted, and did thread
Our eyes, upon one double string;

So to entergraft our hands, as yet
Was all the means to make us one,
And pictures in our eyes to get
Was all our propagation.

As twixt two equal Armies, Fate
Suspends uncertain victory,

Our souls, (which, to advance their state,
Were gone out,) hung 'twixt her, and me.

And while our souls negotiate there,
We like sepulchral statues lay;
All day, the same our postures were,
And we said nothing, all the day. . . .

This ecstasy does unperplex
(We said) and tell us what we love,
We see by this, it was not sex,
We see, we saw not what did move:

But as all several souls contain
Mixture of things, they know not what,
Love, these mixed souls does mix again,
And makes both one, each this and that. . . .

When love, with one another so
Interinanimates two souls,
That abler soul, which thence doth flow,
Defects of loneliness controls.

We then, who are this new soul, know,
Of what we are composed, and made,
For th'atomies of which we grow,
Are souls, whom no change can invade. . . .

So must pure lovers' souls descend
T'affections, and to faculties,
Which sense may reach and apprehend,
Else a great prince in prison lies.

The tantric movement flowered and spread throughout India and neighboring countries during a time when Europe was plunged in the Dark Ages of oppression by religious dogma and feudal power. Later, when Europe's spirit blossomed in the renaissance and enlightenment of science, India sank into a morass of superstition and inertia from which it has still not emerged. Is there some kind of *yin-yang* relationship here?

Interestingly, for centuries, Indian popular religion has known and worshipped only two members of the original trinity, namely Vishnu (more by those with worldly aims) and Siva (by those with spiritual ambitions). Brahma, the Creator, seems to have been forgotten; pundits explain that his creative role is over now, and it's up to the other two. The West, by contrast, has almost exclusively emphasized the

Creator-God, the one who made it all, and has had a very ambiguous relationship to the destroyer-transformer, at times ignoring him altogether, at others grudgingly recognizing his role in the Devil. Vishnu, the All-Quarters Maintainer, is not known at all, except by mystics and students of the occult.

One could argue here that India has made a fundamental mistake in not recognizing the principle of continuous creation: creation is always going on, within and without us, and creative power can be used to solve problems and remove obstacles in the outer and the inner world. The West, playing perfectly its counterpart role, has ignored the archeologist Vishnu, and projected its own destructive tendencies outward onto others, running rampant all over the globe in wanton aggression masquerading as defense. (Note that India has never, in recent centuries, waged a foreign war.)

A planetary synergetic synthesis is called for, here and now. We need to learn the oriental's magnetic receptivity and openness to higher forces; they need to learn our dynamic active creativity in harnessing and adapting the forces of Great Nature. The Orient, as the *yin* side of the planet, has been female oriented, seeking the power of the Mother principle: the "valley spirit" of the Taoists, the Shakti power of the Hindus, the "all-containing void" of the Japanese Buddhists, to the extreme of the Kaliworshippers of Bengal. The West, under the Judaeo-Christian tradition, has expressed *yang* force almost exclusively: our God is Jehovah, or a Father in Heaven (he often has a beard), our goal has ever been the conquest of the forces of Nature, and the patriarchal, autocratic excesses stemming from this orientation are well known to all.

For centuries Western seekers have sought in the Orient the other, missing half of life. Never before now have so many Westerners practiced the ways of *yoga,* or cultivated the exquisite receptivity of Zen. Carl Jung was much pleased by the Papal Bull of 1950, in which Pius XII promulgated the Assumption of the Blessed Virgin Mary. Jung felt this represented a greater acceptance of the feminine element by the most conservative power group in the West, making the Holy Trinity into a quaternity. A new age of union of opposites is at hand: God the Mother-Father, "as above, so below."

Confirming this trend, we see the current re-emphasis and revaluation of the body as the vehicle of inner growth (only very recently could books called *Joy* or *Sense Relaxation* have become best sellers) as part of a modern movement with many features common to the *tantra.* And yet, we cannot simply use the Indian ways, or the Japanese ways of Zen. Our culture is different, our children are programmed differently, our body constitution is different, and the evolution of consciousness has not stood still since the Middle Ages. We need to extract the viable essence from the *tantras* and other ancient ways and convert it to our needs, using what we can, experimentally, in a context of testing and verification.

The new, and yet very ancient, *Agni Yoga* methods of Actualism can provide such a context. In an old Tibetan proverb it was said: "One must learn to protect oneself against the tigers to which one has given birth, as well as against those begotten by others." By bringing light we can discriminate what is ours and what is not, and with consuming fire eliminate the tigers that obstruct our growth.

EXPERIENTIAL EXPERIMENTS

There are innumerable books on *Hatha Yoga* describing in more or less detail the various postures and breathing exercises of that tradition. One cannot recommend studying these methods from a book, they should always be learned from a qualified teacher. In particular, breathing exercises of a complex nature are best avoided unless properly supervised.

However, the mere observation of breathing, without any attempt to control it or influence it in any way, can provide interesting results in terms of "mindfulness." Thus, you simply breathe as normal, but observe the process, and say to yourself, or think, "I am breathing in, I am breathing out." By thinking thus, you amplify awareness of the breathing as a process of energy distribution through the body; at the same time, you begin to learn to direct mental processes, so that the mind's activity is where you want it to be, rather than following random associations as usual. This is the beginning of "mindfulness," or what Gurdjieff called "self-remembering."

This exercise can then be extended to: "I am breathing a long breath in, I am breathing a long breath out," and "I am breathing a short breath in. I am breathing a short breath out." Then, "I experience my whole body, breathing in, I experience my whole body, breathing out," and "I experience serenity breathing in, I experience serenity breathing out." In this sequence, gradually the observation of breathing becomes the observation of more and more physical and mental processes.

A parallel exercise, which also involves only impartial observation and does not interfere with the natural rhythm of breathing, comes from a series of 101 tantric miniature exercises, called Centering (in *Zen Flesh, Zen Bones*, edited by Paul Reps). The myth is that Devi, the Goddess, asked Siva, the Lord of Yogis, "how to perceive ultimate reality, highest truth"; so that his answer might enlighten all men, Siva replied with the 101 ways. Many have to do with breathing: you put your attention on the turning point between in-breath and out-breath; and on the other turning point, when out-breath becomes in-breath. This requires no change, or stoppage, just awareness. In doing this, you get the feeling as if it were possible, at those moments, to slip through the cycle of time; a sudden feeling of lightness and a subtle release is experienced. Another way from the same series, is to visualize the spinal column as a hollow tube, and inside it a hair-fine thread, and then put all one's awareness on that thread—just there.

An extension of this, is to shift your weight while standing, very slowly, from one leg to the other, without lifting, and to note the relationship to the line of gravity, and to attend especially to the precise moment of crossing the central line.

According to tantric theory we are usually breathing predominantly through one nostril or the other, and this alternates in cycles of approximately twenty-seven minutes. It is valuable to begin to observe the different quality of awareness and body feeling when "sun-breath" or "moon-breath" is predominating. You can induce a changeover in a variety of different ways, the simplest of which is to lie on your side, with the breathing side to the floor. Generally, in a few minutes you will observe the shift. The moment of changeover is one in which psychic energy would be flowing through the central *nādī,* and hence you should observe it attentively. It has been suggested that this breath changing is part of the reason for the turning we do in our sleep, which also follows an approximate half-hour cycle.

There are many *mandalas* available commercially as posters and you can experiment with these along the lines of tantric practice. The basic procedure, as stated, is to fixate the center and place one's awareness in the entire field of the *mandala;* then, keeping the central fixation point, gradually move awareness inward from all four sides simultaneously until it is fully concentrated on the seed-point or *bindu,* and then to go through that point. The most striking optical effects, though not necessarily the most valuable in other ways, will be obtained with *mandalas* consisting of closely spaced concentric rings, as in some op art productions.

The use of *mantras,* such as the chanting of *OM,* individually or in groups, can be much enhanced if cognizance is taken of the prevailing sound of the room. Indian musicians always tune their instruments to the "silent sound" of the environment in which they are. Each space has its sound. Also, each individual has his sound, his tonic, and through letting it appear naturally, as part of the outgoing breath, without any attempt to sing or chant, this natural sound can be discovered. To do so, you must start very slowly and softly and allow it to come from within, of itself, without being forced. "The merging of mind is achieved by listening to inner sound," says one tantric text.

To discover and explore the power of sound, with instruments, it is best to begin with those producing very simple, pure tones, rather than the rich and complex mixtures of our orchestral instruments. Thus gongs, bells, large drums, cymbals, or tambouras, are excellent for these purposes. You can make useful discoveries in the perception of sound by following John Cage's procedures of ignoring the distinction between what we consider "sound" and what we call "noise," and allowing everything. You will find, that once divorced from their identity much more will be heard: when "sound of car," "sound of door slamming," or "sound of bird" are separated from their thingness, as it were, in an auditory Mirrorlike Wisdom and instead simply received as sound waves of certain pitch, certain volume, certain timbre, these sounds can be heard in the environment in a way you had not dreamed was possible. Why don't you try it now?

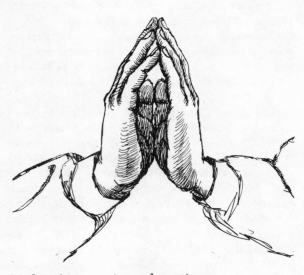

Mudrā *of inner union and greeting.*

The *mudras* of the Dhyānī Buddhas have been described above. In addition, the *mudra* of hands held palm to palm in front of the chest is admirable: a gesture of prayer, signifying the union of opposites within, and used in India as a form of greeting, which says: "The God that I am salutes the God that you are."

To conclude, a few more of the tantric minia-

tures from *Zen Flesh, Zen Bones,* relevant especially to *maithuna:*

"While being caressed, enter the caressing as everlasting life."

"At the start of sexual union, keep attentive on the fire in the beginning, and, so continuing, avoid the embers in the end."

"When in such embrace your senses are shaken as leaves, enter this shaking."

"When some desire comes, consider it. Then, suddenly, quit it."

NOTES AND REFERENCES

1. Shashibhusan Dasgupta, *Obscure Religious Cults* (Calcutta: Firma Mukhopadhyay, 1962), p. 56.
2. *Ibid.,* p. 75.
3. *Ibid.,* p. 89.
4. *Advaya-vajra-samgraha,* in Dasgupta, *Obscure Religious Cults,* p. 26.
5. Mircea Eliade, *Yoga: Immortality and Freedom* (New York: Pantheon Books, Bollingen Series LVI, 1958), p. 201.
6. *Ibid.,* p. 202.
7. *Ibid.,* p. 206.
8. *Ibid.,* p. 202.
9. Quoted in Heinrich Zimmer, *Myths and Symbols in Indian Art and Civilization* (New York: Harper & Row Publishers, Harper Torchbooks, 1946), p. 128n.
10. *Vyakta-bhava-nugata-tattva-siddhi,* in Dasgupta, *Obscure Religious Cults,* pp. 31–32.
11. Lāma Anagarika Govinda, *The Foundations of Tibetan Mysticism* (New York: E. P. Dutton & Co.; London: Rider & Co., 1960), p. 148.
12. See, for example, John Gaito, "DNA and RNA as Memory Molecules," *Psychological Review,* 70 (1963): 471–480; James V. McConnell, "Memory Transfer through Cannibalism in Planarians," *Journal of Neuropsychiatry* (August, 1962): 42–48; Walter Moore and Henry Mahler, "Introduction to Molecular Psychology," *Journal of Chemical Education* 42 (1965): 49–60.
13. W. Y. Evans-Wentz, *Tibetan Yoga and Secret Doctrines* (London: Oxford University Press, 1935; paperback, 1967), p. 324.
14. Lāma Govinda, *Foundations of Tibetan Mysticism,* p. 135.
15. Shafica Karagulla, *Breakthrough to Creativity* (Los Angeles: De Vorss, 1967), p. 125.
16. Robert O. Becker, Charles Bachman, and Howard Friedman, "The Direct Current Control System," *New*

York State Journal of Medicine (April, 1962): 1169–1176.

17. See Wilhelm Reich, *The Function of the Orgasm* (New York: Bantam Books, 1967; orig. pub., 1942); and Ellsworth Baker, "Wilhelm Reich," *Journal of Orgonomy* 1, no. 1 (1968).

18. Lāma Govinda, *Foundations of Tibetan Mysticism*, p. 155.

19. Mircea Eliade, *Yoga: Immortality and Freedom*, p. 239.

20. *Ibid.*, pp. 238–239.

21. Dasgupta, *Obscure Religious Cults*, p. 93.

22. Lāma Govinda, *Foundations of Tibetan Mysticism*, p. 156.

23. Quoted in P. D. Ouspensky, *In Search of the Miraculous* (New York: Harcourt Brace & World, 1949), p. 220.

24. Eliade, *Yoga: Immortality and Freedom*, p. 225.

25. The concentric ring structure of the *mandala* is suggestive of a model of its action in terms of the physiology of the optic system. We know that the light-sensitive rods and cones of the retina are pointed backward so that light is actually received by these receptors through a fine mesh of millions of fibers, similarly to the way we see a scene through a net-covered window. Dr. Gerald Oster has suggested that it is this net of fibers, plus the *moiré* effects which result from its superposition on lattice patterns in the environment, which may account for many of the optical effects induced by psychedelic substances. See G. Oster, "Moiré Patterns and Visual Hallucinations," *Psychedelic Review*, no. 7 (1966). Now, the so-called blind spot in the eye is the point near the foveal center where the fibers converge, and bunched into the optic cable, pass to the brain. Thus, when the *yogi* in the process of *mandala* meditation, gradually moves his awareness from the periphery, through the four doors, to the center, and then passes through the center (*bindu*), or the vanishing point, it may be that his point of awareness at that moment passes literally from the peripheral optic system, which is oriented toward the perception of external objects, to the central brain system, which is more oriented toward the synthesizing and assimilation of perception and inner states.

26. David Villaseñor, *Tapestries in Sand* (Healdsburg, Calif.: Naturegraph Co., 1963), p. 70.

27. Evans-Wentz, *Tibetan Yoga*, p. 93n.

28. Zimmer, *Indian Art*, p. 147.

29. Eliade, *Yoga: Immortality and Freedom*, p. 263.

30. I owe this analogy to Robert Lowe.

31. Evans-Wentz, *Tibetan Yoga*, pp. 204–205.

32. Such methods of compressing a great deal of information into a single formula, whether auditory or graphic, were formerly the object of intensive study, especially in Asiatic countries, and especially before the invention of the printing press. There is, for example, a graphic formula which supposedly contains within it the entire corpus of laws and principles used in Tibetan medicine, with its macro-microcosmic correspondences and relationships. See P. Cyrill von Kowin-Krasinski, O.S.B., *Tibetische Medizinphilosophie* (Zurich: Origo Verlag, 1953). Lāma Govinda's entire book *Foundations of Tibetan Mysticism* is devoted to the explication of the "Great Mantra" *Om mani padme hum*. Eight thousand stanzas of a *Mahāyāna* treatise were contracted into the seed syllable *pram* of the *Prajñā-Pāramitā Sūtra*.

33. Lāma Govinda, *Foundations of Tibetan Mysticism*, p. 119.

34. Mircea Eliade, *Yoga: Immortality and Freedom*, p. 266. Further, more extensive treatments of the tantric approach to sex can be found in Omar Garrison's *Tantra: The Yoga of Sex* (New York: Julian Press, 1964); and from a Taoist viewpoint, in Alan Watts' *Nature, Man and Woman* (New York: New American Library, Mentor Books, 1960). A rather abstruse, but fascinating, discussion is found in Herbert V. Guenther's *Yuganaddha —The Tantric View of Life* (Benares: Chowkhamba Sanskrit Series, 1952).

TAROT

Signposts on the Way

There is no such thing as an immortal work of art. There is one art— the greatest of all, the art of making a complete human being of oneself.

A. R. ORAGE

IN A FAMOUS PASSAGE IN *The Republic*, Plato compares the human situation to that of prisoners chained to the wall of a cave, watching with fascination the shadows cast on the wall in front of them by flickering flames behind; unaware that outside the cave things are seen in the radiant light of the daytime sun, unable to escape because they do not recognize that they are bound. The subtle, yet pervasive, entrapment of man through the illusion-generating processes of sense perception has been a central theme of mystics, prophets, seers, and teachers for as long as mankind has been inquiring into the nature of consciousness.

Contemporary physiologists could amplify this theme by pointing out that the process of sense-perception is much more than simply receiving stimuli from sources in the environment and learning to recognize them as objects. Now we know that in addition to the afferent fibers carrying electrical code impulses from the peripheral sense receptors to the brain, there are efferent fibers carrying signals from the brain to the periphery, whose function it is to screen, select, and filter irrelevant or unnecessary data. Some physiologists estimate that as much as 50 percent of the information reaching the eye does not get beyond the eye. The filtering mechanisms by which the incoming data are screened are genetically and culturally transmitted programs: we see what we are programmed to see.[1] And in this way we are literally bound by our perceptual mechanisms.

The very word *fascination*, indicating intense attractive interest, originally meant spellbinding, and is derived from the Latin *fasces,* which were bound bundles of rods carried before Roman magistrates in the streets as symbols of authority. Fascinating phenomena elicit in us binding images that authoritatively dominate consciousness, or, as the hippies say, they "cop your mind."

Once this subtle trap was recognized, numerous means were proposed to escape from it. In the ascetic tradition of classical Indian *yoga* or Christian monasticism the attempt is to avoid the trap by subduing and denying the function of the physical organs of sensation perception. The argument is that if the outstreaming of psychic energy into fascinating sense-objects is checked, then this energy can be turned to inner attunement with higher forces and lead to liberation. While this argument may have a certain validity, in extreme and deviated forms this tradition degenerates into the life-negating austerities of the Indian fakirs, and the vindictive rage of the puritanical Christian against natural bodily, especially sexual, functions. The alternative path, followed by Taoists, Tantrics, Sūfis, Alchemists, and Actualists is to remember that it is not the body or the organs of perception *per se* which are the trap, but rather the programs and imprints under which they are operating. And so, by means of transformation, by changing the form, they strive to make the body a living temple of the Higher Self instead of a prison, a responsive instrument instead of a cave of phantoms.

We have seen how tantric adepts devised *yantras* and *mandalas* to represent, in graphic and visual form, specific methods and stages of the process of psychic transformation. We find further that in myths and fairy tales ancient schools of wisdom often embodied teachings relating to the stages of the path of transformation. In these myths the inner journey to the discovery and realization of the Higher Self—the trials and obstacles to be overcome as well as the sudden breakthroughs and steps of initiation—are disguised as an outer journey, a hero's quest. And we find that there is always a common pattern to this myth of the hero "with a thousand faces": [2] whether his name is Gilgamesh, Rama, Orpheus, or Siegfried, there exists a communality which

stems from the fact that all these heros are engaged in the same eternal quest.

Indeed, the myth of the hero path is what Jung would call an archetype. Jung derived this concept to explain the recurrence of common themes in world literature, mythology, and in the dreams and fantasies of his contemporaries. "These typical images and associations are what I call archetypal ideas. The more vivid they are, the more they will be colored by particularly strong feeling-tones . . . they impress, influence, fascinate us." [3] The "hero" is an archetype, so is the "shadow," the "anima," the *mandala.* It was one of Jung's significant insights that many of the most dominant and influential images are personifications, either in a negative, distorting, limiting fashion, or in the role of helpful, guiding, messengers: that is, they are self-images, either masks which hide the true self or models that show the way.

Myths and tales may make the valuable teachings of transformation more accessible to the common understanding, and they may communicate to those who would be unable to comprehend the teachings directly. However, they are still culture bound and limited by the linguistic and literary media of the age and time. So it is not surprising that an attempt should have been made to express the archetypes of psychic transformation in direct, visual form; a form that would resonate in the mind and feelings of the perceiver without the intermediary of language or code. To show in images the steps that must be taken, the many phases of the inner work, and thus to ensure the teachings a universality that transcends cultural and linguistic conventions. This is the Tarot.

The set of mythic images which constitutes the Tarot has exercised a singular fascination on the minds and feelings of many persons, particularly those who are consciously engaged in a search for the Way. The emotional resonance and mental interest, which it produces, are in no way diminished by the fact that all attempts to trace the Tarot's origin or history have been amazingly unsuccessful. It presents itself to us as a kind of phenomenon, an unexplained message in the form of images of obscure origin, that by their power to affect us challenge and stimulate, and awaken deep echoes in long-forgotten strata of the psyche. Like the Sphinx, an equally obscure image of equally mysterious origin, the Tarot poses a riddle: what is the meaning? And, since no external explanations that would allow us to categorize it in neat, pre-programmed concepts, come with it, we are forced to look within if we want to solve the riddle. And so it awakens us a little more to the unused treasures, which lie buried within each and every one of us.

The Tarot apparently made its first recorded appearance in Europe around the fourteenth century, as a deck of cards used in games of chance and also by fortune-tellers for divination. Some attribute it to the Gypsies; others argue that decks were already in existence almost a century before the Gypsies first arrived in Europe. Assuredly, the Gypsies took it over and used it for divinatory purposes with undoubted flair and intuition. The association of a wisdom teaching with a divinatory technique reminds us at once of the *I Ching*, which is a similar combination; and the point can well be made that by association with a technique of divination the wisdom teaching most probably survived much longer than it would have without. The ancient sages apparently felt that man's thirst for wisdom and truth was subject to considerable fluctuation over time, whereas his desire to predict the future and have advance knowledge of his fate was a much more stable trait.

The compilers of the Tarot demonstrated an even greater stroke of genius by presenting their message in the form of a deck of playing cards. The nineteenth-century French occult philosopher Dr. Papus proposed (while mysteriously concealing the source of his information) that Egyptian priests, when faced with the imminent destruction of their temples and orders, held a council to decide how to transmit their teachings to subsequent generations:

At first they thought of confiding these secrets to virtuous men secretly recruited by the Initiates themselves, who would transmit them from generation to generation. But one priest, observing that virtue is a most fragile thing, and most difficult to find, at all events in a continuous line, proposed to confide the scientific traditions to vice. The latter, he said, would never fail completely, and through it we are sure of a long and durable preservation of our principles. This opinion was evidently adopted, and the game chosen as a vice was preferred. The small plates were then engraved with the mysterious figures which formerly taught the most important scientific secrets, and since then players have transmitted this Tarot from generation to generation, far better than the most virtuous men on earth could have done.[4]

Although there is apparently no scholarly evidence whatsoever for an Egyptian origin of the Tarot, nor for an Indian or Arabic origin, the story or myth of its origin has a flavor of truth to it.

The strategy of the Egyptian priests succeeded almost too well since the playing deck which has come down to our times as a popular game consists only of the so-called *minor arcana*; and the *major arcana*, or greater trumps, which supposedly contained the most important secrets, were "lost in the shuffle," as it were. But the Gypsies, fortune-tellers, occultists, and perhaps, esoteric schools of adepts such as the Knights Templar and Freemasons, preserved the entire deck to be resurrected now at the dawn of our new age.

It has been proposed that the twenty-two cards which make up the major arcana of the Tarot were, in the Egyptian Mystery Schools, hung on the walls of a gallery in the form of tablets or paintings, along with hieroglyphs and other symbols. The initiate then had to pass through the gallery elucidating the meaning of the symbols, as a kind of test. He would be able to do so only if he had had certain experiences. "Initiation," in other words, was not, as is commonly supposed, a process of imparting secret knowledge but rather a method of testing whether the initiate had experienced certain states of consciousness, and then consolidating and validating that experience by means of a symbol and a rite. It is thus more analogous to the Christian rite of Confirmation, though generally there appear to have been many stages of confirmation-initiation, not just one. In *The Aquarian Gospel of Jesus the Christ,* a version of the life of Jesus supposedly transcribed directly from the akashic record, Jesus is described as passing through such a series of tests in an Egyptian School.[5]

We will explore the meanings of the major trumps later. The minor trumps, which some experts consider to be a totally separate deck, are the ancestors of our playing deck: they consist of four suits of fourteen cards each. Each suit has four court cards, King, Queen, Knight, and Page, one Ace (number one), and cards numbered two through ten. In some versions of these cards, for instance the so-called Minchiate or Florentine set, "the Knights were sometimes monsters of the centaur type, while the Knaves were sometimes warriors and sometimes servingmen." [6] There are also sets in which the Page is replaced by a Maid of Honor, thus pairing the sexes in the tetrad of court cards. The relationship of the court cards to the structure of medieval feudalism is obvious. In divination, the court cards are often chosen as the "significator," the card that represents the questioner; and the other cards are then laid out according to certain schemes to determine "that which crosses him," "where he comes from," "his future," etc.

To arrive at a coherent and consistent interpretation of the numbered cards it would be necessary to go into *numerology,* the use of numbers as symbols for states of consciousness, which would take us too far afield here. Suffice it to say that numbers, like geometrical figures, can be taken to indicate different stages on the path of a man's inner growth and integration.[7] There are several volumes, including *The Pictorial Key to the Tarot* by A. E. Waite, which list the supposed divinatory meanings of the various cards and describe various methods of "spreading the deck."

It is interesting to reflect on the significance of the suits. The wands, swords, cups, and pentacles of the Tarot were changed, for unknown reasons, toward the end of the eighteenth century, to the clubs, spades, hearts, and diamonds of our modern decks. The original symbols were linked by early commentators on the Tarot to the Egyptian caste system, or, as by Grillot de Givry, to the structure of medieval society: "the wand, . . . the weapon of the peasant, stood for agriculture; the cup, or sacred vessel, for the clergy; the sword for the warrior; and the money [pentacles, deniers] for commerce." [8] Yet others, including Ouspensky, link the suits to the four elements that play such a pervasive role in the various symbolic languages of occult psychology: thus wands are used to represent "fire," cups stand for "water," swords for "air," and pentacles for "earth." In the *Tarot for the Aquarian Age,* a recently published version, the correlations are carried a step further in that the elements and suits are linked to the four functions of the Jungian theory of types: thinking, feeling, intuiting, and sensing. This has the virtue of facilitating psychologically more explicit readings or interpretations.[9]

In the chapters on alchemy and astrology below, we shall discuss the actual meaning of the elements as levels of consciousness or higher bodies. For purposes of divination the court cards have been linked to astrological types. Thus, the King of Wands would represent a "fire-sign" male (Aries, Leo, or Sagittarius); the Queen of Cups a "water-sign" female (Cancer, Scorpio, or Pisces), etc. They need not literally be born under that sign, but represent that type or disposition.

However one may choose to think of the four suits in psychological divination, there is one card in the *major arcana* which gives a clue to their inner meaning. This is the *Magician.* The Magician stands holding a wand in his raised right hand, his left hand points down, and in front of him on a table lie a sword, a cup, and a disc with a pentacle on it. Waite calls them the "counters of the adept," and Ouspensky says he is "playing with the four signs of the elements." I know of no commentator who has pointed out the obvious fact that these objects are the tools of the Magician. The Magician in the inner sense is not, of course, a juggler who performs tricks for an audience, rather he is an adept who is aware of and can use laws and principles which ordinary man cannot use. He can change his level of consciousness to both higher and lower, as his upward and downward pointing hands indicate; and he uses tools in his inner work.

The notion of psychic tools can be further elucidated by the following very interesting passage from the *Aquarian Gospel*, in which Jesus, when working as a carpenter with his father Joseph, one day comments: "These tools remind me of the ones we handle in the workshop of the mind where things are made of thought and where we build up character . . . We use the compass to draw circles round our passions and desires to keep them in the bounds of righteousness. We use the axe to cut away the knotty, useless and ungainly parts and make the character symmetrical." [10]

It is quite probable that several of the cards of the *major arcana* contain symbols representing actual tools and methods of psychic transformation. The paradox of such symbolism is that it cannot be explained to someone who has not already understood it in himself. If one has experienced a certain state of consciousness, or the use of a certain method, the symbol becomes an easily remembered, synthetic formula or summary of knowledge; if one has not experienced them, no amount of words can convey the meaning. The meaning is hidden or secret only in the same sense that the meaning of technical terms in physics or electronics is hidden or secret. They are open to anyone willing to take the trouble to learn.

Whether we choose to regard the twenty-two cards of the major trumps as Egyptian initiation symbols, or, as some have proposed, as remnants of still older Atlantean traditions, or, perhaps more plausibly, as a consciousness map which a medieval school grafted onto a deck of Gypsy playing cards, leaving all questions of their origins to the debates of the academicians, we can take them at their face value: that is, we can look at them and see what happens. After all, if, when used as a map or guide to consciousness evolution, the cards work, that is, give results in terms of growth of being and understanding, they will have served their purpose. If they do not work, no harm is done, and perhaps the

seeker will find another system that does work.

Separating the pragmatic value of the cards from the question of the authenticity of their origin is even more necessary if we wish to avail ourselves of the powerfully evocative images of *The Tarot for the Aquarian Age*. This Tarot was obtained, according to the authors, from an unnamed source referred to only as "One," through the Ouija board, in a series of sessions involving a group of four persons and lasting several months in 1962. Such a procedure would tend automatically to make the whole thing suspect, not quite "above board," in the eyes of many persons trained according to the current canons of scientific credibility. I myself have no reason to doubt the authors' veracity, knowing them personally to be sane and honorable persons not given to deceit nor subject to delusion any more than the rest of us. But even *if* the authors had made the whole thing up, had perpetrated a hoax, let us say, in ascribing their discovery to this nonhuman source, its potential value as guide or map can only be evaluated by testing it in use.

In the Aquarian Tarot each of the twenty-two cards, with a new image and new name, is regarded as a progression from a corresponding card of the old deck. The reason for the progression is said to be first, to rescue the Tarot symbols from their degenerate use as fortune-telling cards, and secondly, because we are entering a new phase, the Aquarian phase, of the cycle of human evolution-in-consciousness and new symbols are called for. It does seem that, in some instances, the cards of the Aquarian Tarot represent a kind of unfoldment of the concealed meaning of the old. I should hasten to add here that this is a personal opinion and one not shared by some long-time users of the traditional decks.

It is perhaps pertinent to digress momentarily in order to discuss what is meant by the Aquarian Age. Very slow oscillations in the direction and tilt of the earth's polar axis produce a cycle of approximately twenty-six thousand years. This cycle is divided into twelve periods or ages of about twenty-one hundred years each. The effect known as "precession of the equinoxes" alters the angular relationship of earth, sun, and stars through these ages, as a result of which we are able to plot their time-course by reference to the well-known constellations, Aries, Taurus, etc. Because the constellations differ in width, there is disagreement among astronomers and astrologers as to the precise date of the beginning of the Aquarian Age. For the purposes of the present discussion it is sufficient to note that the twenty-one-hundred-year cycle which we are now leaving, the Piscean Age, was closely associated with the Christian religion. There are in fact many elements in Christianity that support such an association, from the baptismal water rite, to the use of the fish as a symbol among early Christians and Christ's reference to the disciples as "fishers of men." Jung has devoted extensive research to the symbolic connection between Christ and the fish.[11]

The Aquarian Age we are now entering is ruled by the air element, and is already marked by far-reaching explorations of the atmosphere by planes, rockets, and communications systems, much as the Piscean water age was distinguished by the technology of sea power. Astrologically, Aquarius is the birth sign of scientists such as Galileo and Darwin, and is associated with the spread of objective knowledge, discovery, and the revealing of the hidden. The current surge of interest in occult traditions, in mind-manifesting drugs, and in new ways of consciousness growth, are all held to be manifestations of the dawning Aquarian Age.

Consistent with this view is the publication of the *Aquarian Gospel*, which describes, in highly plausible manner, the so-called lost years of Jesus as being spent in studies of oriental wisdom and in Egyptian Mystery Schools. Consistent also is the publication of a new Tarot to mark the new, open phase in the evolution of consciousness. It is important that in the new Tarot, the figures "have abandoned thrones, chariots, robes, and most royal and spiritual paraphernalia and stand forth nakedly." [12]

Before going on to examine the major trumps in detail, in both their old and new versions, it is well to say something about the relationship of the Tarot with the Cabala. Though I would hazard the opinion that much of the attraction of the Tarot is due precisely to its independence from verbal-conceptual systems, there are many who hold that the Tarot, astrology, and the Cabala form an inseparable body of knowledge, and that one cannot be understood without the others. Thus, extensive and elaborate charts and diagrams have been prepared showing the correspondences and correlations between planets, signs, Tarot cards, and Hebrew letters.[13] To me, this seems like a harmless, though useless, diversion. It is like comparing and correlating one map with another map without reference to the territory. Since, in this case, the territory is the human psyche, the maps will agree insofar as the observers are accurate. Distortions and deviations exist undoubtedly in all systems, since error is hard to avoid. But again, at the risk of being repetitive, the map should not be confused with the truth, which can only be validated by experience.

The Cabala is a Hebrew system of theosophy, based on very ancient Jewish traditions, which arose in the Middle Ages. It presents a highly complex cosmology and occult psychology using as its primary symbolic language the twenty-two letters of the Hebrew alphabet. The basis and starting-point is the so-called tetragrammaton, the name of God, Yahweh, composed of the four letters Y, H, W, H. These represent a quaternity which was linked to the four elements of alchemy, the four suits of the Tarot, and other fourfold schemata. In its use of letters, the Cabalistic system is reminiscent of the tantric use of *mantra* syllables; though the letters do not seem to have been used so much as inner tools, but rather as meditative symbols.

The "Tree of Life" in the Cabala is a cosmo-psychic *yantra*, showing God's ten creative emanations or *sephiroth*, which, at the same time, correspond to ten levels of consciousness in man and to parts of the human body. The ten spheres were linked to the planets and the twenty-one paths between them were linked to the cards of the Tarot. The Tarot cards have also been linked to the twenty-two letters of the

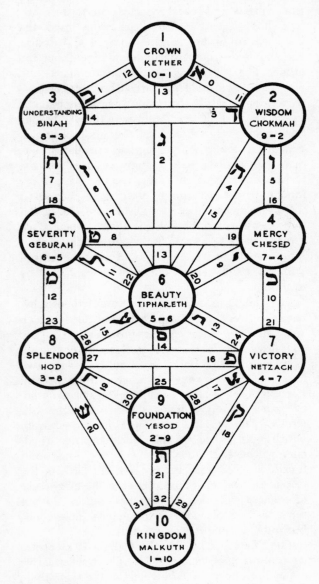

Tree of Life.

Hebrew alphabet, both in medieval and modern times. Paul Foster Case, for example, in his *Book of Tokens* published a beautiful set of Tarot meditations in which each image is seen as revealing the philosophic essence of the corresponding letter.[14]

Other attempts have also been made to order the twenty-two cards according to geometric or numerical principles. Ouspensky proposed that they could be arranged in pairs, 1 with 0, 2 with 21, and so on, down to 11 with 12, and that the pairs had complementary meanings.[15] This seems successful in some instances, not in others. It has also been noted that the cards could be arranged in three sets of seven (not counting the 0 card). Seven has long been considered a sacred number. According to Gurdjieff, it takes seven stages to complete any cycle of transformations. In his system, the Law of Seven is used to explain processes ranging from the digestion of food and the development of higher bodies, to the arrangement of elements on the periodic table and the creation of cosmoses. Conversely, they could also be grouped as seven triads; and the threefold principle of activity, rest, and balance has universal application, as we have noted. A numerical sequence can also be constructed as follows: beginning with one (1), proceeding to duality (2 and 3), to the triad (4, 5, and 6), to the tetrad (7, 8, 9, and 10), the pentagram (11, 12, 13, 14, and 15), and the six-pointed star (16, 17, 18, 19, 20, and 21) and returning to unity or zero (0).

It is doubtful whether any of these arrangements add significantly to the message contained in each individual card; perhaps because distortions and deviations have already heavily altered the content. There is no agreed upon sequence and each person has to make his own. Like a multilayered spiral, one can enter the series at any point and proceed upward or downward or sideways, as the need dictates, trying to follow the inner guide who knows the way and knows how to read the signs on the way. What follows here is in no way the "true" interpretation of the cards; they are merely my own subjective responses and associations, inevitably limited by my level of understanding.

The major arcana

The so-called zero card, the *Fool,* is placed at the beginning of some decks, at the end of others, or assigned a free floating place, not unlike the joker in our playing decks. In many games the joker is a card that can assume any value; in games of chance he is supreme, he is "lucky." But in the Tarot path he has no place, no number, and is not on the path. He is usually depicted as a carefree young man, wearing a richly embroidered tunic; with his face up in the air, he is about to step off the edge of a precipice. He is caught in dreams and images, self-created fantasies preventing him from seeing the world as it actually is, which *may* plunge him to his death. Note that he has not yet fallen off the precipice; but he may very well unless he wakes up. He carries over his shoulder a staff with a bag; some say the bag contains the tools of the magician, the suits of the Tarot, which he does not use. He is not actualizing his potentials, and he is blind to the positive as well as the negative possibilities confronting him. In some decks he is called *le mat,* the materialist, and indeed his sumptuous clothes indicate great interest in externals. Surface beauty attracts him, though he is asleep to what he does not want to see. His dog, a faithful creature (symbolizing his creature body), is barking and trying to wake him up.

Some have tended to idealize the Fool, partly because of the association with *aleph,* the potent first letter of the Hebrew alphabet. He has been called the "mystic fool," the "fire of mind." P. F. Case says, speaking as the Fool, "For what thou callest ignorance and folly is my pure knowing, imperfectly expressed through an uncompleted image of my divine perfection." [16] His is the folly of innocence and naiveté, not that of knavery and stupidity. He seems to have something of the protection that court jesters enjoyed; the sun is shining brightly on his path, and he has not yet stepped off the precipice; he can still make it. "Youthful folly has success," says the *I Ching.*

The Fool as the unawakened man may be compared with the Magician as the initiate: they are ego and Higher Self, Arjuna and Krishna, the childlike dreamer and the God within. William Blake said: "If the fool would persist in his folly, he would become wise"; [17] because he would learn eventually, and awaken to the fact that there is a purpose to his life, and his aim must be to discover that purpose and fulfill it. He then reaches the stage where he knows he must find something, but he does not know what. He becomes the Nameless One of the Aquarian Tarot. Here he is shown naked, leaving a dark hole with bones behind. He has emerged from the precipice, given up his gaudy clothes, and is proceeding along, reading a scroll which he is carrying. He is studying ancient maps of consciousness, just as you are, dear reader. Over his head hangs a spider: he has become aware of the web of thoughts and images, which we

0   THE FOOL

NAMELESS-ONE

1 | THE MAGICIAN

CHANGER

spin and in which we live, and he is determined to find his way out, to resolve his tangled fate. For this reason he is also called "the resolver." He has made a beginning, perhaps it was a rude awakening, but he is on the path. "By asking the question 'Whom am I?' he commences the journey . . ." [18]

The Magician, as already indicated, is the knowing, Higher Self, and has attained that state that is as yet only potential in the Fool. As the Magician he has come into his own: he is able to move his consciousness to higher or lower levels, he can use the tools of psychic transformation. He is at home equally in the inner universe and in the outer world of the earth. The former is indicated by the infinity symbol, ∞, over his head; the latter by the luxuriant flowers and plants growing round him. Exoterically, he is the juggler, the name of this card in some decks, who performs sleights of hand and tricks of magic; but his true nature is much greater. He is reminiscent of Amogha-Siddhi, the Tibetan Dhyani Buddha of the All-Accomplishing Wisdom, who brings the diamond fire of higher wisdom into the outer world of action, and who, like the Magician, carries a double sceptre (*vajra*), signifying the double direction of awareness. Ouspensky says of this card: "I saw that he was changing all the time. Innumerable crowds seemed to pass and pass in him before me . . . at the same time I saw myself in him, reflected as in a mirror, and it seemed to me that I was looking at myself through his eyes." [19] He is the "shape-shifter," the "mirror of form," who reflects but does not identify with the "innumerable crowds" of false self-images that dominate our normal consciousness, which, to the God-Magician within, are fleeting and insubstantial. He has the mobility of consciousness enabling him to enter into and withdraw from these images at will so he does not get caught in them. In Actualism, this mobility is referred to as "standing firmly on a moving point."

Appropriately, in the Aquarian Tarot, the transmuted Magician, now called the Changer, is standing upon a rolling sphere. His arms are stretched out from his sides, as if to indicate he is balancing on the neutral point, the flexible posi-

tion of the impartial observer. In one hand he holds a flower, from the other flows running water. In his flowing mutability he evokes the myth of Proteus, the prophetic sea god, who lived among the seals by the shore, and who would evade questioners by changing in rapid succession into lion, serpent, panther, bear, running water, leafy tree. If one could hold him fast, one could get him to prophesy. We might translate this, if one can maintain steady awareness through the shifting flux of images, then the Immortal Self will vouchsafe revelation. In the alchemical symbolism, the Magician-Changer is related to mercury, the "philosophic substance," the elusive essence that enters into all forms, but, like quicksilver, cannot be grasped by the mind.

The *High Priestess*, the *Empress*, the *Hierophant*, and the *Emperor* form a tetrad of masculine and feminine figures representing spiritual and worldly orientations. To the modern con-

2 HIGH PRIESTESS

MOTHER

THE EMPRESS.

sciousness, the ecclesiastic associations evoked by the High Priestess and the Hierophant are no longer relevant; rather we would see them as representing the inner search and growth in consciousness. Similarly, the Empress and Emperor, instead of worldly authority figures, become symbols of external reality activity and attitude.

The *High Priestess* is usually shown as a robed figure seated between two columns in front of a veiled entrance. She holds a book and the crescent moon is at her feet; a cross of light hangs on her breast. She was called Isis, the Guardian of the Mysteries, the Spiritual Bride, the Cosmic Mother; she was also identified with Sophia, the Divine Wisdom. In the Aquarian Tarot she is called simply Mother and the veils of Isis, the images that veil the truth from our understanding, have been removed: she stands pregnant, with open robe, but eyes closed, *on* the pillars instead of between them. The cross of light on her breast has become a blazing star. As

Isis she is man's mediator with the hidden truth which she conceals from the uninitiated. As Mother, akin to the Hindu *Sakti,* she is creative energy, inwardly absorbed in the process of generation.

The *Empress* is wearing a flowery robe and a star-studded diadem, seated on a throne among corn fields, waterfalls, and blossoming trees. Where Isis is the Cosmic Mother, associated with the moon and with divine secrets, this is Demeter, the Earth Mother, symbolizing the nourishing fruitfulness and thousand delights of earth. She is all-loving, radiant, universal femaleness. In the Aquarian deck she becomes the Feeler, who stands with arms stretched out to embrace, her golden hair encircling naked breasts. She is called "prime mover," and it is indeed *e*motions that stimulate us to movement and activity. The Sign of Cancer, a watery, emotional, maternal sign, is over her head linking her back again to the moon goddess, sea mother.

The *Hierophant,* literally "he who shows sacred

FEELER

5 HIEROPHANT ٦

SPEAKER

things," is the male counterpart of the High Priestess; sometimes he is called the Pope. In some decks these two are known as Jupiter and Juno, the Olympian Father and Mother. His association with ecclesiastic authority has led to an obscuring of his true nature. He is expressive while the Priestess is conservative; he reveals and teaches, she preserves and contains. In the Aquarian deck he is shown as the Speaker. From his mouth shoot forth birds (winged thoughts) and lightning bolts (inspiring sparks of energy); volcanoes erupt, the land shakes, waters spout. The words of power which he speaks are dislodging structures, bringing forth fire from earthform, activating emotional torrents. His heart is blazing with light, like that of the Mother; like her, he is naked, unadorned.

The *Emperor* is armored, sitting on a throne or cube decorated with rams' heads (symbols of the Arian Age that preceded the Piscean?). He is the executive ego acting in the external world. Formerly seated on a throne, a "seat of power," his contemporary descendant is the chairman. His armor is indicative of his defensiveness, the usual feature of this type. Reich would call him "the armored individual." In the Aquarian deck, he still has defenses, but he takes them on or off at will: he becomes the Actor, the mind that performs acts. He is depicted holding a mask in front of his face. He has quit his throne, his seat of authority, he is less concerned with maintaining or defending power. He is now on a stage, consciously participating in the tragedies and comedies of life. He knows that his personality is but his *persona,* his mask used for relating externally (*per-sonare,* "for sounding").

One of the most mysterious and intriguing cards of the Tarot is the one known as the *Hanged Man.* It shows a man hanging upside down, tied by his right foot to the top of a T-shaped tree cross. His left leg is folded behind his right, his hands are tied behind his back, he has a halo. He is a being of light, but he is inverted, bound. He reminds us of Prometheus, who was chained to a rock as a punishment for stealing fire from the gods and giving it to mankind. So we have a divine being, an immortal, imprisoned in matter, bound to the cross of reality. But was it punishment? Or is that a fable, invented by guilt-plagued men? For Prometheus is the divine creator of man, he does not suffer, he cannot be punished. In Actualism, it is taught that we suffer pain only if we identify with the body, the creation, instead of with the divine creator within (Prometheus). He is the bringer of light, the teacher-

knower. In the myth, Prometheus is released from the rock when an immortal voluntarily surrenders his immortality; that is, when the bound man recognizes and remembers that as Immortal Self he voluntarily created and entered "this mortal frame," he will be free (again).

Thus the Hanged Man is truly "hung up" in his *karma*. But it is not his fault (or anybody's fault), he is not being punished. Karma, from the Sanskrit root *kr*, "to do," simply refers to the consequences of actions. As long as he is identified with his mortal ego he is bound to the task of paying off old debts and "unravelling the web of fate." But as Immortal Higher Self he can "do" without being involved and getting caught, which is the meaning of *Karma Yoga*. And also as Higher Self he can undo the tangled knots

of fate and he can redeem his birthright, which he (as ego) has sold "for a mess of pottage." Hence Christ, who also was hung up on a cross, is called the Redeemer. And in the new Tarot, the significance of the Hanging Man is said to be "redemption." This Hanging Man stands spread out with his feet on two separate buildings, with a man and a woman hanging from his wrists, the woman upside down. Tears are streaming down his face with grief at the separation of the male and female aspects of his own nature. When he unifies them, he will be redeemed; and then he will be free to engage in creative activity, instead of having his hands tied.

The *Chariot* card is usually related to conquest and defense, yet most commentators have

7 THE CHARIOT ⊓

VICTORIOUS-ONE

felt that the conquest involved was not actual, or only partial. It shows a princely figure in a chariot in front of which sit a black and white sphinx. It seems to have generally escaped notice that the sphinxes are not in a shaft or harness, nor does the driver have reins. Following an ancient Eastern allegory we can see the driver as the mind, the sphinx-lions as the emotions (positive and negative), and the chariot as the body. Gurdjieff pointed out that to achieve unity, not only must the different parts of this complex organization be brought into harmony, and under the direction of the "master," the "I"; but the connections also must function well. The driver (mind) must hear and understand the master (the I); he must learn to guide the lions (feelings) with reins; the lions must be properly harnessed to the carriage (related to the body).[20] In this card, the connections are absent; each center or level of consciousness, though *apparently* they are together, is in fact separate and

independent from the other. A good allegory of our usual condition.

In the card of the Victorious One, the Aquarian Tarot's version of this image, the self has overcome this disorganization. The chariot, which now has both harness and reins is in the background; the man is walking with right foot sandaled, earth-grounded, and left foot winged, ready to fly. He is leading the black and white lions by a leash. A brilliant sun over his head guides him, and an eagle protects him. Birds are holding up a transparent veil, behind which wolves are snarling and fighting. That is, though the conflict of passions and instincts continues, it no longer affects him or deviates him from his path; he is not *in* it. One can sometimes see one's own psychic components with this kind of translucent detachment under psychedelic chemicals.

The Actualist interpretation of the Chariot card brings out yet another perspective: here, the princely figure represents Actual Self, the

Immortal One within all that is external. The chariot represents the exterior form aspects within and from which the Actual Self observes, without reservation or restraint or involvement. The absence of reins or harness indicates free will is given to the personality self, to choose between inner or outer orientation. The leonine bodies of the two sphinxes represent the animal-creature body of the human; the human heads represent the human structures and functions with consciousness centered in the forebrain. The black sphinx is the mysterious, magnetic, female aspect of the nature; the white is the known, dynamic, male aspect. The sphinxes are reclining: the personality self, comprised of human and animal natures, is immobilized with respect to the inner worlds, it is unawakened. However, the open eyes indicate that its orientation is outward, toward the external world of material realities.

Another kind of relationship between man and his creature-instinctive nature is shown in the *Strength* card: a woman, with an infinity symbol over her head, is allegedly either closing or opening the mouth of a big lion. My guess is that this is an error, and that the "Strength is the higher nature in its liberation," as Waite, who has her leading the lion with a chain of flowers, points out.[21] She is the female counterpart of the Magician, as the infinity symbol over her head indicates, and her strength is feminine-magnetic, the power of love and understanding. In the Aquarian Tarot, Strength becomes the Deliverer: lion and woman have become very close, he stands tamed behind her, in front of them is a vat of fire. It was said of this: "She is not the Deliverer—nor is he. The flame is."[22] But this fire is not the fire of earth—it is electric fire. It is the inner fire in its consuming aspect, purifying and eliminating unnecessary debris, as taught in *Agni Yoga*.

Fire as purification, with the purpose and goal

of liberation from obstructions and psychic wholeness, is purgatory; fire which merely burns, unwanted and without promise of end, is hell. In the former case we have destructuring, for the purpose of change and the creation of new form, for trans-formation; in the latter we have senseless destruction seeking only to exercise and increase its own power. This is the realm of the *Devil*. In Goethe's *Faust*, Mephisto introduces himself as "the spirit who always negates." Pure negation, "just for the hell of it." In the Tarot, he is shown in the classic medieval manner, as bearded, horned goat-demon with bat's wings, the planetary symbol of Mercury on his hairy navel, an inverted torch in his left hand. Two human figures, male and female, are chained to the "altar" on which the Dark One squats. Typical is Waite's interpretation: "Hereof is the chain and fatality of the material life." They are

analogous to the two figures in the Lovers card, where they are presided over by an angelic figure. Love is apparently either paradisal or infernal, sacred or profane. In some older versions of the Lovers card, this good-bad polarization of love was even more graphically shown: a man had to choose between a naked, sensuous woman, and a clothed, chaste one. Cupid was flitting blindly overhead, up to his usual tricks.

The Devil, whose Greek name *diabolos* means "the slanderer," performed one of his most cunningly deceitful tricks in getting himself associated with sex. Generations of Christians have suffered both external and internal torments over so-called sins of the flesh, over the powerful impulses of generation. By separating the body's instinct toward unification into numerous double-concepts of lust and love, carnal and spiritual, dirty and proper, he has made it into its opposite

—a factor that divides people within and thus keeps them from truly uniting with each other. And yet, though his lies and false concepts actually block and negate the free flow of generative energy with mechanisms of shame, guilt, vanity, fear, he has acquired the reputation of "suggesting it," of "tempting" one, of leading one astray into the ways of the flesh—in short, of being "a sexy devil." A downright falsehood of course, since actually the devil negates sex just as he negates everything else. The "horny goat" is a devil's mask; for as Blake put it, "the lust of the goat is the bounty of God." [23] The Devil's effect is separative, divisive, and binding; the Lovers are bound, but to him, not to each other.

But who is the Devil? He is the slanderer, the liar, the false images and concepts we have invented that would deny our divinity. In the Aquarian Tarot, this card is named the Thinker, and shows a cross-legged figure with a chain around his head; a heart is hanging from one end of the chain, a male-female pair is pulling on the other end. "The man and woman bind his thoughts to thoughts about duality, passion and sensuality. The bleeding heart weights these thoughts by thoughts about compassion. The Thinker is not passionate, nor compassionate." [24] He is in error.

The solution to the conflict is shown in the Aquarian Tarot's version of the Lovers card, now called Unity. On it, there is a circle with two winged fish swimming-flying in ocean-air inside: the Piscean image of the union of male and female within, the alchemists' *conjunctio oppositorum*. Around the outside of the circle are a naked man and woman, not touching but not apart, facing in the same direction. That is, unity between two individuals must be based on and proceed from unity within. Then they will no longer be opposed to each other in the constant seesaw of attraction-repulsion. They share the same goal, and "by this understanding of alignment, there exists only constant merging and emerging." [25]

The *Hermit* is a cloaked, hooded man with a staff, carrying a lamp. His eyes are closed, as if in meditation. He is the solitary seeker, absorbed in the search for the Self. He guards his light, but he keeps it outside, as if his goal could be found in the external world. A well-known Sūfi story refers to this situation: Nasrudin, the great teacher, was found by one of his disciples one night looking for something under a street lamp. "What are you looking for?" asked the student. "My purse," said Nasrudin. "Did you lose it here?" asked the student. "No," said Nasrudin, "but where I lost it, I cannot see; so I'm looking here, where it's light." The corresponding figure in the Aquarian deck, the Seeker, is shown naked with a blindfold, reaching out. A huge fire is blazing on top of the mountain toward which he is groping his way. As Goethe said: "The most difficult thing of all is to see what lies before your eyes."

The Cabalistic meditation on the *Star* card, which pictures a large blazing star and seven smaller ones surrounding it, is: "Thinkest thou, O seeker for wisdom, that thou bringest thyself in the Light by thine own search? Not so. I am the hook, cast into the rivers of darkness, to bring men from their depths into the sphere of true perception. . . . Men think they seek me, but it is I who seek them." [26] We think we are saving the soul by seeking the light; actually, the light of the soul radiates starlike and lifts us out of the depths. In this card, a young, naked girl is pouring water from two pitchers onto the earth and the water. If we are receptive with innocent purity, the blessings of the light of the stars pour abundantly into earth-body and emotional waters. This is the card of Aquarius, the water bearer, showering stars upon the earth. The mind receptive to illumination goes on to become an illuminator for men. "But they

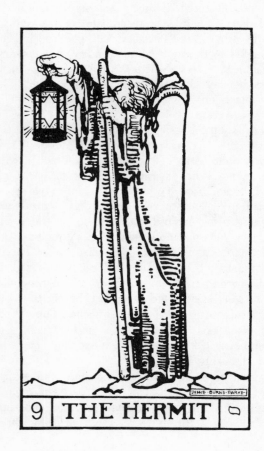

must have the light before they can reveal the light." [27] In the Aquarian deck a man looks down from the heavens, double rays of light shine from his eyes, a star is behind his head; there is a glittering city, a waterfall, a rainbow, an inverted cup from which many hued streams are flowing down. They are all aspects of the inner work of transformation-illumination. He is called the Way-Shower. A cock crows, announcing the dawn of the new age, and the arrival of the Light. "That which is above is showering down, golden, upon that which is below; and the way is being shown." [28] One might say this is a breakthrough.

A powerful winged androgynous being holds two pitchers and pours water from one to the other in such a way that the flow is simultaneously from left to right and vice versa: *Tem-*

17　THE STAR

WAY~SHOWER

perance. This word is used here not in the sense it has in temperance societies, but in the original meaning of the Latin *temperare,* "to mix properly," as in tempered steel and well-tempered clavichord. By the judicious mixing of right-hand and left-hand, dynamic-male and magnetic-female energies one produces "temperament" that is resilient and harmonious. A bad "temper" is simply the inharmonious blending of what alchemist-psychologists called the humors, the emotional fluids. In some versions of the Temperance card the cosmic androgyne is tempering the elements of personality with slightly different emphasis: water pours down on the right, fire on the left; a lion is on the right, an eagle on the left. The water of feeling and the fire of perception is being blended with the creature body and the bird of thought. In the Aquarian deck's corresponding Reverser, the metasexual consciousness being with a blazing sun over his head is similarly engaged in bringing water down on his right side and grounding fire through his left. He is able to "correctly channel flow." He is the offspring of the Unity, the "son who has become his own father and mother, and who is also the Sun." Like the tantric *Siva Ardhanarisvara,* he is horizontally balancing sexual polarity, and vertically integrating with respect to his several bodies. Astrologically, he is the centaur-archer Sagittarius, who unites man and creature within himself and aims at the perfect center.

This is another aspect of the connecting done by the Victorious One and his Chariot. And it is also the bringing down of energy done by the Star who is the Way-Shower. Man as a cosmic being acts like a "step-down transformer," who brings higher frequency energy to lower frequency systems in order to enlighten them and lift them up. This activity is anti-entropic, regenerative; it counteracts the running down of energies, the degeneration which occurs in closed systems. The great planetary closed system of reciprocal feeding known to the ancients as the Wheel of Life keeps us chained to the alternating ebb-and-flow of its changing seasons and fortunes. But if we become an open system

with the awareness of the Magician tuned to both higher and lower levels, and a finely tempered instrument which channels and transmutes cosmic energies, we can liberate ourselves from the Wheel and fulfill our function as gods.

The *Sun* and the *Moon* cards form an antithetical pair comparable to the Magician and the Fool. The Moon, it is interesting to note, is the only card in the Tarot, besides the Wheel of Life, that does not have a human or humanoid figure on it. There is a path winding through a gate into the distance. The moon is above. A dog and a wolf are looking up at it, as if magnetized. An amphibious shell-fish creature is climbing out of the water on to the land in the foreground. In Greek mythology Selene, the Moon, was the offspring of Earth and Sun. This is not unlike one modern theory of the moon's origin as a torn-off fragment of earth. Is the moon's magnetism, its "sucking" of the fluids on the earth's surface and in the biosphere, like the nourishing of a child by its mother? Some esoteric doctrines assert it is: "Organic life on earth feeds the moon," according to Gurdjieff.[29] In Greek myth, Selene was said to be beloved by Pan, the world of nature. The dog, the wolf, and the amphibian, the instinctual nature within us, are drawn to the moon. The path through the gate of consciousness lies ahead, but they are not on it.

The moon as a symbol represents our evolutionary tail, the mammalian, amphibian, and cellular imprints in our consciousness. This is why the moon is sometimes erroneously said to be "the unconscious"; it is below our usual range of awareness, but it is not at all unconscious, as is evidenced by the fact that one can experience those levels, with psychedelic substances for instance, and by the fact that we still have feelings triggered by those imprints. We "react" to lunar forces. The Aquarian version is called the Reacter, who is "not the Actor." In this card a naked babe with two keys is coming through seven gates; behind in the distance is the moon. He is moving away from the moon, he has opened the gates of awareness with the keys of love and understanding. In ancient times the

TEMPERANCE.

REACTER

18   **THE MOON**

19 THE SUN

DOER

way of liberation was often called "escape from the power of the moon."

The *Sun* card shows a wall with a garden of sunflowers behind it. The benign face of the sun radiates life-warmth above. Two small children are playing in front, or sometimes a small child with a banner is shown on a horse. Speaking of the child, Waite says: "When the self-knowing spirit has dawned in the consciousness above the natural mind, that mind in its renewal leads forth the animal nature." [30] The children have walked through the wall which enclosed the garden of "the sensitive life." Having dropped their defensive armoring and "become like little children," they can pass through the barriers to enter the kingdom within. For "the kingdom is within you and it is without you." [31] And the sun shines equally on all and knows no distinctions.

The Aquarian version shows a seven-year-old child standing in a sun-filled garden of flowers

and endless vistas. With one hand he holds a meek, black horse by a loose tie; on his other side a white horse is rearing up high, standing on a skull. Death is overcome, darkness is tamed. The child holds a book, open to the viewer. "Each reader of the book sees his needed sign." The card is the Doer of "right activity." "There is only one thing to do: be as you are, . . . be it openly, and let the sun shine." [32] And, it should be noted that the Sun is not the sun in the sky, but the eye of lighted consciousness. Thus it was said in the uncanonical gospels: "If thine 'I' be single, thy whole body will be full of light."

It is worth relating that two of the individuals who were the medium for bringing through the Aquarian Tarot once gave me a reading. The card which came up as the significator, the basic current trend of probability, was the Doer. This was a helpful, inspiring clue and guide for inner development. But the reading also included a definite prediction that I would be writing. Now this was over a year ago, when I had no thoughts of a book of this nature. So here was a rather literal, explicit indication even of the kind of writing (though I did not see this at the time): I am holding up a book, a set of ancient books, for you, friend reader. "Each reader of the book sees his needed sign."

The *Judgement* card shows the archangel Gabriel raising the dead from their graves: with upstretched arms they joyously ascend. The idea of the Last Judgement in Christian mythology has usually been associated with notions of separation (of the good from the bad) and of punishment. "Dies irae, dies illa"—that dreadful day of final accounting. But again we must recognize this as a distortion. For it is in the ordinary state of fixed-pattern responding according to conditioning factors that we are constantly judging our experiences: this is a bad or good thought, this feeling is right or wrong, this sensation is nasty or nice, etc. As we judge ourselves, so we judge others—and distort the meanings and values of our experiences and others' actions. The day when we are finally able to give up this judgementalizing tendency completely will be the day of the *last* judgement—and it will be a joyous day indeed, for it will signal the realization of the True Self; and those aspects of our nature that we have rejected and locked away will arise from their graves, reborn, to join at last in the feast of the gods with love and joy.

Modern methods using imagery

There is in exoteric psychological practice a number of methods which also use images, and it may be useful to briefly explore the similarities and differences between these methods and the Tarot. The well-known ink-blot test, beloved of court-room and TV psychologists, was developed by Herman Rohrschach on the basis of the Freudian theory of projection. An ink-blot pattern is shown to the patient or client and from his responses inferences are made to his "unconscious" impulses and fears. Thus if he sees a phallus in the ink blot, a strong sex drive is inferred; if he sees blood and gore,

destructive urges and hidden rage may be seething below the surface. The notion of "fantasy-substitution" is prevalent in this school of clinical psychology: an individual will fantasize doing something if his fears or outside forces prevent him from doing it. And experiments have been done which indeed show that if, for example, an individual is prevented from moving physically, the number of "M" responses, that is responses showing human figures in movement on the Rohrschach, will increase; and conversely, after vigorous callisthenics, "M" responses will be less.

While these theories may be correct enough on one level, though they are gross simplifications, note the *purpose:* the psychologist is trying to probe, like a kind of psychic X ray, beneath the defenses of the patient. What the patient wants is beside the point, though it is always supposed to help him somehow. With the Tarot, there is no question of probing; rather, it is taken for granted that the "inquirer" wishes to see through his own defenses and understand himself better. Therefore, instead of supposedly neutral blots, into which he projects his mental contents, he is shown powerfully evocative images which can and sometimes do elicit strong emotional reactions, positive as well as negative, and by observing these the inquirer is able to increase his understanding of himself. The "reader," if there is one, may also get to know the inquirer better, but this is secondary. The compilers of the Tarot knew that man has sex drives and destructive drives; they were interested in helping man increase his understanding of these drives within him. So they have a naked couple, and a skeleton mower. And they ask: how well do you know *that* in you?

The so-called Thematic Apperception Test (T.A.T.), developed by Henry Murray and his associates, is a good deal more sophisticated than the Rohrschach. Here the subject is shown a series of drawings and is asked to tell a story about each of the drawings. Thus there is a picture of a little boy looking at a violin on a table in front of him. The story may be about how the boy hopes to become a great violinist; this would be scored for "level of aspiration" or "need for achievement." Or the story may be about how the boy is worried about his lesson ("fear of failure"), or how he is mad at his mother for making him practice ("need for independence"). Most of the drawings commonly used have typical family figures in characteristic family situations; they are used to determine patterns of family relationships as they appear to the client. The more cosmic and mysterious cards are related to the kinds of images Jung said came from the "collective unconscious."

A similar principle is used in the techniques known as "guided daydream" or "psychosynthesis" developed by Desoille in France, Leuner in Germany, Assagioli in Italy, and Gerard in the United States. Here a series of images is presented to the client verbally and he is asked to elaborate, describe, fantasize, and develop this image. For example, he may be asked to visualize a house, to describe its outside, and then its inside. Often, there is a remarkable correspondence between the description the client gives of his house and the images he has of his own personality. He may not be aware of the similarity until it is pointed out to him. In a context of therapy, the client may be asked to enter the basement, or attic of his house, and there to open a trunk he has not opened before, or look at an old, dusty book. With this method, revealing insights can often be gained by the client into some of the more obscure and disguised programs which are affecting his emotional responses. Needless to say, such methods must be handled with care, trust, and understanding.

With these methods, we are not too far from the meditative, associative-synthetic approach of the Tarot. In fact, there are some advantages to the verbal presentation of an image over the visual: it allows the client-seeker to produce an image more corresponding to his own inner state. The main difference is that the Tarot, as it has come down to us, has built into it certain ideas and conceptions of what a human being is; and what man's function in the cosmos is; and what possibilities for development are open to man; and how these possibilities may be realized.

The symbols and images used in the method

of the "guided fantasy," as well as those of the Tarot, are thought of as being *archetypal*. According to Jung, these are part of the common psychic structure of mankind, much as hands and feet are common physical structure. But it is important to realize that the images and ideas themselves, though derived from, are not archetypes: they are imitations. As Jung put it: "Archetypes are not determined as regards their content, but only as regards their form. . . . Its form . . . might be compared to the axial system of a crystal, which as it were, preforms the crystalline structure in the mother liquid, although it has no material existence of its own. This first appears according to the specific way in which the ions and molecules aggregate. The archetype in itself is empty and purely formal . . . a possibility of representation." [33]

Thus the various images of a path that appear in the Tarot, or are used in guided fantasy methods, or appear in dreams and visions, though directed toward evolutionary growth—are still images and must eventually be eliminated. Images of transformation, of "the way," may be helpful in finding the way, but having found it, it is necessary to go on it; and then the image becomes an obstacle. This is why it was said by a Zen Master: "If you meet the Buddha on the road, kill him." Because the Buddha you meet on the road is not the Buddha, but an image—going in the opposite direction.

EXPERIENTIAL EXPERIMENTS

It is good first to look at the various Tarot decks and find one that appeals the most, or relates to something experienced. Then lay out the various cards of the major trumps and simply look at them, if possible without preconceptions. Pick out one that evokes the strongest positive reaction, and put that one up on the wall, in a place where it will be seen often in the course of daily activities.

I found that when looking at a card intently, expecting something to happen, nothing did; but if, when I was thinking about something else, or absentmindedly going about business, I would suddenly chance to see it a flash of recognition could come. Gradually, over a period of time, the image began to work itself into deeper layers of consciousness, as it were. I might begin to dream about it or suddenly think of it in other contexts. It might work subtle transformation on prerational, highly charged complexes of ideas and emotions, changing them from anxious fixations, to enlarging, life-affirming visions.

Perhaps even more dramatic results can be obtained if you "work" in this manner with a card to which the initial reaction is strongly negative. Trying to determine the nature of the resistance, you can learn much: if not the origin of the conflict, at least some knowledge of the subtleties of your defenses. After a while, you may then be drawn to another card, which might represent the next stage. It is important to let yourself take the cards in any order, to make "your own way."

It is valuable also to try to internalize the energy symbolism of the cards. For example, while writing the portion of this chapter dealing with the Temperance card, I woke up one morning with that image in my mind, and as I held it, there occurred a shift in awareness such that "I" was no longer just the body-personality, but expanded into the consciousness of the "field."

You can make the experiment of standing and imaging yourself as the Reverser, with "watery energy" flowing down from above into your upturned right hand; and "fiery energy" flowing down from your left hand into the ground. Try to perceive what this "water" and "fire" is, inside, and what its effects are. Similarly you can *be* the Changer and think of yourself standing firmly on a rolling sphere, to get that feeling in the body.

Also, the images can be used as starting points for exploratory fantasy trips. For example, you can visualize yourself as the Fool, and then complete the fantasy: what happens? Does he fall off? If not, how so? If yes, then what happens? And the Nameless One? What happens to him in the desert? Following the images, and then tracing the *source* of the images, one can learn much.

Spreading the cards. Once you have obtained,

by such methods, some feeling for the meaning of the different cards, you can begin to use them to obtain readings. Like the *I Ching,* the cards of the Tarot offer an independent perspective on a given situation or cusp of choice, a perspective that allows higher intuition to come into play. Essentially, the reading is done for oneself; considering the unavoidable subjective biases, I see little value in doing readings for another, or in having another interpret one's cards.

The following lay-out relates to the astrological map of the 24-hour cycle and uses the basic form of the cross. It also corresponds in part to the "celtic method," described in Waite's book. Only the twenty-two major arcana are used; after shuffling while concentrating on the question, five cards are laid out in the order shown.

(1) represents *what is coming,* what is becoming stronger in influence, the developing trend of the immediate future, the direction of growth. It corresponds to the *ascendant* in astrology: the sign or planet rising over the horizon (of awareness), the morning-time. In the celtic method it is called "what is before him."

(2) represents *what is passing,* what is declining in influence, a waning factor of the recent past, or something that ties us to the past. It corresponds to the *descendant* in astrology: the sign or planet sinking below the horizon (of awareness), the evening time. In the celtic method it is called "what is behind him."

(3) represents *what is manifesting,* what is now being openly expressed in relation to the world and others. It corresponds to the *zenith* (or mid-heaven, M.C.) in astrology: what is culminating in the sky, the highest point, the noon-time. In the celtic method it is called "what crowns him."

(4) represents *what is hidden,* an unexpressed factor in the situation, latent yet active below awareness, an unmanifest tendency. It corresponds to the *nadir* (or *imum coeli,* I.C.) in astrology: the point opposite the zenith, on the nether side of the earth, the midnight-time. In

the celtic method it is called "what is beneath him."

(5) is the *key card,* the integrating factor, that which is needed or indicated to bring these four

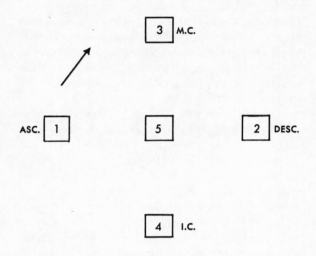

tendencies or influences into balance: the primary focus for understanding the situation.

Each card represents an inner factor, or state of consciousness, or quality. The four "principal actors"—High Priestess, Hierophant, Emperor and Empress—can be taken to refer to dynamic and magnetic aspects of one's own nature, as described above; or they may refer to external males or females if the question or situation pertains to them.

It should be remembered that such a reading is only one sample out of a constantly evolving pattern of change. The cross rotates in a clockwise direction; so that what is now on the ascendant will eventually culminate or be fully manifest; and what is now hidden below awareness will emerge into the light of day. As with the *I Ching,* a given reading should always and only be taken to indicate the probability patterns *as of the moment,* always subject to change.

There are of course no fixed interpretations. The cards laid out can be pondered as indications, or hints—signposts on the way.

NOTES AND REFERENCES

1. "A large number of experiments have been done to show that the organism's input channels and even the sensory receptors themselves, are subject to efferent control by the central nervous system. A recent series of studies performed in my laboratories demonstrated corticofugal influence as far peripherally as the cochlear nucleus and optic tract, originating in the so-called association areas." Karl H. Pribram, "The New Neurology and the Biology of Emotion," *American Psychologist* 22, no. 10 (1967): 834.

E. Lester Smith, writing in *Science Group Journal* 10, no. 2 (London: March, 1966), referring to recent electron microscope studies of retinal structure, says: "This makes the retina look like a piece of peripheral brain, and justifies regarding it as an extension of the brain on the end of the optic nerve. It is now believed, accordingly, that the retina not only acts as an amplifier with a gain of about 10^6, but also processes the information it receives before passing it on to the brain."

2. Joseph Campbell's *The Hero With a Thousand Faces* is a superb compilation of these myths (Cleveland: World Publishing Co., Meridian Books, 1956).

3. Carl Jung, *Civilization in Transition*, quoted in Carl Jung, *Memories, Dreams and Reflections* (New York: Random House, Vintage Books, 1961), p. 392.

4. Dr. Papus, *The Tarot of the Bohemians*, rev. ed. (London: Rider & Son, 1919), quoted in P. D. Ouspensky, *A New Model of the Universe* (New York: Alfred A. Knopf, 1943), p. 201.

5. Levi, *The Aquarian Gospel of Jesus the Christ*, "Transcribed from the Akashic Records" (Los Angeles: De Vorss & Co., 1969; orig. publ., 1907). The akashic record, known to the Buddhists as *alaya vijnana*, "store consciousness," is, according to esoteric doctrine, the record of *all* words, deeds, and thoughts that can be read by certain sensitives and psychics. Edgar Cayce, for example, supposedly read it to obtain medical diagnoses and cures for thousands of people. Whether or not one chooses to believe the story of its origin, the *Aquarian Gospel* is a document of uncommon interest and extraordinary beauty, which in highly plausible manner describes Jesus' years of searching in the Orient and Egypt, as well as those portions of his life known from the other gospels.

6. A. E. Waite, *The Pictorial Key to the Tarot* (New York: University Books, 1960; orig. publ., 1910), p. 40. Waite's book contains descriptive bibliography of the earlier commentaries on the Tarot.

7. See, for example, P. D. Ouspensky, *In Search of the Miraculous* (New York: Harcourt, Brace & World, 1949), p. 281.

8. Grillot de Givry, *Witchcraft, Magic and Alchemy* (Boston: Houghton Mifflin, 1931), p. 282.

9. John Cooke and Rosalind Sharpe, *The New Tarot. The Tarot for the Aquarian Age* (Kentfield, Calif.: Western Star Press, 1969). This version, originally published only as large meditation posters, has now also been published as a deck, with the minor arcana, and a divination game, using the Royal Maze card as a game board.

10. Levi, *Aquarian Gospel*, p. 55.

11. Carl G. Jung, *Aion: Researches into the Phenomenology of the Self*, vol. 9, II, *Collected Works* (New York: Pantheon Books, Bollingen Series XX, 1959).

12. *Ibid.*, p. 7.

13. See, for example, Mayananda, *The Tarot for Today* (London: Zeus Press, 1963).

14. Paul Foster Case, *The Book of Tokens. Tarot Meditations* (Los Angeles: Builders of the Adytum, 1968).

15. Ouspensky, *A New Model of the Universe*, p. 205.

16. Case, *Book of Tokens*, p. 9.

17. William Blake, *The Marriage of Heaven and Hell*.

18. Cooke and Sharpe, *Aquarian Tarot*, p. 11.

19. Ouspensky, *New Model of the Universe*, p. 203.

20. Ouspensky, *In Search of the Miraculous*, p. 91.

21. Waite, *Pictorial Key to the Tarot*, p. 103.

22. Cooke and Sharpe, *Aquarian Tarot*, p. 93.

23. William Blake, *The Marriage of Heaven and Hell*.

24. Cooke and Sharpe, *Aquarian Tarot*, p. 58.

25. *Ibid.*, p. 39.

26. Case, *Book of Tokens*, p. 161.

27. Levi, *Aquarian Gospel*, p. 39.

28. Cooke and Sharpe, *Aquarian Tarot*, p. 50.

29. Ouspensky, *In Search of the Miraculous*, p. 85.

30. Waite, *Pictorial Key to the Tarot*, p. 147.

31. *The Gospel According to Thomas*, (Leiden: E. J. Brill, and London: Collins, 1959), p. 3.

32. Cooke and Sharpe, *Aquarian Tarot*, p. 53.

33. Carl Jung, *The Archetypes and the Collective Unconscious*, vol. 9, I, *Collected Works* (New York: Pantheon Books, Bollingen Series XX, 1959), pp. 79–80.

THE

HERMETIC MUSEUM

——

RESTORED AND

ENLARGED.

Title page from The Hermetic Museum. *Note Athena and Hermes, at top left and right respectively; the four elemental spirits at the sides; the Sun and Moon at bottom left and right; and the Light of Nature leading the short-sighted alchemists, bottom center.*

ALCHEMY

The Chemistry of Inner Union

*Turn inward for your voyage! For all
your arts*
*You will not find the Stone in foreign
parts.*

ANGELUS SILESIUS

THE HISTORY OF ALCHEMY IS INTI-
mately connected with the history of the so-
called secret societies of the European Middle
Ages. The secrecy of these groups was in part a
political survival necessity. Their teachings,
which involved liberation from false concepts
and preprogrammed designs, if openly declared,
would have aroused the opposition of the
established church. In part, also, the need for
secrecy is inherent in the nature of the work of
schools of inner transformation, as we have seen.
It is the secrecy of a technical language, not the
secrecy of an attempt to gain political or com-
mercial advantage, although this was precisely
the accusation leveled against them.

The secrecy factor makes it difficult to recon-
struct the history of these psychological schools
with any accuracy, especially since much of the
information about them derives from the defama-
tory distortions of the churchly opposition. It
seems reasonably certain though that throughout the period when Europe was dominated by
the power of the church these schools of psychological transformation continued to arise. To
what extent there was an unbroken continuity
of tradition, reappearing in different guises, and
to what extent new teachings were formulated
in concepts derived from ancient, semimythical
sources in order to facilitate their acceptance, is
difficult to say. The alchemists and other groups
tended to emphasize that their teaching was the
same as that taught by the "ancient sages": the
first teacher was always Hermes Trismegistos,
an Egyptian initiate, whom Egyptians identified
with Thoth, the scribe of the gods, and the

Greeks identified with Hermes, messenger of the gods. Numerous works of anonymous medieval Latin alchemists were simply attributed to Hermes. Other ancients, whom the alchemists cited as initiates in their tradition, include Solomon, Pythagoras, Socrates, Plato, and Anaxagoras; and among medievalists, Avicenna, Albertus Magnus, Roger Bacon, Raymond Lully, and others.

The pattern observable in this tradition is somewhat as follows: the initial school or college of adepts is established teaching the techniques of transformation and the associated knowledge of man's psychophysiological constitution. Around a nucleus of usually anonymous teachers grows a community or brotherhood, which, in order to exemplify and externalize the teachings and at the same time generate the material resources to support itself, specializes in one or another of the arts or sciences. Thus the Freemasons were originally a group of adepts who were also master architects and builders, and who studied the laws of geometry and proportion and the nature of materials in order to build temples which would inspire and raise the consciousness even of those who knew nothing of their purpose.[1]

Others, such as the Rosicrucians (the Brothers of the Cross of the Rose) and the Brotherhood of the Golden Cross, specialized in the natural sciences and studied the workings of God and Nature in the cosmos (astrology) and in the composition of matter (alchemy). Yet others investigated herbs and pharmacy and developed new approaches to medicine and healing. The seventeenth-century German alchemist Paracelsus, for example, was the first to develop the concept of chemical specificity, still one of the cornerstones of modern therapeutics. The Knights Templar, which probably began as an attempt by a group of adepts who were members of the military caste to convert the warriors to a spiritual orientation, channeled their external activities into commerce and cultural exchange, and were responsible for bringing much material and scientific wealth to the West from the Arabic and Greek worlds.

The commonly accepted view of alchemy among contemporary scientists is that though their researchers had the merit of paving the way for the development of modern chemistry, yet they were regrettably steeped in the useless and superstitious quest to make gold. This despite the repeated and insistent statements of the alchemists that *aurum nostrum non est aurum vulgum*, "our gold is not the common gold"; and that "our" mercury is *not* the common mercury. Thus, the anonymous author of an alchemical tract entitled "An Open Entrance to the Closed Palace of the King" says: "I have spoken about mercury, sulphur, the vessel, the treatment, etc.—and of course, all these things are to be understood with a grain of salt. You must understand . . . that I have spoken metaphorically; if you take my words literally you will reap no harvest." [2]

Here, and elsewhere, it is clearly stated that the language of chemistry employed by the alchemists is a metaphor for the inner work, the *opus*, of psychic transformation. The transmutation of "base metals" into "gold" is the transmutation of psychophysical elements within man from an impure, obstructed state to a fine state of responsiveness to high-frequency energy. The precious metals were regarded as the most evolved members of the mineral kingdom; so, by analogy, to "make gold" by "our art" was to make oneself into a more highly evolved member of the human kingdom.

And this was not an exclusive, separative endeavor: when the alchemists say "our gold," they do not mean ours as opposed to yours, but the gold that is within us, as opposed to the gold of the goldsmiths. There is in the writings of the alchemists an intense, almost poignant ambivalence between their desire to share the valuable knowledge and art they have learned and the knowledge that this sharing is possible only to a very limited degree, because of the possible danger both to the art and to the individual, if premature information came into the wrong hands. "For the matter is so glorious and wonderful that it cannot be fully delivered to any one but by word of mouth." [3]

The genuine alchemical adepts were aware of course that their teachings were being distorted and abused by charlatans who claimed to be able to make physical gold, and who preyed on the concupiscence of the ignorant. They denounced the "huffers and puffers" who said they could "multiply metals"; and pointed out, quite logically, that if these imposters really were able to make gold, they wouldn't be wandering around boasting of it, and "cheating the credulous out of their money." Yet their protestations were in vain, and the low reputation, which alchemy acquired as the result of the activities of fraudulent imitators, has prevailed to this day.

Although modern scientists accuse the alchemists of trying to make money, and believe that by pursuing science for its own sake they have arrived at more exact and comprehensive knowledge, this is actually a quite false and idealized picture. The majority of modern scientists work for industry and government, for money; the determination of the goal or purpose of the scientific experimentation is often left to politicians and businessmen. Consequently, the researches of modern chemists and physicists, originally started by alchemists as an aid to man's own evolution, have become quite separated from this purpose. Using chemistry to make money, which is what the alchemists were accused of trying to do, is what the modern chemists and their patrons actually do.

In modern times the study of alchemy has received a new infusion of interest due to the work of Carl Jung. In his autobiography, Jung relates how during a period of several years in the middle of his life, he was exposed to a "confrontation with the unconscious," that is, images, dreams, and fantasies which were both very strange and very powerful rose up uncontrollably into his awareness. He had a dream in which he felt that he was "caught in the seventeenth century." Soon he began to notice that "analytical psychology coincided in a curious way with alchemy." [4] The dream symbols and images he encountered had numerous parallels in the alchemical literature. This discovery was extremely important to Jung because it indicated to him that the psychic experiences he was undergoing were not purely personal-subjective, but had collective, historical antecedents. Jung

had no external teacher or companion explorers with whom to verify his experiences, and he found himself in an extremely isolated position without such external confirmation. For this reason, Jung regarded his work in alchemy as that which gave his psychology "its place in reality and established [it] upon its historical foundations." [5]

Jung made pioneering advances in recognizing the importance of the alchemical tradition and its continued relevance to modern man's quest for self-understanding and individuation, yet he was not able to step outside the role of the scholar. "I worked along philological lines, as if I were trying to solve the riddle of an unknown language." [6] The actual experimental practice of the art of alchemy eluded him, because, as they themselves repeatedly said, this could only be taught by word of mouth, by a teacher. In this way, despite his sincere and persevering efforts in the realm of scholarship, Jung fell victim to the inherent trap of the intellectual approach: that of assuming that mental knowledge is true understanding. Hence he accuses the alchemists of "incredible naïveté," in projecting their "fantasies" into matter; although the contradiction between this and the great psychological wisdom with which he credits them, seems to escape him. A mere projection of fantasies into matter would not have lasted a thousand years with such profound effects on all areas of European life and culture.

Jung's blind spot regarding the role of the body led him to miss the point that the transmutation of substances took place within the psychophysical organism, even when the alchemists say this explicitly. Thus, when Paracelsus says, "The microcosm in its interior anatomy must be reverberated up to the highest reverberation," Jung interprets this as, "While the artifex heats the chemical substance in the furnace he himself is morally undergoing the same fiery torment and purification." [7] Yet Paracelsus is quite literally referring to an actual process of raising the vibratory rate of structures in the "interior anatomy" by means of "fire" ("reverberation is ignition"). It is not just a "projection" of a "moral" purification, or becoming "uncon-

The evolution of awareness, in seven stages from the fixed plant stage to the mobile human stage, through the transforming power of lightning-fire.

sciously identical" with a process going on in an external furnace, as Jung would have it.

Perhaps this difference of interpretation can best be made clear by relating a personal experience. A short while after having begun to study the Yoga of Fire, which has many points in common with the alchemical work, I interrupted a yoga session in order to brew myself a cup of tea. While waiting for the water to boil, I sat down in the kitchen and continued to work with the "fire." Shortly I became aware of the sound of the water beginning to heat up. As I was attempting to increase the heat of the inner fire, a linkage was spontaneously set up between the internal and the external heating. When the water reached the boiling point, there was a definite discontinuous energy change internally, experienced subjectively as a kind of release. In other words, the external heating provided a kind of support to the inner work, akin to the role of *mandala* in visual meditation. There was no projection of images, or identification going on here; I was fully aware of both processes and the difference between them.

This experience suggested to me that where the alchemists actually employed physical apparatus in their experiments, which was not necessarily very often, they were perhaps working with this type of procedure. They might have been setting up laboratory analogues of internal transformation processes, and using these

analogues as supports for inner work. In the text entitled "The Sophic Hydrolith, or Water-Stone of the Wise," there is a passage which seems to refer to this procedure: "We saw that in our chemical operation the regulation of the fire, and a most patient and careful tempering of its heat, was of the greatest importance . . . we also spoke of the 'fire of the Sages' as being one of the chief agents in our chemical process, and said that it was an essential, preternatural and Divine fire, that it lay hid in our substance, and that it was stirred into action by the influence and aid of the outward, material fire." [8]

Another author makes a careful distinction between the "truly secret furnace, which a vulgar eye never saw," and the "common furnace, made of potter's earth." [9] One of the essential requirements of the latter was that "you must be able to keep up in it a fire for ten or twelve hours, without looking to it"; which suggests that it was used as an external support to the inner or "living fire" that burns in "our vessel."

The alchemists were adepts first and natural scientists second. That is, their goal and purpose and main endeavor was evolutionary transformation of man's total being. Their methods were taught by direct contact between teacher and student. Yet they believed that since man is a microcosm, the processes they observed and studied internally could also be found externally, in Nature, and vice versa. "If, therefore, we wish to exercise the fine Art of Alchemy, we must imitate the method by which Nature does her work in the bowels of the earth." [10] Alchemical texts are laboratory manuals for the great experiment of Nature, which we carry out in our own nature: self-transformation.

It is impossible at this date to determine to what extent actual physical experimental setups were used by the alchemical adepts. Many were evidently distressed at and disapproving of an increasing trend to use external materials. One author, quoting Nature, writes: "Let me tell you that your artificial fire will never impart my heavenly warmth." [11] And continues later: "All you want is leisure, and some place where you can be without any fear of interruptions." Another author emphasizes: "There is but one vessel, one method, and one consummation." [12] Yet another implores: "Relinquish the multiplicity of methods and substances, for our substance is *one*." Clearly, the setting up of laboratory analogues as aids established a tendency for some of the alchemists to concern themselves more and more with the nature and composition of external elements and thus lose track of the original goal. This is essentially the birth of modern chemistry, which, in the course of time, then proliferated into numberless specialized subdisciplines.

The alchemists often referred to their method as the "spagyric" art, a compound word made up from Greek roots meaning "to take apart" and "to bring together." Thus it was a combination of what is today called analytic and synthetic chemistry, in the interior sphere: the separation of elements, the extraction of gold from ore, on the one hand, and the synthesis of finer substances, the combining of elements, on the other. Analysis probes, goes into, takes apart: it is a masculine, dynamic fuction. Synthesis contains, combines, encloses: it is a feminine, magnetic function. The fusion of male and female energies, known as the *conjunction,* is the central process of alchemy. Many of the illustrations of the work show a man on the right and a woman on the left performing various operations in the vessel, in the center. They are preparing what

was called "the chemical wedding," the marriage of chemicals within.

The hermetic vessel, called by some "the root and the principle of our art," that in which all the operations of alchemy are performed, is the human body, or rather the whole organization of bodies and fields considered under the aspect of regenerative inner work. Jung writes: "The Hermetic vessel is a uterus of spiritual renewal or rebirth"; [13] and this is half the picture. For the renewal is physical as well as spiritual. The vessel is said to be circular, or egg-shaped, corresponding to the shape of the organizing field seen by sensitives around human beings. The use of the word *vessel* recalls early Christian mystics who saw the body as the "vessel of the spirit," in which the "second birth" of regeneration takes place. The alchemical "Liber Quartorum" ("Book of the Four") says, "like the work of God is the vessel of the divine seed, for it has received the clay, moulded it, and mixed it with fire and water." [14] The rebirth of the new man, or second Adam, following the work of regeneration through fusion of male and female (sometimes called the spagyric birth) brings forth the son of the wise, that is the actual, knowing Self, the hermaphroditic One, the unified being.

For the proper mixing of chemicals to take place the alchemists emphasized the importance of keeping the vessel sealed. This so-called *hermetic seal* is like a protective field which the adept establishes around himself, to prevent "air" from coming in, that is, extraneous thought-forms which could be destructive to the process, as well as to prevent "air" from leaking out, that is, to prevent mental energy from being dissipated in outward projections. This latter aspect recalls Patanjali's definition of *yoga* as "the restriction of the fluctuations of mind-stuff."

The four elements

Central to the thinking of the alchemical philosophers is the idea that macrocosmic Nature and man, the microcosm, are made up of the four elements: fire, air, water, and earth. This notion is not at all far-fetched when it is remembered that 99 percent of the atoms of proteins,

The salamander as the spirit of the living fire. "This is the reiteration, gradation and amelioration of the Philosopher's Stone; the whole is called its augmentation."

The alchemical masculine and feminine aspects of the nature, mixing chemicals in the vessel (within), until finally the sun, the power of transmutation, bearing the golden flower, appears.

the chief ingredient of living matter, are constituted of the elements carbon, oxygen, hydrogen, and nitrogen. Perhaps this is one aspect of what the alchemists meant by the four elements.

Another aspect is what we nowadays call the states of matter. Molecules bound into relatively fixed, immobile structures are solid; within the body, bones, muscles, cartilage, connective tissue, and cell structures are the "earth elements" of our nature. The alchemists say: "Elementary earth is like a sponge, and the receptacle of all other elements." [15]

With a rise in temperature the movement of molecules in a substance increases and matter enters the liquid state; our organism is 70 percent liquid, with its circulating blood and lymph systems, hormones, and intracellular fluids. The alchemists refer to this fluid medium of life as the *aqua permanens,* the "permanent water," or as *mare nostrum,* "our sea." Through its connection with the endocrine system, "water" is associated with the emotional nature. The bloodstream, it has been said by Rodney Collin, is "an index of man's being." [16]

The gaseous state of matter is marked by still higher temperatures and degree of activity; the molecules are in ceaseless, random motion. The alchemists said air "contains the vital spirit of all creatures . . . it nourishes, impregnates, conserves the other elements." [17] It is hardly necessary to point out that the consistent oxygenation of the blood is a vital part of the continuing life process, and particularly of cerebral processes. Or, as the alchemists put it, "We see that water becomes foul and unwholesome without a supply of fresh air."

The breath of life is the carrier of energy in the process of creation, as God breathed life into the form of Adam; it is also intimately involved in all systems of *yogic* regeneration, or re-creation; and metaphorically, we find it in the "inspiration" of artistic creativity. The very words *spirit* and *psyche* come from Greek and Latin words meaning "to breathe." In most esoteric philosophy and in the symbolism of many dreams and fantasies, "air" is associated with the thinking nature, the "wings of thought."

The statements of the alchemists concerning

fire are less easily interpreted in terms of states of matter. Knowing what we do now about the electromagnetic wave properties of matter, and the interchangeability of the wave-energy aspect and the particle-matter aspect, one could say that electricity is a fourth state of matter, and identify it with the sensory-perceptual nervous system in the body, which functions electrically. However, the alchemists either did not possess this information or did not write about it; they were concerned mostly with fire in its aspect of purifying energy.

"Would you know the perfect Master?" asks "The Ordinal of Alchemy." "It is he who understands the regulation of the fire, and its degrees." [18] The author goes on to describe thirteen different kinds of fire and when to use them. Another text, entitled "The Glory of the World," states that "without this fire our Art can not be brought to a successful issue. . . . It is the most precious fire that God has created in the earth, and has a thousand virtues. . . . It has the purifying virtue of Purgatory." [19] Yet others identify fire with spirit or soul. Although sometimes the alchemists identify their "fire of the Sages," with the fire of hell or purgatory, when describing its purifying aspects, yet mostly they emphasize that the art is to be carried out with "gentle cooking."

Yet another aspect of the doctrine of the four elements is that this may be a metaphor for the subtle bodies which we encounter in all esoteric philosophy. These bodies are held to differ in material density, or in frequency of vibration. The earth body, which is the one we perceive with our physical senses, is the densest, and has the lowest frequency. "Water" then refers to the emotional body, also known as the astral body. This is a different level of consciousness which links into but is not identical with the fluid components of the physical, earth body. Similarly, "air" refers then to the mental body, also known as the causal body, the mental level of consciousness, which links into but is not identical with the brain systems.

The work of alchemy consisted in integrating and transmuting these elements, these levels of consciousness. They need to be integrated because in the normal condition of man they are in a state of conflict and confusion and are programmed by low-level images and imprints. The alchemists referred to this initial state as "chaos," or a "confused mass," or *nigredo*, "blackness." It was essential to recognize this state of inner chaos, the constant warfare of what Gurdjieff called the "many 'I's," before the work of transformation could begin.

"The elixir is composed by the reconciling and mutual transmutation of the four elements," says one alchemist.[20] Another text explains: "When corruptible elements are united in a certain subject, their strife must sooner or later bring about its decomposition . . . if the pure elements are then once more joined together by the action of natural heat, a much nobler and higher form of life is produced."[21] The integration of the bodies or levels of consciousness was often described by analogy with the chemical processes of "solution" and "coagulation": the former turns a solid into a liquid, the latter does the reverse. "The whole thing is done by a simple process of heating, which includes the solution and coagulation of bodies," writes the author of "The Only True Way."[22] "Dissolve and coagulate" became one of the oft-quoted maxims of the alchemists.

The integration of levels of consciousness was seen also as the spirit becoming body and the body becoming spiritualized. In "The Glory of the World" is a fascinating passage which unites many of these metaphors: "The gentle inward heat which changes it (the body) into water, and yields two waters, viz., the distilled spirit, and the dissolved body. These two waters are again united by slow and gentle coction, the distilled spirit becoming coagulated into a body, the dissolved body becoming a spirit. The fixed becomes volatile, and the volatile fixed, by dissolution and coagulation."[23]

In one of the strange quirks of linguistic history the term *distilled spirit*, having lost its connection to the process of psychological transmutation, became the name for a type of chemically processed beverage prepared by the liquor industry; a beverage notable for its effect of blunting the spirit. The original alchemical "dis-

tillation of the spirit," was described as thousandfold and as circular; reminiscent of the "circulation of the light" of Chinese alchemy, and of the "thousand petal lotus" of the Hindu and Tibetan *Tantras*.

"Separation of elements" was another frequently employed and as frequently misunderstood metaphor. Paracelsus wrote: "The impure animate body must be purified through the separation of the elements," and he goes on, "which is done by your meditating on it."[24] In other words, it is clearly specified that the separation is in awareness. In the initial state of "confused mass," we are not aware of several bodies; our awareness gradually becomes more discriminating, and is able to separate the elements, that is, to distinguish the different levels of consciousness.

Some alchemists became very involved in describing the various inner changes that resulted from the work in chemical terms. As the image-factors obstructing clear consciousness are burned out by the inner fire, various processes analogous to "calcination," "putrefaction," "decomposition," "sublimation," etc., might indeed take place. Yet again some authors were dismayed by this trend toward multiple terminology, which they saw as a distraction from the basic simplicity of the method. In "The Only True Way," it is said the "substance" needs no special treatment, "except that of digestion by gentle heat. . . . For while you heat, you also putrefy, or decompose . . . Again when you heat, you also sublime."[25] And indeed, this author is evidently quite correct in pointing out that the various chemical processes named are all the *results* and *effects* of heating. So that we may regard them as names for different stages of one process.

Sometimes, the purification or transmutation of elements was described as a process of ascent, followed by descent. In the "Emerald Tablet" attributed to Hermes, it was said: "It ascendeth from the earth to heaven, and descendeth again to the earth, and receiveth the power of the higher and the lower things. So wilt thou have the glory of the whole world."[26] The ascent is of course not in physical space but rather in levels of consciousness, in frequency rate, through the four elements and higher states; and the descent is the return journey, which brings something of the quality of the higher levels into the lower. Thus, Gerhard Dorn, a seventeenth-century alchemist writes: "This earthly spagyric birth clothes itself with heavenly nature by its ascent, and then by its descent visibly puts on the nature of the centre of the earth, but nonetheless the nature of the heavenly centre which it acquired by the ascent is secretly preserved." This birth conquers the "subtle and spiritual sickness in the human mind and also all bodily defects, within as well as without." [27]

The medical, healing properties of the "stone," the goal of alchemy, are often emphasized: it was called "tincture," "panacea," "elixir of life," "spagyric medicine." Again, with the exception of certain of the physician specialists, it must not be supposed that the alchemists were preparing actual physical medicines. Rather, the transformation of self into a unified being in whom Immortal Self actualizes its highest potentials involves in part the ability to heal one's own earth-body, and to a certain degree the bodies of others. The great teachers have always been healers as well, not miracle healers or faith healers, but healers with higher energies.

As one might expect, the reputed or actual ability to heal sometimes got the alchemists into trouble from those who mistook the inner powers of the alchemist as being due to an external material. This was an additional reason for their secrecy, as is illustrated in the following story told by the author of "An Open Entrance": "It was only a short time ago that, after visiting the plague-stricken haunts of a certain city, and restoring the sick to health by means of my miraculous medicine, I found myself surrounded by a yelling mob, who demanded that I should give to them my Elixir of the Sages; and it was only by changing my dress and my name, by shaving off my beard and putting on a wig, that I was enabled to save my life, and escape from the hands of those wicked men." [28] This is why "fear closes our lips, when love tempts us to open ourselves freely to a brother." Mankind has ever tended to respond to the message of light with fear, greed, rage, envy, ingratitude, and destructive hate.

The alchemist-teachers required the highest qualities of character and devotion from their students because the difficulties of the work were such that without these qualities it could not be carried through, and because they were unwilling to have the techniques fall into the

In the state of "chaos" the king (the higher nature) is lifeless, his body being devoured by predatory images (cf. Prometheus). But as the fire consumes the wolfish images, the king is liberated.

hands of those who would misuse them for their personal advantage.

By and large, the alchemists seem to have been extremely devout and sincere individuals. In their "laboratory manuals" the phrase *Deo concedente*, "if God be willing," was appended to the descriptions of their experiments and their art. Though they knew that many of their doctrines, especially the emphasis on Nature as the revealer of truth, were anathema to established Christianity, which held that church and priest were the only guardians of truth, yet they saw themselves as followers of Christ, and as "Godfearing men." Carl Jung has devoted considerable research and scholarship to pointing out the many parallels between alchemy and early Christian mysticism, especially the Gnostic school and Manichaeism; and he has also suggested that the philosophers' stone was in many ways synonymous with what the Christians called "the Christ," or "Christ-consciousness," or "the body of Christ."

The following passage, from the treatise entitled "The Sophic Hydrolith," is typical of the alchemists' attitude:

In the first place, let every devout and Godfearing chemist and student of the Art consider that this arcanum should be regarded, not only as a truly great, but as a most holy Art (seeing that it typifies and shadows out the highest heavenly good). Therefore, if any man desire to reach this great and unspeakable Mystery, he must remember that it is obtained not by the might of man, but by the grace of God, and that not our will or desire, but only the Mercy of the Most High can bestow it upon us. . . . When you have thus devoted yourself to God and learned to appreciate justly the aim and scope of this Art, you should, in the first place, strive to realize how Nature, having been set in order by God the Triune, now works invisibly day by day, and moves and dwells in the will of God alone. For no one should set about the study of this Art without a just appreciation of natural processes. Now Nature may truly be described as being *one*, true, simple, and perfect in her own essence, and as being animated by an invisible spirit. If therefore you would know her, you, too, should be true, single-hearted,

"Hear without terror that in the forest are hidden a deer and an unicorn. In the body there is soul and spirit."

patient, constant, pious, forbearing, and, in short, a new and regenerate man.[29]

The counsel of patience is ubiquitous in the alchemical literature. They warned that undue haste could be destructive to the work, an explosion could wreck the "furnace" and wipe out many months of effort. By explosions the alchemists presumably meant explosions of anger, or rage, which, if let out, could upset the delicate balancing of internal chemistry, which the art was trying to bring about. Gurdjieff used to say one moment of anger cost him three pints of blood.

Besides haste, the other main obstacle the alchemists warned of was despair or discouragement. As an antidote to this, "The Ordinal of Alchemy" counsels that "you should take care, from time to time, to unbend your mind from its sterner employments with some convenient recreation; otherwise your spirits might be weighed down with melancholy and despair, and you might lose heart for the continuation of the work."[30]

The three forces

We have seen how the principle of integrating four aspects of the nature of man is of central importance in alchemy. Most often the four are designated earth, water, air, and fire. Sometimes the process is said to be one of the correct adjustments of the four qualities dry, moist, hot, and cold, which were related to the four humors, or psychophysiological dispositions to be sanguine, melancholic, choleric, or phlegmatic. The common-sense psychology of everyday speech still recognizes these four types, even though rational minds consider them outmoded: we all know the "dry humor" of the sanguine character, the melancholic's "dampening" effect on our spirits, the "hot temper" of the choleric, and the "cool" of the phlegmatic.

Besides the principle of four, the quaternity, the alchemists also attached great importance to the trinity, the duality and the singularity. In the treatise "The New Chemical Light," by Michael Sendivogius, the three principles "sulphur," "salt," and "mercury" are said to arise from the interaction of the four elements. And then, "as the three principles are produced out of four, so they, in their turn, must produce two, a male and a female; and these two must produce an incorruptible one, in which are exhibited the four elements in a highly purified and digested condition, and with their mutual strife hushed in unending peace and goodwill."[31]

In other words, the work is here described as beginning with the mutual balancing and harmonizing of the four bodies or levels of consciousness, from which arises an awareness of the three primary forces, and when these are polarized as male and female (sun and moon, king and queen), they can be united in the chemical wedding, and from this conjunction will come the philosophers' stone, the "elixir of the Sages."

The trinity sulphur, salt, and mercury, at least in the later alchemical writings, is conceived as a trio of forces interacting in everything. "That universal thing, the greatest treasure of earthly wisdom, is one thing, and the principles of three things are found in one. . . . The three things are the true spirit of mercury, and the soul of sulphur, united to a spiritual salt, and dwelling in one body."[32] This is comparable to the *yang, yin,* and *Tao* of Chinese philosophy, and the Hindu trinity of Brahma, Siva, and Vishnu. We recall also Gurdjieff's formulation of the Law of Three: that everything is a product of the interaction of affirming, denying and reconciling forces. For the alchemists, sulphur is the active, dynamic principle; salt is the female, magnetic; and mercury or quicksilver is double-natured, ubiquitous and fluid, like the water of the Taoists. (It must be said though that in some texts only two forces are described, in which case sulphur is active and mercury passive.)

Sulphur is related to sun, the male aspect in the conjunction. According to Gerhard Dorn, "The male and universal seed, the first and most potent, is the solar sulphur, the first part and most potent cause of generation".[33] It is also referred to as "the homogeneous sperm," as "living fire," which "quickens and matures lifeless substances," and as "the spirit of gen-

The four, the three, the two, and the one. (Squaring the circle.)

erative power, who works in the moisture." In its crude, untransmuted form, sulphur, if excessive, is the "cause of corruption," it is of an "evil, stinking odour and not much strength"; but, transmuted, it becomes, "the virtue of all things," and is compared to a rainbow.

The change undergone by sulphur, the male principle, in the course of the work, is indicated in "An Open Entrance," where it is said that "the coagulating sulphur, which in the corporal gold was turned outwards, is turned inwards";[34] this inward turning comes about when sun and moon are united. In other words, inner unity is brought about by the male principle seeking its own female consort *within* the nature, rather than externally.

Salt, because of its association with the sea and hence the moon, was seen as a feminine, lunar principle. It is referred to as the "permanent radical moisture," as the "concentrated centre of the elements," as "common moon," and as the "white water." In its initial, impure state, it is "bitter" and "harsh," also "black and evil-smelling." Transmuted, it is called *albedo,* "whiteness," it is the tincture that coagulates all substances, even itself. "The salt alkali is hidden in the womb of magnesia," says "The New Chemical Light." [35] And in "The Golden Tract" it is said that "he who works without salt will never raise dead bodies . . . he who works without salt draws a bow without a string." [36] Thus,

salt is the structural, feminine, magnetic principle; also the wisdom principle. "And the Light was made Salt, a body of salt, the salt of wisdom," [37] according to the alchemist Khunrath.

The association of salt with wisdom is ancient, and is found in the Gospels, where Jesus refers to his disciples as "the salt of the earth," and admonishes them to "have salt in yourselves." The colloquial expression "with a grain of salt," still carries this meaning. Wisdom, as an aspect of the feminine half of the nature, is embodied by Egyptian mythology in the figure of Isis (the High Priestess of the Tarot), by Greek myth in the figure of Athena, and by American myth in the concept of *alma mater,* literally "nourishing mother." The preservative qualities of common salt may have contributed to its choice as the metaphor for the sustaining mother-principle.

Just as the attempt to define *Tao* led Lao-tse into his most mind-baffling paradoxical statements, so the attempt to describe the nature of *mercurius* caused the alchemists to produce some of their most fantastic formulations. Here for example is a passage from "The New Chemical Light," in which Nature, in response to a question from the Alchemist, describes Mercury, her son: "Know that I have only one such son; he is one of seven, and the first among them; and though he is now all things, he was at first only one. In him are the four elements, yet he is not an element. He is a spirit, yet he has a body; a man, yet he performs a woman's part; a boy, yet he bears a man's weapons; a beast, yet he has the wings of a bird. He is poison, yet he cures leprosy; life, yet he kills all things; a King, yet another occupies his throne; he flees from the fire, yet fire is taken from him; he is water, yet does not wet the hands; he is earth, yet is sown; he is air, and lives by water." [38]

In a German version of the well-known tale of the genie in the bottle, the name of the imprisoned spirit is Mercurius. A little boy finds a bottle (the "hermetic vessel") in the forest, and a spirit within, calling to be let out. When he lets him out, Mercurius grows to the size of a giant tree. Later, as a reward, Mercurius gives the boy something that both heals and turns metals into silver.

We would say mercury is consciousness; consciousness exists on many different levels (elements), can assume many guises, be male or female, young or old, bird or beast; normally, it is restricted, "bottled up," though it has the potential of a giant, of a tree. The mobile, elusive fluidity of quicksilver make it an apt choice of metaphor for consciousness.

Mercury is described as "dry water," as "root moisture," as "invisible fire," and "scintillating fire of the light of nature"; as "stone uplifted by the wind" and as "winged and wingless dragon." [39] Even more graphic is his characterization as the dragon Pantophthalmos, who is covered with eyes all over his body, and sleeps with some open and some closed. He is also called "duplex," "inconstant," "changing his skin," a "hermaphroditic monster," "good with the good and evil with the evil." These designations are suggestive of the image-producing power of consciousness, the polymorphous perversity of ever changing, shape-shifting images with which consciousness is programmed. Mercury is everywhere, goes everywhere, to the highest and the lowest, the lightest and heaviest, earth and heaven, strong and weak; he is akin to the Godhead, yet he is found in sewers. He is referred to as *terminus ani*, "end of the anus," but also as "carbuncle of the sun."

Mercury's role as the mediator between sul-

phur and salt, between male and female, between spirit and body, is clearly indicated when he is called *anima media natura*, "soul of intermediate nature" or "intermediate substance." Probably the most concise summary of his nature and role is "Mercurius is the medium of the conjunction." [40] Inner unification takes place in the medium, the neutral field of consciousness. "Living mercury . . . promotes fusion . . . it is full of affinity, cleaving faithfully, and is the medium by which tinctures are united, for it mingles most intimately with them, penetrating into their inmost part, for it is of the same nature." [41]

The two opposites

The "union of opposites" in alchemy is most often described as the "conjunction of sun and moon," also called "gold" and "silver." "Gold, then, being the most precious of all the metals, is the red tincture, tinging and transforming every body. Silver is the white tincture, tinging other bodies with its perfect whiteness." [42] The text goes on to explain that gold and silver are not meant here in their "metallic form"; no other tincture is meant "but our own." "There is no acid but our own, no other regimen, no other colours." Sun is described as a "living fire," "ruddy and burning." The "philosopher's gold" is a "quickening ferment" which must be sown into the "earth." Alternatively, the "living gold" must be extracted from its "ore," which is the "earth." It is called "regenerate gold," whose red color is due to the admixture of copper. In the alchemical drawings, the sun is usually shown above and to the right of the adept, or sometimes he is standing upon it. The moon is above and to the left, or, sometimes, the female has the moon below her feet.

"Gold," or "sun," or "red tincture" would seem to be names for an aspect of inner work: a tool of transmutation, of purification, and transformation. The transmutation takes place in consciousness, at least to begin with, and is brought about through the action of fire. Mercury multiplies gold, but "in virtue, rather than in weight." [43] In other words, consciousness amplifies the transformative power.

"A wolf and a dog are in one house, and are afterwards changed into one."

The transmutation of animal aspects of the nature by "gentle cooking" in the hermetic vessel. Note the lingam-yoni symbolism on the vessel.

"Moon" in alchemy is the source of moisture, of "hidden dew," also of "appetites" and emotions such as anger and desire. It is said that "the realm of the perishable begins with the moon," [44] and the moon is said to be the "contriver of bodies." "Hence the body, or moon, has been well designated the female principle, and the water, or sun, the male principle." [45] Lunar mythology is associated with animals such as dragons, serpents, scorpions, toads; lions, bears, wolves, dogs; eagles and ravens. Reptiles, mammals, and birds appear in awareness, in approximately this order, as a result of the conjunction of sun and moon. The "moon" is regarded as the preserver of past evolutionary tendencies and imprints. If these animal, lunar, consciousness factors usurp the human level of consciousness, "lunacy" results. But when the transformative power of the "red-gold sun" is brought to bear upon them, these animal forms will appear in consciousness and be transmuted.

The alchemists were much concerned with the animal aspects of our nature, or what in Actualism would be called the creature-body

level of consciousness, which has powerful residual imprints and images left over from past evolutionary stages. One alchemical drawing shows a wolf and a dog fighting with fury and jealous rage. (The wolf and dog appear also in the Moon card of the Tarot.) This is the struggle between the wild and the domesticated animal nature, fighting the evolutionary battle for survival. Hermann Hesse wrote of this conflict in *Steppenwolf*. Fritz Perls called it the struggles between "top dog" and "under dog." For the alchemists, when these two are changed into one, they become "the most great and precious medicine." The transmutation of animal, lunar consciousness is also indicated in the frequent verbal and visual references to crowned serpents, crowned birds, or winged mammals, or mammals with human heads.

The conjunction of opposites was described in many different ways under different aspects. One might say the union has to take place on all levels of consciousness. On the level of the animal, creature body, we find representations of the lion and the lioness. Or, it was said one should

The conjunction of male and female creature body levels of consciousness. "Here you behold a great marvel—two lions are joined into one."

Union of Fire and Water.

mate the "corascene dog" and the "armenian bitch." The marriage of king and queen is the union of transmuted male and female energies. The English alchemist John Pordage described it as the union of Mars, "the fiery life," and Venus, "the gentle love-fire." [46] It was also seen as the marriage of spirit and body, the integration of the highest and the lowest, that is, high-frequency and low-frequency levels of consciousness, fire and water. In the words of Avicenna, "Marriage is the mingling of the subtle with the dense." [47]

In a series of drawings illustrating stages of the conjunction, the *hierosgamos* or "sacred marriage," one can see how the alchemists conceived the gradual, progressive unification of the male and the female within. [48] At first, there is a man on the right with a sun beneath his feet, and a woman on the left with the moon beneath her feet. They are giving each other their left hands, and with their right hands are holding crossed branches. Centered above is a star, and a dove is descending, holding another branch. A first, awkward, "gauche" contact has been made between the two halves of the nature, with the help of the bird of peace and the light of the star.

In the next picture, the couple is naked, they confront each other more openly, undisguised and undefensive. Each one is holding the branch from the opposite hand of the other, indicating greater interrelatedness. Sol, the male, solar force, says: "O Luna, let me be your husband." Luna, the female, lunar force, says: "O Sol, I will be receptive to you."

In the following picture, the man and woman are immersed in the bath. They are being bathed, purified, heated; impurities, factors obstructing the union, are being dissolved out. "Our stone is to be extracted from the nature of the two bodies," says the accompanying text.

In the next picture, solar king and lunar queen are mating. They are under the earth and in the water: the conjunction takes place in the "earth-body" and in the emotional "waters of life." The pictorial version of this stage shows them each with a pair of wings, indicating even more clearly the multidimensional nature of this conjunction: in earth, in water, and in air. Sol says: "O Luna, through my embrace and sweet love, you become beautiful and strong as I am." Luna says: "O Sol, though your light is the brightest, yet you need me as the cock the hen." The text says, "In the hour of conjunction the greatest marvels appear." And "The new light is begotten by them."

In the following picture, king and queen have fused into a single being with two heads. They are shown in a tomb, because the old has died, and the new is yet to be born. "The death of one is the generation of the other." This is the classic theme of regeneration through death and rebirth. This is by no means the end of the process: in subsequent pictures the soul is shown ascending, leaving the body, the body is

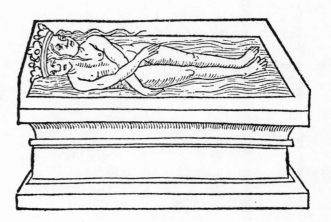

further purified, by dew from above, and the soul returns into the new, lighted, unified, androgynous body. This being was called "son" or "daughter" of the philosophers. "Now is the stone shaped, the elixir of life prepared, the love-child or the child of love born, the new birth completed, and the work made whole and perfect." [49]

No aspect of the teaching of alchemy, or of esoteric philosophy in general, has been as misunderstood as the concept of the conjunction or royal marriage. The difficulty of communication stems from the fact that we are dealing with an *experience*, and a rare one. To one who has not had the experience, or anything like it, the words are sheer fantasy. In addition, the alchemists themselves were most allegorical and reticent about this aspect of their work. In the *Rosarium Philosophorum*, it was said: "So I have not declared all that appears and is necessary in this work, because there are things of which a man may not speak." And: "Such matters must be transmitted in mystical terms, like employing fables and parables." [50]

There is another reason why it is so difficult to communicate and understand this process of inner union of male and female. There are very strong psychic image-factors and imprints which prevent us from coming to a just appreciation of this most vital secret. There are internal defense screens which block us from perceiving and experiencing this union. It is precisely for this reason that the art has been so difficult: all kinds of false interpretations of the meaning of this marriage are superimposed on the actual meaning, which Higher Self knows.

Typically, the union has been interpreted externally rather than internally. The Christian Church, which received the teaching of the mystic union from the early Christians, interpreted it as the union of Christ and the church. Thus, Christ had taught, clearly enough: "Make the male and the female into a single one, so the male shall not be male and the female not be female." [51] Yet, St. Gregory and others of the Church Fathers taught that "When the only-begotten son of God wished to join his divinity with our human nature, he decided to take unto himself, as his bride, the Church." [52] The union is no longer inner, but outer.

Jung himself, in spite of his lengthy and profound study of the alchemical texts and his high sensitivity and intuition, did not really grasp this point. In his book *Psychology of the Transference* he interprets the conjunction in terms of the transference relationship between doctor and patient; again, an external union rather than the inner.

Freud's theory of the "primal scene" is another image-distortion of the actual inner union. Freud held that most children at some time see their parents copulating and this implants a traumatic fearful image of sexual union. From the esoteric or alchemic point of view, we can see the whole notion of the traumatic primal scene taking place "out there" as a defensive fantasy screen, preventing awareness of the potential creative union of the divine Father and Mother within. For, as the *Rosarium* says: "When my beloved parents have tasted of life, . . . and have embraced each other in my bed, they shall bring forth the son of the moon, who will excell all his kindred." [53] Or, in the words of Paracelsus: "When the heavenly marriage is acomplished, who will deny its superexcellent virtue?" [54]

The one stone

When the offspring of the inner union has been tested, purified, tempered, and strengthened by repeated ascents and descents, by distillation and sublimation, the long sought-after philosophers' stone is produced, "the most ancient, secret, natural, incomprehensible, heavenly, blessed, beatified, and triune universal Stone of the Sages." [55] "This child of the two parents, of the elements and heaven, has in itself such a nature that the potentiality and the actuality of both parents can be found in it. What will remain there till today, save the stone in the spagyric generation?" [56]

But what is this stone? "It is called perfect because it has in itself the nature of mineral, vegetable and animal. For the stone is triple and one, having four natures." [57] "It is called a stone, not because it is like a stone, but only because, by virtue of its fixed nature, it resists the action of fire." [58] According to the "Emerald Tablet" attributed to Hermes, "The Sun is its Father, the Moon its Mother, the wind bears it in its womb, and it is nursed by the earth." [59] Thus the stone would seem to be a power, or ability, which is acquired in the alchemical art, through conjunction of sun and moon; this power grows at first in the air element, the mental level of consciousness; it is nourished and strengthened in the earth element, the physical body. It is called the "flower of gold," *i.e.*, it is the product (flower) of the transmutation process (gold).

And where is the stone to be found? "Our stone is found in all mountains, all trees, all herbs, and animals and with all men. It wears many different colors, contains the four elements, and has been designated a microcosm." [60] It is ubiquitous, it enters into everything, it involves a synthesis of elements, of bodies, or levels of consciousness. "This stone is under you, and near you, and above you, and around you." [61] But mostly, it is within you: "This thing is extracted from you, for you are its ore; . . . and when you have experienced this, the love and desire for it will be increased in you." [62]

Russell Schofield said that "The philosophers' stone is not a magical object, it is the magnificent condition resulting from reaching the objective." [63] The stone is the ability to be objective about fact, to perceive and know the "hard" fact of a given situation as it actually is, without preconceived ideas and images distorting the fact. Hence, the stone was said to be one, though it could be infinitely multiplied: a fact is unitary, immutable; yet the ability to know the fact, once it has been acquired, can be infinitely extended to all situations—all mountains, all herbs, etc. It was also said that the stone is water: to know the fact from all aspects one must maintain fluidity of perspective. "Standing firmly on a moving point" is an Actualist phrase for this perceptual mobility.

To know objectively is to know with the certainty that one knows. It is to know the essence of the fact from all levels of consciousness, all four elements; hence the stone was called the "fifth essence," the quintessence or perfect manifestation. The alchemist Geber said: "It illumines all bodies, since it is the light of the light, and their tincture." [64] This stone, this "father of miracles," is acquired through a process analogous to mining: the "bedrock" of truth has to be separated from the ore. The superimposed distortions have to be dissolved, until only that which cannot be dissolved remains: the "rock-bottom," the "stone."

One may ask why the alchemical adepts went to such extraordinary lengths to conceal in metaphor and parable something as straightforward as the ability to be objective. Why not just say it the way it is? Because to do so would be to invite misunderstanding. "Our substance is openly displayed before the eyes of all, and yet is not known." [65] "Learned doctors . . . have it before their eyes every day, but they do not understand it, because they never attend to it." [66] It is misunderstood primarily because people do not realize that the work of finding the stone has first and foremost to be performed within. "We cannot be resolved of any doubt save by experiment, and there is no better way to make it than on ourselves," wrote Dorn.[67] Both the obstructions to truth and truth itself lie within us.

We cannot be objective about anything external until we can be objective about ourselves. To be objective means to be whole. "The goal of our art is not reached until Sun and Moon are conjoined, and become, as it were, one body." [68] This body is akin to the "diamond body" of the Buddhist *Tantras*, the "immutable wisdom" of the "adamantine essence." It is indeed a totally transmuted body, a whole, illumined, multidimensional, objective consciousness. "When the pure and essential elements are joined together in loving equilibrium, as they are in our Stone, they are inseparable and immortal like the human body in Paradise." [69]

The new alchemy

The wisdom of the alchemists was very ancient and timeless. It was, in essentials, the same teaching that has arisen at other times and places: the wisdom of wholeness and how to attain it. Their metaphors and symbols were suggested by the concepts of the science of their day. In this new age, a new alchemy will undoubtedly arise, that will take into account everything the chemists have learned, and will provide more comprehensive and satisfying formulations.

This will come about when individuals among the natural scientists awake to the simple yet momentous fact that everything that can be studied "out there" can also, and better, be studied "in here." For the barriers to scientific objectivity lie within, the doubts have to be resolved by inner experiments, and the evolutionary purpose can only be understood and accomplished within. Afterwards it can also be externalized. If it be asked how I can be so sure of this, I will answer, like the alchemists, that I know it by experiment and experience.

Gurdjieff attempted to formulate a revised alchemy. In his "table of hydrogens" described in Ouspensky's *In Search of the Miraculous*, he set up a scale of "matters" of different densities or frequency rates, from the highest to the lowest. A segment of this spectrum was the range of matters that involved man. "The chemistry of which we speak here studies matter on a different basis from ordinary chemistry and takes into consideration not only the chemical and physical, but also the psychic and cosmic properties of matter." [70]

A new alchemy is particularly necessary for the true understanding of psychedelic substances, which are substances whose cosmic and psychic properties are startlingly evident. These substances were not unknown to the old alchemists. Paracelsus in particular makes many allusions to herbs and drugs. Cheyri (the yellow wallflower, *Cheiranthus cheiri*) "fortifies the microcosmic body . . . so that it must necessarily continue in its conservation through the universal anatomy of the four elements." [71] Thereniabin, or oil of manna (*pinguedo manna*), also known as honeydew, was said to be "heavenly food," and "assist sublimation." [72] It has been suggested that since honeydew is the secretion of certain kinds of fungus, particularly the

ergot fungus *claviceps purpurea*, which contains alkaloids of the LSD family, it is not impossible that this "manna" had psychedelic properties. [73] Other "arcane remedies" mentioned by Paracelsus include Nostoch, a gelatinous algae, also known as "star jelly" or "witches' butter"; and Melissa (*melissa officinalis*), a "balm" that was said to have the power of "supracelestial conjunction." These four are called *aniada*, and are said to produce "exaltation in both worlds," and to promote longevity.

From a chemical point of view it has often been proposed that psychedelic substances act like catalysts in the nervous system; that is, they facilitate a chemical change in the fluids surrounding nerve cells so that these cells will respond with increased rate of flow of electrical impulses. The heightened perceptual sensitivity is equivalent to a reduced firing threshold of neurons. This increased responsiveness could lead to a temporary release from neurophysiological imprints. As one alchemist said: "The drug being ignited, the shadow of the dense body is to be stripped away." [74]

Most catalysts are reversible, and they will equally well facilitate the reaction from A to B as the one from B to A. This appears to be true of LSD. If the prevailing current, metaphorically speaking, is to clear existing programs, it will facilitate this clearing. If, on the other hand, the consciousness field is dominated by mental or emotional imprints, these will be magnified. Psychedelics can heighten clarity of perception and flow of awareness; or they can still further intensify the muddiness of clouded viewpoints and amplify negative feelings. They can "cleanse the doors of perception," or obscure them still further. This is why LSD is only a tool for amplication. It is not *by itself* a reliable guide to direction or purpose or means of attaining wholeness.

The psychedelic drugs have proved for many people to be powerful awakeners to the possibilities of consciousness to the Promethean potentials that are chained, immobilized, and unactualized in most of us. Thus, the discovery and synthesis of psychedelics is in the true alchemical tradition of studying Nature to find aids for man's evolutionary growth. Among physicians, the Naturopaths and Homeopaths who use natural remedies and endeavor to strengthen the body's own innate regenerative powers are the inheritors of the alchemical tradition. The extraordinary potency of LSD, which far exceeds that of any other known drug, suggests that the mechanism of its action may be similar to what the Homeopaths refer to as their "dynamized serial solutions." [75]

In the new alchemy, current knowledge of biochemistry and psychopharmacology would be integrated into an experimentally verifiable understanding of the psychophysiological energy systems, rather than being, as now, a mass of separate, unsynthesized data. It will be found, as it was found by the old alchemists, that there are certain laws that are operative at every level of energy organization and corresponding level of consciousness.

The modern theory of acid-base regulation in the bloodstream is not unrelated to the alchemists' conception of sulphur and salt. Acids carry a positive charge in aqueous solutions, bases a negative charge. "Acid and base in solution react to form a salt" by a process of "neutralization." [76] By maintaining the hydrogen ion concentration of the blood, the balance of acid and base has an important effect on the psyche. It is known that excessive positive ionization of the atmosphere, as found today in our polluted cities, reduces the energy charge of the total organism, whereas a predominance of negative ions, as found in the country, increases the charge-carrying capacity of the organism and produces a feeling of vitality and buoyancy. Acid-base regulation is the "conjunction" of positive and negative energies on the molecular level.

The old alchemists frequently referred to the need for "digestion" by "gentle cooking" with "living fire." We are dealing here with what Sir Julian Huxley called "psychometabolism": the processing of experience-information by the brain and nervous system parallels the processing of food by the digestive system. Experiences that are not digested, that "can't be stomached,"

leave residues obstructing the free flow of energy. On the emotional level we recognize these residues as "traumatic complexes." On the physiological and nervous level they are experienced as "crystallizations." In body-work of the Rolfian or Reichian type these crystallizations can be literally felt, producing sharp pain when probed.

Much harder to reach are the imprint structures and image-factors, which through long-term hereditary and cultural conditioning processes, have become crystallized in the brain. It is part of the art of alchemy to dissolve these crystallizations so that consciousness can function unobstructedly, so that higher frequency energy systems can appear more solidly in awareness. "Dissolve and coagulate."

Again and again the alchemists returned to their theme of studying the "possibilities of Nature," and following Nature in her simplicity; of making experiments in order to resolve any doubts. They counseled that books should be studied, but only to a limited degree, for they can lead astray, whereas Nature does not. So "rend the books lest your hearts be rent asunder." [77] Alchemy is not armchair philosophy or speculative science. It is the *practice* of inner union on all levels of consciousness, separately and conjoined. "Many strive to accomplish this separation and conjunction; but few succeed in bringing about a union which can stand the test of fire." [78]

EXPERIENTIAL EXPERIMENTS

The methods of the alchemical adept of course cannot be described. However, it is possible to develop a sensory-physical understanding of their ideas. By reading, the mind can only know about something. True understanding however involves "standing," the earth-body and the cells must know it by experiencing it.

We can try to get a sense of what the elements are within us. What is the aspect of our consciousness that feels earthy, solid? Can we feel those structural elements throughout? Can we let ourselves sink into earth like into a receptacle?

And water—can we let ourselves dissolve into the fluid medium of life? Can we feel the liquid motion of emotion, as it washes through us? Can we distinguish the sharp spurting of adrenaline in the emotions of fear and rage; and the slow, expansive melting of soothing joy; the salty bitterness of waves of grief; and the balmy sweetness of pleasure?

It is worth trying to experience the mixing of these aspects of consciousness. Fluid feeling becoming volatile thought, fiery energy sinking into earth structures. An idea condensing into a feeling, or subliming into a tangible solid, like a snow crystal. "Make the fixed volatile, and the volatile fixed."

An experiment can be set up analogous to the one described: an external fire, or candle, is lit. Here it is best to use whatever form of meditation the person has found most efficacious. Let that internal focal point link up with the sound or visual aspect of the outer fire. The "I" becomes an observer or witness.

It is fruitful also to observe the differences, if any, between the left and right side of the body. The alchemical androgynous consciousness, as his tantric counterpart, is polarized dynamic male on the right and magnetic female on the left. By observing differences in body sensation in the two halves of the earth-body, we can learn about attitudes, feelings, and images that the two halves of our nature have toward each other. And we can also begin to see how these attitudes, feelings, and images are projected out onto external individuals in male or female form.

One minute of such experimental self-observation is worth several hours of reading. And that's true.

NOTES AND REFERENCES

1. The Freemasons had members of their brotherhood among the founding fathers of the American nation. They left one of their secret insignia, an eye enclosed in a triangle, on that most universal American artifact, the dollar bill.

2. *The Hermetic Museum,* restored and enlarged, trans. from the Latin (London: James Elliot & Co., 1893; orig. publ., Frankfort: 1678). Introduction by A. E. Waite. This is one of the outstanding anthologies of later alchemical texts, mostly anonymous, published in English in a limited edition of two hundred and fifty copies. The sentence quoted is found in volume 2, p. 183. Jung gives extensive quotations from this and other alchemical anthologies not accessible to this writer. Hence, his five books on alchemy are the main reference source used here, besides the work mentioned above.

3. "The Ordinal of Alchemy," *Herm. Mus.,* vol. 2, p. 12.

4. Carl Jung, *Memories, Dreams and Reflections* (New York: Vintage Books, 1961), p. 205.

5. *Ibid.,* p. 221.

6. *Ibid.,* p. 205.

7. Carl Jung, *Alchemical Studies,* vol. 13, *Collected Works* (New York: Pantheon Books, Bollingen Series XX, 1967), p. 138.

8. *Herm. Mus.,* vol. 1, p. 108.

9. "An Open Entrance to the Closed Palace of the King," *Herm. Mus.,* vol. 2, p. 183.

10. "The Only True Way," *Herm. Mus.,* vol. 1, p. 155.

11. "A Demonstration of Nature," *Herm. Mus.,* vol. 1, p. 130.

12. "The Glory of the World or Tables of Paradise," *Herm. Mus.,* vol. 1, p. 210.

13. Jung, *Alchemical Studies,* p. 73.

14. *Ibid.,* p. 86.

15. "The New Chemical Light," *Herm. Mus.,* vol. 2, p. 131.

16. Rodney Collin, *The Theory of Celestial Influence* (London: Stuart, 1954), p. 151.

17. "The New Chemical Light," *Herm. Mus.,* vol. 2, p. 136.

18. *Herm. Mus.,* vol. 2, p. 64.

19. *Herm. Mus.,* vol. 1, p. 198.

20. "A Demonstration of Nature," *Herm. Mus.,* vol. 3, p. 135.

21. "The New Chemical Light," *Herm. Mus.,* vol. 2, p. 14.

22. *Herm. Mus.,* vol. 1, p. 158.

23. *Ibid.,* p. 219.

24. Jung, *Alchemical Studies,* p. 137.

25. *Herm, Mus.,* vol. 1, p. 153.

26. "Glory of the World," *Herm. Mus.,* vol. 1, p. 210.

27. Quoted in Carl Jung, *Mysterium Coniunctionis,* vol. 14, *Collected Works* (New York: Pantheon Books, Bollingen Series XX, 1963), p. 220.

28. *Herm. Mus.,* vol. 2, p. 175.

29. *Herm. Mus.,* vol. 2, p. 74.

30. *Herm. Mus.,* vol. 2, p. 35.

31. *Herm. Mus.,* vol. 2, p. 143.

32. "The Golden Tract," *Herm. Mus.,* vol. 1, p. 14.

33. Jung, *Mysterium Coniunctionis,* p. 113.

34. *Herm. Mus.*, vol. 2, p. 165.

35. *Ibid.*, p. 107.

36. *Herm. Mus.*, vol. 1, p. 22.

37. Jung, *Mysterium Coniunctionis*, p. 250.

38. *Herm. Mus.*, vol. 2, p. 135.

39. These descriptions were collected by Jung in his essay "The Spirit Mercurius," in *Alchemical Studies*, pp. 191–250.

40. Quoted in Jung, *Mysterium Coniunctionis*, p. 461.

41. "The Golden Tract," *Herm. Mus.*, vol. 1, p. 27.

42. *Ibid.*, p. 33.

43. "An Open Entrance," *Herm. Mus.*, vol. 2, p. 176.

44. Jung, *Mysterium Coniunctionis*, p. 145.

45. "Glory of the World," *Herm. Mus.*, vol. 1, p. 210.

46. Quoted in Carl Jung, "Psychology of the Transference," *Practice of Psychotherapy*, vol. 16, *Collected Works* (Princeton: Princeton University Press, Bollingen Series XX, 1954), p. 298.

47. Carl Jung, *Aion: Researches into the Phenomenology of the Self*, vol. 9, II, *Collected Works* (Princeton: Princeton University Press, Bollingen Series XX, 1959), p. 167.

48. These drawings and the texts accompanying them are from a text entitled *Rosarium Philosophorum* ("The Rosary of the Wise"), which Jung quotes and uses to illustrate his (to me, incorrect) thesis that the "conjunction" referred to an external relationship. "Psychology of Transference," pp. 211–270.

49. John Pordage, quoted in Jung, "Psychology of Transference," p. 301.

50. Jung, "Psychology of Transference," p. 288.

51. *Gospel According to Thomas* (London: Collins, 1959), logos 22.

52. Jung, "Psychology of Transference," p. 286.

53. *Ibid.*, p. 284.

54. Jung, *Alchemical Studies*, p. 163.

55. "The Sophic Hydrolith," *Herm. Mus.*, vol. 1, p. 77.

56. Gerhard Dorn, quoted in Jung, *Mysterium Coniunctionis*, p. 482.

57. Hortulanus, quoted in Jung, "Psychology of the Transference," p. 204.

58. "Three Treatises of Philateles," *Herm. Mus.*, vol. 2, p. 249.

59. "Glory of the World," *Herm. Mus.*, vol. 1, p. 209.

60. *Ibid.*, p. 209.

61. Jung, *Mysterium Coniunctionis*, p. 51.

62. Morienus, quoted in Jung, *Aion*, p. 166.

63. Russell Schofield, "Agni Yoga as Taught in the School of Actualism" (Los Angeles, 1969).

64. *Herm. Mus.*, vol. 1, p. 210.

65. "The New Chemical Light," *Herm. Mus.*, vol. 2, p. 108.

66. "The Glory of the World," *Herm. Mus.*, vol. 1, p. 173.

67. Jung, *Mysterium Coniunctionis*, p. 270.

68. "The Glory of the World," *Herm. Mus.*, vol. 1, p. 210.

69. "The New Chemical Light," *Herm. Mus.*, vol. 2, p. 141.

70. P. D. Ouspensky, *In Search of the Miraculous* (New York: Harcourt, Brace & World, 1949), p. 176.

71. Jung, *Alchemical Studies*, p. 135.

72. *Ibid.*, p. 153.

73. Ruthven Todd, "Coleridge and Paracelsus; Honeydew and LSD," *London Magazine* (March, 1967), 52–62.

74. Jung, *Alchemical Studies*, p. 160n.

75. Brian Inglis, in his book *The Case for Unorthodox Medicine* (New York: G. P. Putnam's Sons, 1964), p. 98, wrote: "Perhaps the most striking confirmation of the homeopathic theory has come out of recent investigation into hallucinogens, and in particular into LSD." For an account of the action of homeopathic preparations in terms of polymer structures in the fluid component of biological systems, see G. P. Barnard and James H. Stephenson, "Fresh Evidence for a Biophysical Field," in *Main Currents of Modern Thought*, 24, no. 5 (1968): 115–122. The authors conclude that "what the homeopathic physician is attempting to do is to match the pure quantized informational content of particular chemicals to the informational needs of his patients and, at the same time, to take account of the individual capacity of the patient to process information at a given rate."

76. "Salt," *Van Nostrand's Scientific Encyclopedia*, 4th ed. (Princeton: Van Nostrand Co., 1968), p. 1561.

77. *Rosarium Philosophorum* in Jung, "Psychology of Transference," p. 274.

78. "The Book of Alze," *Herm. Mus.*, vol. 1, p. 264.

ASTROLOGY I

The Celestial Scenario

The cause, dear Brutus, lies not in the stars,

but in us.

SHAKESPEARE, AMENDED

THE STUDY OF PLANETARY COSMIC CY-cles and their relationship to life on earth has been a central interest of man since the beginnings. Some of the earliest known fragments of inscriptions remaining from ancient civilizations are records of planetary positions. Among the Egyptians, Babylonians, Chaldeans, Persians, Indians, and Chinese there were always members of the scholar-priest caste who specialized in investigations of cosmic phenomena and sought to relate their observations to the needs of community and individual. It is only in very recent times that this branch of learning has atrophied so that the contemporary scientist-priest caste concerns itself exclusively with the precision of quantitative measurement of cosmic cycles (astronomy); while the study of the relationship of these cycles to biological and psychological processes on earth (astrology) is dismissed as "pseudo-science" and left indiscriminately to undisciplined fortune-tellers and only a few serious students.

Up to the times of Johannes Kepler and Isaac Newton, a mere three hundred years ago, this was not the case; and these two fathers of astronomy were interested in and proficient at astrology, and motivated in their researches in part by the attempt to understand its scientific basis. Kepler, in his *Tertius Interveniens*, wrote that "it should not seem incredible that from the stupidities and blasphemies of the astrologers a new, healthy and useful learning may arise." His laws of planetary motion were discovered as a result of persistent efforts on his part to verify the Pythagorean concept that the cycles of the planets were related to each other in the manner of the notes of a musical octave—the doctrine of "the music of the spheres." It is an intriguing question in the history of science why Kepler's astronomical successors failed to share his interest in astrology.

The result of this split has been that astrological practice, with few exceptions, has not kept up with developments in astronomical knowledge, and the symbol systems used by astrologers are largely based on obsolete information. As a consequence, there is much dispute among astrologers as to the best zodiac and the best house-system, and this disagreement is adduced as proof of astrology's unscientific nature by the sceptical orthodoxy. The fact that similar far-reaching disagreements exist among the cosmological theories of orthodox science does not seem to alter this evaluation. The reason for the discomfort of the rational, scientifically trained mind at the thought of astrology seems to be basically two-fold: astrology seems to eliminate free will or choice; and there is no presently known way to account for the supposed effects.

The notion that astrology does not allow for free will is one for which the commercialized fortune-tellers and their overcredulous clients are responsible. It is ever the path of least resistance to attribute our mishaps and difficulties to external causes, whether another person, or, more conveniently, since they won't talk back, the stars. Yet sophisticated astrologers have always pointed out they are dealing not with compelling influences, but with tendencies; not with forces, but with inclinations; with *probabilities* to behave, think, feel in certain ways, which the individual could follow or not as he chose.

Kepler himself was quite clear on this point: "There is no evil star in the heavens, . . . for the following reasons: it is the nature of man as such, dwelling as it does here on earth, that lends to the planetary radiations their effect on itself; just as the sense of hearing, endowed with the faculty of discerning chords, lends to music such power that it incites him who hears

it to dance." [1] Kepler is pointing here to what we might call the response factor, which is not often brought out by modern astrologers: namely, that astrological forces or influences are subject to great individual variability, just as is responsiveness to music. The same astrological configuration or aspect may be very influential in one person and not another, depending on response factors.

Albertus Magnus, the medieval churchman, alchemist, and astrologer, explained the free will question as follows: "There is in man a double spring of action, namely nature and will; and nature for its part is ruled by the stars, while the will is free; but unless it resists it is swept along by nature and becomes mechanical." [2] This is very similar to Gurdjieff's notion that the attempt to develop consciousness and being means to exert will in a direction contrary to nature, to struggle against natural habits, if one is not to remain a machine.

The great modern clairvoyant and prophet Edgar Cayce formulated the effects of the planets also in just this way: "For will is the factor which affords the opportunity to choose what is for development or for retardation. . . . Each soul chooses its manifestations. . . . Use such directions [from the planets] as stepping-stones and do not let them become stumbling stones in thy experience." [3]

The idea that astrology precludes free will is a complete inversion of its original function, as developed by the Chaldean and Egyptian schools of adepts. These schools charted planetary cycles and observed their characteristic effects on the different human types, and then invented symbols to indicate what some of the influences and factors were, that a man had to deal with. In other words, astrological symbolism was designed to help man in his evolutionary development; help him to liberate his higher will by making clear what some of the factors opposing it are.

The problem of free will arises only if astrology is considered separately from the purpose of evolutionary growth and development. In the context of growth, planetary "aspects," like hereditary or acquired characteristics or experiences encountered in life, become factors to work with, to assimilate and transmute for the goal of individuation. For this reason esoteric philosophy has taught that there are two kinds of astrology, or two kinds of horoscope: the astrology of man "on the wheel," and the astrology of man "on the path"; or the horoscope of "personality," and the horoscope of "individuality." The latter could only be constructed by an astrologer who was also a teacher and who could accurately determine the level of development of being of the person.

Astrological theories

The question of *how* astrological influences work is, of course, the other major stumbling block to academic acceptance. Science is notoriously resistant to accepting observations it cannot explain; and the highly indeterminate and probabilistic nature of astrologers' observations has not made this any easier. Early attempts to make systematic observations of supposed astrological effects were spectacularly unsuccessful; largely because they were based on naive assumptions about astrology. Through the use of modern statistical methods of analysis and high-speed computers, data are beginning to be collected which can provide a more empirical base for the new astrology. Some of these empirical findings will be reviewed below.

It should be remembered though that statistically valid data are not enough for scientific credibility, as the fate of J. B. Rhine's ESP experiments clearly shows. The data have to be somehow integrated into the framework of the current scientific paradigm. I hope to be able to indicate, with necessary brevity, that certain basic astrological premises are quite compatible with the most recent scientific theories and observations.[4]

The nature of the linkage between planetary and other cosmic cycles on the one hand and processes on earth, particularly in man, on the other, has been conceptualized in a number of different ways which can be roughly grouped into five categories: (1) material-physical theo-

ries, which state that there are forms of radiation and force fields that affect earth; (2) the theory of "planetary heredity," which postulates a synchronization between cosmic and biological cycles; (3) Jung's theory of "synchronicity," which assumes a noncausal linkage between material and psychic processes; (4) theories which consider the relationship between cosmic and human factors as purely symbolic or metaphorical and ignore the causal question; and (5) theories which attend to astrological factors primarily as an evolutionary map, a kind of script or scenario designed by the incarnating entity or soul as it chooses the time, place, and conditions of its life on earth.

These theories are not mutually exclusive. In fact it is my belief that they all contain aspects of the truth, and I propose to discuss them as such in what follows. The survey is by no means exhaustive and is intended merely to stimulate thinking and suggest possible lines of research.

Physical Theories. Two major research interests of present day biology are directly relevant to the perspectives of traditional astrology. *Ecology,* the science of the interrelations of life forms and environments, when extended beyond the planet to include the entire solar system, becomes the study of the reciprocally interacting field forces of sun and planets. This has been called *biocosmology* or *cosmo-ecology.*[5] The study of *circadian rhythms* has gained increasing importance in recent years, and much research now exists demonstrating the susceptibility of plants and animals to the twenty-four-hour cycle of the earth's rotation.[6] Extended to sun, moon, and other planets, this branch of learning coincides with some facets of astrology.

Frank Brown, a biologist at Northwestern University, has carried out numerous experiments on behavior and physiological process in small animals, unicellular organisms, and plants showing not only that they are of a periodic nature, but that their rhythmic functioning is due to their sensitivity to subtle but pervasive physical stimuli.[7] They have been shown to be responsive to very weak magnetic fields of the order of strength of the earth's own; to electrostatic fields; to ultrashort and very long electromagnetic waves; and to changes in the gravitational field of their environment. Sea animals show rhythms correlated to lunar phase, even when shielded from external stimuli; when moved to a different locality, still under constant conditions, they can reset their cycles to correspond to the new local lunar phase.[8]

Brown postulated that organisms have a mechanism which acts as "a harmonic analyzer for solar and lunar geophysical rhythms and under some circumstances becomes a variable frequency transformer." [9] The capability of biological life forms, and especially man, to act as energy transformers is one of the key concepts of esoteric philosophy and is implicit in astrology.

The gross effects of solar and lunar cycles on the earth's oceans, on the atmosphere, and on climate has been observed and studied for some time. Michel Gauquelin, in his book *The Cosmic Clocks,* has summarized much of this work, showing the relationship of the eleven-year sun-spot cycle (which is going through its maximum phase this year, 1970), as well as monthly and daily fluctuations in solar magnetic activity to processes as varied as physical and psychic epidemics, revolutions, accidents, heart and lung diseases, psychiatric diseases, blood counts, and even molecular chemical reactions.[10]

Thus the influence of the sun on all manner of processes on earth is demonstrable. The influence of the moon, particularly on the fluids of the earth, namely tides and rainfall, has also been demonstrated.[11] The combined influence of sun and moon on female fertility and sex of offspring has been the subject of intensive investigation by the Czechoslovakian gynecologist and psychiatrist Eugen Jonas. He has been able to show, in studies now covering thousands of cases, that a woman's fertile period recurs each month on her "lunation birthday," when sun and moon repeat the same angular relationship they had when she was born; and that the sex of offspring conceived depends on the position of the moon at this time—if the moon was in one of the positive fields of the ecliptic, a male child will result

and if in one of the alternating negative fields, a female. Jonas explains his findings by postulating that the ovum's receptivity to sperm with XX chromosomes (female) or XY chromosomes (male) varies with cyclic variations in the polarity of the lines of force of the sun's field.[12]

Traditional astrology teaches that this field polarity alternates through the twelve divisions of the ecliptic, called the signs of the zodiac. Thus Aries is positive, Taurus negative, and so on. The sun passes through these fields in one year; the moon passes through them in a month. Recent satellite studies of the interplanetary magnetic field have confirmed the presence of periodic reversals of polarity in this field. When positive, solar energy is streaming from the sun; when negative, the flow is reversed.[13]

Dr. Jonas' results, if they can be confirmed, obviously have enormous practical relevance. In the first place, they give a way of determining a woman's fertility cycle, and thus a method of contraception that does not involve mechanical or chemical intervention, both of which are subject to medical as well as religious objections. Secondly, a family could choose the sex of its offspring, which can be of great value in unbalanced families. Since no mechanical intervention is involved, only the *timing* of conception to accord with the positions of cosmic bodies, the worst that could happen is that a child is born whose sex is opposite of what was wished for. And, as Jonas points out, this happens all the time.

Potentially of equal, or greater importance, is some preliminary work Jonas has done on the effect of certain planetary positions on the viability of embryo. This, if confirmed, introduces a whole new perspective on the question of eugenics: namely the possibility of heredity control without the spectre of genetic manipulation.

Satellite observations of the interplanetary solar magnetic field have found it to lie close to the plane of the ecliptic, to have a spiral form, and to rotate with the sun in a twenty-seven day period.[14] We see in these observations confirmation of some classical astrological assumptions: the so-called signs of the zodiac (not to be confused with the constellations bearing the same name) is a twelve-fold division of the ecliptic, a map of the earth's path around the sun. The rotation of the sun's field, plus the movement of the earth in its orbit, would generate an approximately twelve-fold variation in the interacting field relationships of earth and sun.

Evidence has been found that the sun's magnetic and gravitational fields are modulated by changes in planetary positions. In 1954, J. H. Nelson, who was employed by RCA to research factors interfering with the propagation of radio waves through the ionosphere, found that predictable disturbances occurred when three or more planets were either aligned with the sun (in *conjunction* or in *opposition*), or formed angles of 90° (astrologically *square*). Angles of 30° and 60° and their multiples were also disturbing, and the more planets thus related the greater the effect. The planet Mercury (traditionally associated with communications) was involved in the greatest number of interferences. The angles though were heliocentric (sun-centered), not the geocentric (earth-centered) aspects of classical astrology.[15] The planets' positions, through their effects on the sun's gravitational field, also influence solar flare activity.[16] This in turn affects weather as well as biological and psychosocial processes on earth, as noted above.

Angular positions of the planets have been shown to effect indices of activity in the earth's magnetic field. In particular, inferior conjunctions of Venus (when Venus lies in a straight line between earth and sun) consistently and significantly reduce magnetic storm activity on the earth.[17] Since such magnetic activity has been related to physical, psychic, and social disturbances, these data are an interesting confirmation of the traditionally "benign" effect of the planet Venus.[18]

These findings are all suggestive of a model of solar-planetary interaction in which the planets, through their interacting gravitational and magnetic fields, modulate the basic radiation channeled by the sun. The entire solar system functions like a gigantic frequency transformer in which the energy generated by the sun, or received by it from outside cosmic sources, is transmitted to the planets, each modulating its intensity and frequency in characteristic ways according to the angular relationships between them.

On such a hypothesis, the different frequency rates channeled by the planets at different intensities are linked to various biological, psychological, and social processes on earth. In particular, man as a microcosm has a system of glands, each of which is assumed to be responsive to a particular frequency or type of energy. Intensity of activity of the various glandular systems in various combinations can certainly be related to personality and temperamental variations. Although several sets of correlations of planets and glands have been proposed, there is only little agreement among them. This is an area awaiting empirical research.

A somewhat different and intriguing kind of direct physical linkage has been proposed by the physicist H. Prescott Sleeper. He has pointed out that the resonant frequency of the ionosphere is 8 cycles per second, which corresponds to the frequency of the alpha ryhthm of the human brain. Thus, the pulsating ionosphere is thought of as "driving" the brain waves. Variations in the interplanetary magnetic field and other parameters could thus affect human thinking and behavior directly through their effects on the pulsing of the ionosphere.[19]

Planetary Heredity. The French statistician and psychologist Michel Gauquelin has performed large scale investigations, involving thousands of cases, of the birth patterns of persons in different professions. There was no tendency for the births to cluster in the twelve houses of traditional astrology, but there were significant relationships between professions and which planet was rising over the horizon, or culminating in the sky, when he was born. Thus successful physicians were more likely to be born when Mars or Saturn were either rising or culminating. Successful scientists, athletes, or career officers were also likely to conform to this tendency. Painters, musicians, or writers were less likely to be born at such times. On the other hand, the rising or culminating of Jupiter was associated with high frequency of births of politicians, actors, and journalists, though not of scientists and physicians.

To explain these findings Gauquelin postulated an inherited mechanism, responsive to planetary action, which affects the onset of labor and hence the time of birth. "The organism of the child is controlled by the laws of heredity; and it is possible, because of these laws that it will be sensitive to the action of the celestial bodies exactly in the same way that his parents were at their birth. The crisis of birth, already gathering itself, would unfold when all the favorable conditions have been attained; among these, the planets might have their role." [20] In other words, a child inherits from his parents a tendency to be born when a given planet rises or culminates, just as he inherits the color of his hair. To check this hypothesis it was necessary to demonstrate that there are similarities between the positions of the planets at the parents' birth and that of their children. Analyzing the records of over thirty thousand parents and their children, significant correlations were found.

The postulated ability of the foetus in the womb to perceive extremely small changes in the interplanetary environment is remarkable, though not inconceivable if we remember Frank Brown's findings of the high sensitivity of organisms to the subtle synchronizers from space. According to this interpretation, the position of the planets does not *cause* the person to have a certain type of career. Rather they *reveal* a genetic factor which predisposes him toward this career.

It is worthy of note that Johannes Kepler arrived at a very similar hypothesis of the action of the planets, which he published in his *Tertius Interveniens* in 1610: "When a mother is great with child and the natural time of delivery is near, nature selects for the birth a day and hour which correspond, on account of the heavens (i.e., from an astrological point of view), to the nativity of the mother's father or brother, and this not qualitatively, but astronomically and quantitatively." [21]

Synchronicity. Carl Jung, in an attempt to explain the apparently inexplicable successes of J. B. Rhine's ESP experiments, which showed effects independent of time or space parameters, as well as looking for an understanding of the *I Ching*, astrology, and serial coincidences too unusual to attribute to chance, postulated an "acausal connecting principle," which he termed synchronicity. In effect, this states that a link may exist between two events or phenomena which is not material-casual, but rather of a psychic nature, a subjective meaning aspect. Applied to astrology, this would seem to say there is this kind of synchronicity between the calculated horoscope of a person's birth and the psychological factors in his make-up. The link is the astrological "meaning."

Jung compared the horoscopes of several hundred married couples with those of unmarried pairs, and found the astrologically expected relationships. The most frequent combinations in the married couples were one partner's moon conjunct the other's sun; or the two moons conjunct; or one's moon in opposition to the other's sun. Although the frequencies found were not statistically significant, Jung was inclined to regard the whole experiment as a demonstration of synchronicity.[22]

An important consideration emerges from this point of view: like the *I Ching*, the Tarot, palmistry, and other mantic procedures, astrological horoscope casting is in one way a framework for intuitive perception. I know of one clairvoyant astrologer who simply looks at the actual horoscope diagram and then begins to "see" the inner life, the thought forms, and emotional patterns of her client, almost as if she were gazing into a crystal ball.

Jung's work on marriages has not, to my knowledge, been pursued further though it would be of the utmost interest to do a comparison of successful and unsuccessful marriages in order to have an empirical base for marital counseling. In this area and in vocational counselling, an empirically grounded astrology has enormous practical potential.

Symbolic Theories. The majority of practicing astrologers adopt what is called a pragmatic point of view, which says: "I use it because it works"; and do not concern themselves further with questions of *how* or *why*. The more sophisticated ones see astrological planets and signs as symbols or metaphors for psychological functions; they analyze the pattern of relationships of the symbols in a chart and hence infer the pattern of relationships of the associated psychological functions.

Thus, Dane Rudhyar, in his *The Practice of Astrology,* writes that "Astrology, as I understand it, has no concern with whether a conjunction of planets causes some things to happen to a person or nation; it only *indicates* the possibility or probability of a certain type of event's occurring in a certain place at a certain time." [23] What Rudhyar and the majority of astrologers do is to regard the planets and signs as metaphors for psychological processes just as the alchemists took sulphur and salt as metaphors for internal energy processes. The metaphorical meaning is derived in part from the ancient sources, in part from their own experience and intuition, and in part from the astronomical facts. Thus, for example, the meaning of Mars and Venus in a chart is partly derived from the Greek myths of the gods Mars and Venus, partly from experience of seeing the role of Mars and Venus in many charts, and partly from the position of the planets Mars and Venus on the outward and sun-ward side of the earth respectively.

This approach undoubtedly will give some results as long as the empirical, factual basis is not ignored altogether. There are surely distortions and deviations in the traditional meaning-attributes of the astrological symbols, and these must be verified anew. In addition, since we are entering a new age in which the planetary and sidereal relationships are different, it must be assumed that the actual functional patterns of effects on earth are changing. They will have to be established on fresh empirical observations for the new astrology.

Astrology as an Evolutionary Map. The new astrology will be new because it will incorporate modern astronomical knowledge; it will also be very old because it will recover what has been lost, the significance of astrological factors as guidelines for individual growth and develop-ment. It is this which distinguishes astrology from other existing models of personality or typologies: it has an inherent growth factor enabling a person to determine not only what he is, but what he can become.

If for example we ask why the twelve zodiacal types have the symbolism they do, simplistic answers in terms of the visual appearance of the constellations will clearly not do. We could see anything we want to in a pattern of lights. Is it not rather, as Gurdjieff suggested, that the adepts in very ancient times who devised this typology, chose for each type a symbol that represents that person's "chief feature"? It is difficult to imagine an arbitrary symbol system having the extraordinary longevity and popularity that the zodiac signs have enjoyed. Something about them "fits"; and by seeking to discover how it "fits" one learns to observe oneself and becomes more aware.

Each sign has positive and negative manifestations: inhibits growth in some ways, enhances it in others. Buddha was a Taurus; and so was Hitler. One can be "stubborn" in one's habits; or "persevering" in one's efforts to free oneself from habits. "Chief feature" is also, in one way, "chief obstacle to l:beration," as Gurdjieff phrased it. And the chief feature represented by the sun sign is, of course, modulated by the aspect relationships of the planets, and in the course of life, by the aspects made by planets in "transit" to the natal chart.

According to the viewpoint of esoteric teachings the basic linkage between the psyche and the cosmic factors mapped out in the natal horoscope is not causal, or even synchronous, but *purposeful.* The Higher, Immortal Self chooses a particular life pattern for incarnation, for the purpose of learning and growing; or rather, to provide opportunities for learning and growth while in the particular personality and physical vehicle of that incarnation. Higher Self writes a script for itself, as it were; which personality ego then discovers, deciphers, and plays out in order to "re-member" its essential unity with the Immortal within.

This, it is taught, is the situation of one who is

on the path of conscious evolution. He "has to become consciously aware of the planetary influences and begin to use them for the carrying out of soul purpose." [24] This is a statement from *Esoteric Astrology* by Alice Bailey, a work said to be the record of telepathically transmitted teachings of a Tibetan initiate. In this work it is also stated that for the average man, the man not consciously searching for purpose, man "on the wheel," the planetary influences condition the major trends of personality and outer life circumstances. However, "the moment that a man becomes aware of his own soul and is endeavoring to control his own 'path in life', the influence of the planets, per se, definitely weakens and steadily becomes less and less." [25] He then becomes more receptive to the forces flowing *through* the planets, rather than the forces *of* the planets, and to the subtler and higher energies of the solar system.

From this point of view, the physical-causal factors reviewed earlier and the synchronization of biological clocks with the planetary clocks are the *means* by which the evolutionary script is concretely put into material form. We could say, for example, that the incarnating entity, having chosen to enter as a physician, will adjust the timing factors of the birth process to synchronize it with the rising or culmination of Mars or Saturn. Thus, the soul's "life plan" can be read off from the planetary patterns at birth, because it is *purposefully synchronized* with the cosmic cycles to which biological life on earth is subject. As Edgar Cayce put it: "The period of the entrance [birth] is not *ruled* by the position [of sun and planets] but may be *judged* by the position, as to influences." [26]

According to Cayce's readings of the akashic record, planetary influences in an individual come about as a result of what he called the "entity's sojourns" in the fields of other planets between material incarnations on Earth. "Not that an entity may have manifested physically on such planets; but have manifested in that consciousness of that environ." [27] These sojourns between earth incarnations in the consciousness of other planets may explain the feeling one

sometimes gets that an individual one meets is "from another planet." Cayce specified further that experiences in other planetary fields between earth sojourns produced mental factors or thought forms. These act as "inclinations and not impelling forces," in present life. An individual's spiritual growth would depend on how he responds to the experiences thus induced in life: "No urge surpasses the will of the entity—the birthright given each soul so that it may know itself to be itself, and by *choice* becomes one with the Creator." [28]

What the precise nature of the linkage between cosmic cycles and human cycles is remains to be discovered in future investigations; whether it is by means of glandular activity rates, or by genetic synchronization, or by imprinted thought-forms—or by means of the "centers" (*cakras*) and higher bodies. A full understanding of the nature of astrological forces can, I believe, only come after the actual design of man has been clarified and experienced in the context of the practice of methods of expanding awareness and extending perception.

In other words there is a zodiac within, and factors corresponding to the signs and the planets within, because man is a microcosm organized according to the same designs that operate in the macrocosmos. With extended perception one becomes increasingly aware of what the inner correspondences of planets and signs are; and only then can one correctly evaluate their influence.

This is why the alchemist Agrippa said: "For the planets, spheres and elements in man work more truly and powerfully through the revolution of their zodiac than foreign bodies or the higher bodily signs." [29] Kepler was even more explicit, in his book *Harmonices Mundi:* "Inasmuch as the soul bears within itself the idea of the zodiac, or rather of its centre, it also feels which planet stands at which time under which degree of the zodiac, and measures the angles of the rays that meet on the earth; but inasmuch as it receives from the irradiation of the Divine essence the geometrical figures of the circle and (by comparing the circle with certain parts of it) the archetypal harmonies (not, to be sure, in purely geometrical form but as it were overlaid or rather completely saturated with a filtrate of glittering radiations), it also recognizes the measurements of the angles and judges some as congruent or harmonious, others as incongruent." [30]

Kepler is here describing an experience of direct knowing and perceptual awareness of planetary aspects *from within*. Another example would be: once one becomes aware, within oneself, what "Mars" is and what the "sun" is, one can then also know directly their relationship ("aspect") without having to consult one's horoscope. The latter may be a useful beginning. For some people.

The circle of houses and the four angles

The language of classical astrology is a set of three interlocking symbolic alphabets: the planets, the houses, and the signs of the zodiac. The signs represent the cycle of the earth's orbit around the sun—a period of one year, divided into twelve equal segments. The houses on the other hand represent the cycle of the earth's rotation on its own axis—a period of twenty-four hours, also divided into twelve sections of about two hours each. Thus the natal horoscope actually consists of two superimposed maps showing the positions of the planets in these two cycles, at a given moment of birth.

The circle of houses, which corresponds to what contemporary biologists call the *circadian* cycle, is computed from two points: the *ascendant* and the *mid-heaven*. The ascendant (or *rising sign*) is the part of the sky rising over the horizon at the moment of birth; and the mid-heaven (or *zenith*) is the part of the sky which is directly above at the moment of birth.[31] These two points, and their opposites, are astronomically fixed. They represent what are called the four "angles." To subdivide the cycle further into eight houses, as Greek astrology did, or twelve, as modern astrology does, requires interpolation —and the different methods of interpolating yield several different house systems, about which there is much dispute in astrological circles.[32]

While the details of these systems or the meanings of the houses need not concern us here, it is interesting to note that contemporary research in biological rhythms has discovered a metabolic and brain activity cycle of about 90-100 minutes, which is superimposed on the twenty-four-hour circadian rhythm.[33] Such a one-and-a-half-hour period is not far from the two-hour houses utilized in astrology.

The rising sign and the sun sign are generally considered the two most important indicators in a horoscope. In classical astrology the sun sign is said to represent Self, or basic life orientation; and the rising sign is the projected personality, the outward appearance, the mask seen by others.

In esoteric astrology as formulated by Alice Bailey the emphasis is significantly different: here the sun sign is said to indicate "the integration already achieved . . . the responsiveness or lack of responsiveness to the soul . . . the present point of unfoldment of soul qualities, the present available equipment, the present life quality. . . . fundamentally, the forces here are indicative of the line of least resistance." The rising sign, on the other hand, indicates the "immediate soul purpose for this incarnation, . . . the intended life. . . . it can produce right relationship between soul and personality in any one incarnation." [34]

The difference between these two views of the sun sign and the rising sign is representative of the difference between astrology seen as a typology and astrology seen as an evolutionary script. For man on the wheel, the sun sign indicates his basic nature, his chief feature. For man on the path, solar chief feature is what he already has accomplished, what is given; and the ascendant shows the direction of growth. Sometimes the sun sign was called the "sun of probability" and the rising sign the "sun of possibility." Our Journey to the East begins when we turn to face the rising sun of possibility.

The work of Michel Gauquelin referred to above showed a relationship between vocational prominence and the presence of planets on or near the ascendant and mid-heaven (M.C.). By considering these two points, or angles, and their opposites, the descendant and the *imum coeli* (I.C.), we obtain a quaternity, or circle, the center of which is the observer on earth at the moment of birth.

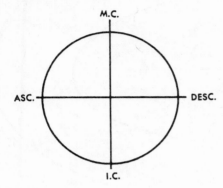

To the east is the ascendant, rising above the horizon of awareness, indicating the direction of future growth and development. Sun, moon or any planets on the ascendant are rising: their influence is becoming more prominent in the personality. Directly opposite, in the west, is the descendant, sinking below the horizon, representing waning influences of the immediate past. The descendant, and the planets that are "setting" with it, may however also represent past factors or ties that hold one back from further growth; they are in "opposition" to the ascendant.

The M.C., or zenith, indicates the highest point, corresponding to the sun at mid-day. It represents the outer manifestation, the most prominent feature or mask presented to others, what Jung called the *persona*. This interpretation is consistent with the usual position of the M.C. at the cusp of the ninth house of religion and the tenth house of profession. Opposite the M.C. lies the I.C., or nadir, below one's feet on the other sides of the earth, corresponding to the midnight phase of the circadian cycle. It represents what is hidden below awareness, and planets on this point can be thought to be important but latent influences. They exert "opposition" to the factors represented by the M.C., until this axis is transformed into a creative polarity, making a cross with the asc.-desc. axis.

In studying a horoscope it is often useful to

begin by plotting out these four angles, along with the planets that are on them, weighting the prominence of the angle by the number and closeness of planets. (Not every horoscope has planets on the angles, in which case we can use only the signs and their elemental significance, as delineated in the following chapter.) Cyril Fagan has suggested the angles and angular planets are like the figure in a figure-ground *gestalt*. By placing oneself mentally in the center of the figure and then thinking of the four directions, east and west, above and below, and the planetary consciousness factors indicated there, one can get a feeling for the prominent features of one's personality structures as mapped by the horoscope.

To do this also enables one to recognize some of the parallelism between the macrocosmic earth-body of the planet and the microcosmic earth-body of man. Both have a central vertical axis, and both a right (west) and left (east) side. The eastern half of the planet, like the left half of man, is polarized magnetic-feminine; the western half of the planet, like the right half of man, is polarized dynamic-masculine.

The two zodiacs and the
cycle of precession

There are in use among astrologers two quite different zodiacs. One of these is the *tropical* zodiac, which is a map of the movements of the various planets around the sun as seen from the earth. Earth is the center and the two axes are defined by the equinoxes and solstices: 0° Aries and Libra define the horizontal axis, 0° Cancer and Capricorn define the vertical axis. The twelve signs simply represent the division of the circle into sectors of 30° each.

The *sidereal* zodiac refers to twelve constellations or groupings of stars outside of the solar system. The stars in a constellation may be of different sizes and at different distances. It is possible to chart the movements of sun and planets by reference to these constellations, but the difficulty is that there is no exact way to tell where one ends and another begins, and they are of quite varying widths.

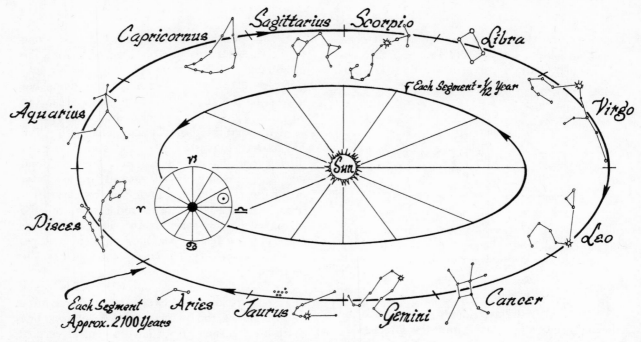

The two zodiacs in Astrology: The small circle with Earth at its center is the tropical zodiac of most horoscopes. It is a map of the elliptical orbit of the Earth around the Sun, through the Sun's field. The outer ellipse is the zodiac of constellations, against which is measured the grand cycle due to precession. Note that 0° Aries is in the constellation Pisces.

It seems fairly certain that in the early history of astrology the cycle produced by the changing earth-sun relationships in the period of one year was mapped by means of the sidereal zodiac, i.e. by reference to the gigantic circle of constellations.[35] When Ptolemy published his *Tetrabiblos* (140 A.D.), which became the foundation for classical astrology as still practiced by the majority of astrologers today, he advocated the use of the tropical system, defined by equinoxes and solstices, which is the logical system to use for mapping earth-sun relationships, and is the system used by astronomers.

Confusion arises because the tropical zodiac moves when compared to the constellational zodiac. This is due to the phenomenon known as precession of the equinoxes, which is a slow, swinging motion of the earth's axis of rotation caused by the tilt of this axis in relation to the ecliptic (orbit). Precession has two effects: it

changes the direction of the polar axis; and it moves the position of the equinoxes in reference to the constellations.[36] Precession is a very slow cycle of approximately twenty-six thousand years; thus it takes about twenty-one hundred years, or one-twelfth of this, for the equinoxes to move through one constellation. At the time of Ptolemy, around the birth of Christ, the vernal equinox coincided with 0° Aries. It has been moving backward through the constellation Pisces, and is now entering the constellation Aquarius. Hence the Aquarian Age, which follows the Piscean Age associated with Christianity.

The changing direction of the polar axis means that the earth's north pole points to different "pole" stars during this twenty-six-thousand-year great cycle. Whereas now it points to the star Polaris in the constellation Ursa Minor, thirteen thousand years ago it pointed to the star Vega; this will again become the pole star around 14,000 A.D. Esoteric astrology teaches that the earth's north pole is the receiving end of cosmic rays, and this great cycle is believed to change the star source, and presumably the nature, of the radiation input from the far reaches of the galaxy.

Some astrologers propose that the starting point of the "grand cycle," or "polar cycle," is when the earth's axis points exactly toward the star Polaris, which will occur between 2000 and 2100 A.D.[37] If this is valid, then not only are we entering a new twenty-one-hundred-year phase, the so-called Aquarian Age, but we are also completing and beginning anew a whole round of the grand cycle. Of course the dates do not have exact significance, since there are probably transition periods of several hundred years between ages and an even longer transition period for the grand cycle.

The shift in the direction of the earth's axis through the long twenty-six-thousand-year polar cycle may also account for the changing of the areas of concentrated evolutionary activity over the surface of the planet. It seems that at different times in the earth's history one or another area may be the primary focus: in the past it has been Atlantis, Egypt, India, China, Persia, the Mediterranean. Perhaps as the axis turns, different parts of the surface of the globe are exposed to sidereal radiation which stimulates evolutionary energy transformation.

This grand cycle may also be related to long-term evolutionary processes, in which the whole of humanity is engaged. The changes in consciousness occurring now as we enter the Aquarian phase have often been described and are well known. In esoteric astrology it is said that "in the greater cycle of man's many incarnations, he . . . passes through the zodiacal circle from Pisces to Aries"; [38] that is, man evolves along with the rest of humanity through the grand cycle. The moment he begins to consciously participate in his own evolution, he "reverses the wheel" and follows a progression from Aries to Pisces, in a counterclockwise direction (though not necessarily in a sign by sign order).

In addition to these cycles, there are undoubtedly other cycles in which we, as human beings living on earth, are involved. The solar system as a whole revolves around the center of the galaxy, a cycle that must take millions of years; it has also been proposed that there is a galactic sun of intermediate size around which our entire solar system revolves, in a cycle of several hundred thousand years. Sirius, Aldebaran, Arcturus, and other stars have been suggested for this role, though astronomers have not in general accepted this view. It is well known, however, that we in our solar system are the recipients of innumerable kinds of cosmic radiation, all varying in rhythmic cycles; channeled, filtered, transformed in various ways as they reach earth.

Esoteric astrology teaches that as we free ourselves more and more from planetary influences, we gradually become more and more aware of, and receptive to, finer and higher frequency radiations from other stars and suns. "As man evolves the mechanism of response or the vehicles of consciousness likewise steadily improve. His reactions, therefore, to the planetary influences and to the energy of the various constellations change." [39]

An example of this change in responsiveness to certain kinds of radiations may be found in considering the "eye signs." [40] It was pointed out that modern astrologers are almost unanimously agreed that the presence of a planet or cusp on one or more of the three fixed stars Pleiades (28° Taurus), Ascellus (6° Leo), and Antares (8° Sagittarius) is indicative of serious eye trouble, even blindness. Further analysis showed that these signs were also found in a number of individuals with a high degree of perception. In other words, the same star or sign in the natal horoscope may indicate more sight or less, depending on the response "vehicle of consciousness."

The nature of our changing relationship to the zodiac and the constellations as we evolve was vividly expressed by the great Paracelsus: "Constellations are subordinate to the wise man; they have to follow him, not vice versa. Only a man still on the animalistic level is ruled by the planets, just as a thief cannot escape the gallows, a murderer cannot escape hanging, a fisher cannot escape the fishes, a hunter cannot escape the animals. But this stems from the fact that such a man does not know himself, and does not know how to use the forces that lie within him, and does not know that the 'constellations' also are within him, that the microcosm and all its powers are within him. Justly he must be regarded as unwise and be in bondage to all earthly mortal factors." [41]

The key, as always, lies within.

NOTES AND REFERENCES

1. From *Mysterium Cosmographicum,* quoted in an excellent article, Wolfgang Pauli, "The Influence of Archetypal Ideas on Kepler's Theories," in Carl Jung and W. Pauli, *The Interpretation of Nature and the Psyche* (New York: Pantheon Books, Bollingen Series LI, 1955), p. 181.

2. From *Mineralium,* quoted in Rupert Gleadow, *The Origin of the Zodiac* (New York: Atheneum, 1969), p. 51.

3. Margaret Gammon, *Astrology and the Edgar Cayce Readings* (Virginia Beach, Va.: A.R.E. Press, 1967), p. 18.

4. Much of this research has been well summarized in Michel Gauquelin, *Cosmic Clocks,* part II (New York: Regnery, 1967).

Professor W. R. Fairbridge of Columbia University, in discussing the eleven-year and the eighty-year sunspot cycles stated: "A direct correlation between oceanography, climate, solar activity, and celestial mechanics thus seems to be probable. Since planetary motions are rather well observed and cyclic in character, it should be possible to correlate and predict climatic-oceanic events, and thus certain critical environmental factors in human history, with planetary arithmetic. There emerges the intriguing possibility of a partial justification of some aspects of classical astrology, shocking as it may sound." In: "Geological and Cosmic Cycles," *Annals of the New York Academy of Sciences,* 138 (1967): 435.

5. See, for example, Oliver Reiser, *Cosmic Humanism* (Cambridge, Mass.: Schenkman Publishing Co., 1966).

6. W. Wolf, ed., "Rhythmic Functions in the Living Systems," *Annals of the New York Academy of Sciences,* 98 (1962).

7. "It has become increasingly evident in recent years that all organisms are rhythmic systems. Whenever adequate data have become available about virtually any biological phenomenon, appropriate analyses have always revealed its periodic nature . . . living things are not only universally rhythmic but the major periods of the rhythms of plants and animals are normally synchonized with the major periods of their external physical environment." In F. A. Brown, "Extrinsic Rhythmicality," *Annals of the New York Academy of Sciences,* 98, (1962): 775–787.

8. See Gauquelin's *Cosmic Clocks,* for detailed descriptions of this research. For a description of the work of Charles F. Stroebel on the twenty-four-hour cycle in human physiological processes consult: Charles F. Stroebel, "The Importance of Biological Clocks in Mental Health," *NIMH: Mental Health Program Reports,* no. 2, (1968): 323–351. Dr. Stroebel's research has shown that most metabolic processes exhibit twenty-four-hour rhythmicity. Lack of synchronization between the cycles of different processes is found in psychosomatic and many "mental" illnesses. The instinctual, "gut-level" processes are locked into the circadian cycle more than cerebral processes. Drug reactions differ according to the phase of the cycle at which the drug is given.

9. F. A. Brown, "Extrinsic Rythmicality," *Annals of the New York Academy of Sciences,* 98 (1962): 785–786. "It seems reasonable to postulate that a solar and lunar frequency transformation became a functional characteristic of living systems during early evolution in the littoral regions of the oceans where the organisms for millions of years were regularly buffeted by the day-night cycles and the ocean tides."

10. The Russian historian A. L. Tchijevsky published, in 1934, studies in which he showed that, over the period from 500 B.C. to A.D. 1900, years of high sun-spot activity coincided with periods of political unrest and with great epidemics, such as the medieval plagues and the Chicago smallpox epidemics. Tchijevsky claimed that what he called "psychic epidemics" coincided with solar activity peaks.

Friedman, Becker, and Bachman of New York State University, Syracuse, have published data showing, over a period of four years, significant correlations between psychiatric hospital admissions and indices of solar magnetic storm activity. "Geomagnetic Parameters and Psychiatric Hospital Admissions," *Nature,* 200 (1963): 626.

Gauquelin has reviewed studies by Japanese, Russian, and European investigators relating monthly and daily fluctuations in solar activity to typhoons and other climatic changes; to the floculation index of blood serum; to the percentage of lymphocytes in the blood, which decreases when solar activity is high; to the incidence of cardio-vascular infarctions and deaths from tuberculosis; and to mining and traffic accidents.

The Italian chemist Piccardi has shown that the speed of certain chemical reactions in an inorganic colloid and the molecular structure of water are affected by daily and long-term fluctuations in solar activity. See M. Gauquelin, *Cosmic Clocks,* and G. Piccardi, *The Chemical Basis of Medical Climatology* (Springfield, Ill.: C. Thomas, 1962).

11. In 1962 Bradley et al. reported an analysis of fifty years of precipitation records in over fifteen hundred weather stations. They found a marked tendency for heavy rainfall to occur four days after full moon, and four days after new moon; minimal rainfall occurred following first and last quarter. The pattern was exactly reversed for the southern hemisphere, presumably due to the fact that the circulation of the atmosphere in the southern hemisphere is a mirror image of the pattern north of the equator. "Lunar Synodical Period and Widespread Precipitation," *Science,* 137 (1962): 748–749.

Thus the moon, in combination with the sun, exerts a potent effect on the liquids of the oceans and the atmosphere. But, as Rodney Collin has pointed out in his book, *The Theory of Celestial Influence* (London: Stuart, 1954), "the tidal effect of the moon works on liquids incorporated in organic matter as it does on those which are free. In fact, the effect is evidently much stronger, for the minute capillaries through which organic liquids move break them up into masses so small that they obey molecular rather than mechanical laws, and are thus infinitely more sensitive than the large bodies of water with which we are more familiar" (p. 110). There have been a number of empirical studies investigating the legendary effect of the moon on the menstrual cycle; the results here have been inconsistent, some investigators finding an effect, others failing to do so.

12. This work has extended over a period of ten years and is currently being carried out with government support and the use of computer facilities. The only English-language report of the work has appeared in an astrological journal, F. Rubin, "Lunar Sex Cycle," *American Astrology,* 36, no. 5 (July, 1968): 3–11. In this report the results of four separate studies are given, totalling over four hundred cases and yielding 83–87 percent accuracy of prediction of sex. This lunar fertility cycle is evidently independent of the menstrual cycle which is used in calculating the fertile period according to the so-called rhythm method. Dr. Jonas stated in the above-mentioned article, that "according to the present scientific view, the ovum's metabolic condition is the factor which results in the attraction by chemotropic means of one or the other of the spermatozoa to the ovum . . . why should it seem unimaginable that this material process may be influenced in some way by the moon's position? The research workers who used electric current to separate the two types of sperm and influence their movement have not yet found an explanation of the migration of one type to the anode and the other to the

cathode. . . . The cyclic variation of the influence of the fields of the ecliptic is connected with the earth's rotation. This is a factor which may in some way affect the chemotropic processes taking place in the mother's system." In view of the demonstrated sensitivity of primitive organisms to magnetic, electric, and gravitational fields, as well as ultrashort and ultralong electromagnetic radiation, it is certainly not impossible to conceive of a sperm or an ovum being similarly sensitive.

13. R. Lust, "The Properties of Interplanetary Space," *Solar-Terrestrial Physics,* ed. J. W. King and W. S. Newman (New York: Academic Press, 1967). "The interplanetary field is highly organized on a 27-day basis into four segments within each of which the direction of the field is, most of the time, either positive or negative," (p. 20).

14. W. I. Axford, "Interplanetary Magnetic Field," *New Scientist,* 29 (July, 1965): 262–264. "The interplanetary magnetic field comprises part of the magnetic field of the sun. . . . the radial form of the field is more reminiscent of what would be expected from a single magnetic pole . . . the reason for this . . . is that we are dealing not with a magnetic field in a vacuum, but with a field which is embedded in a fully ionized gas—a plasma—with a high electrical conductivity. . . . It is believed that the field extends for at least some thousands of millions of miles, to the region where the solar effects run into and merge with the interstellar medium."

Sidereal astrology postulates that the sun's relationship to sources of radiation from the constellations or fixed stars' changes—and this also is confirmed by these new observations. To quote Axford again: "The co-rotation of the interplanetary magnetic field with the sun must affect cosmic rays arriving from the remote regions of the Galaxy" (p. 263).

15. J. H. Nelson, "Radio Weather Forecasting Techniques," *Transactions of the Institute of Radio Engineers,* CS-2, no. 1 (1954).

16. Rex Pay, "Position of Planets Linked to Solar Flare Prediction," *Technology Week* (American Aviation Publications Inc., May 15, 1967): 1. "Although their gravitational effects are many orders of magnitude less than that of the sun itself, the time rate of change of the resultant planetary field vector appears to have some triggering effect on the release of solar flares. It appears therefore that solar flares can be predicted from the positions of the planets."

17. E. K. Bigg, "Lunar and Planetary Influences on Geomagnetic Disturbances, *Journal of Geophysical Research,* 68 (July 1, 1963).

J. A. Jacobs and G. Atkinson, "Planetary Modulation of Geomagnetic Activity," *Magnetism and the Cosmos,* ed. W. R. Hindmarsh et. al. (New York: American Elsevier, 1967), pp. 402–414.

J. Houtgast and A. van Sluiters, "The Geomagnetic

Activity Around Conjunction and Opposition of Planets," in *Magnetism and the Cosmos*, pp. 399–401.

18. Axel Harvey, "The Planets and the Earth's Magnetic Field," *Correlation*, no. 3 (Research Publication of International Society for Astrological Research, 1969).

19. H. Prescott Sleeper, "The Pulsing Ionosphere: A Link Between Human Beings and the Universe," Appendix in Oliver Reiser, *Cosmic Humanism*, p. 571. Also described in Rex Pay's article annotated in reference 16.

20. Gauquelin, *Cosmic Clocks*, p. 205.

21. J. Kepler, *Tertius Interveniens*, quoted in C. Jung, "Synchronicity: An Acausal Connecting Principle," *The Structure and Dynamics of the Psyche*, vol. 8, *Collected Works* (New York: Pantheon Books, Bollingen Series XX, 1960), p. 497.

22. *Ibid.*, pp. 417–531.

23. Dane Rudhyar, *The Practice of Astrology* (Netherlands: Servire/Wassenaar, 1968), p. 11.

24. Alice A. Bailey, *Esoteric Astrology* (New York: Lucis Publishing Co., 1951), p. 23.

25. *Ibid.*, p. 16.

26. Gammon, *Astrology and Edgar Cayce*, p. 19.

27. *Ibid.*, p. 5.

28. *Ibid.*, p. 8.

29. *Theatrum Chemicum V*, quoted in Carl Jung, *Alchemical Studies*, vol. 13, *Collected Works* (New York: Pantheon Books, Bollingen Series XX, 1967), p. 125.

30. Quoted in Pauli, "The Influence of Archetypal Ideas on Kepler's Theories," Jung and Pauli, *Interpretation of Nature and the Psyche*, p. 182.

31. Though it is technically inaccurate, in the strict sense, to equate the mid-heaven with the zenith, and the I.C. with the nadir, the difference does not affect the main point of the present formulation.

32. It is not possible, or necessary, in this chapter, to go into the technical aspects of casting horoscopes. These can be found in any textbook on the subject, such as Margaret Hone's *A Modern Textbook of Astrology* (London: Fowler, 1969). This book also discusses the different house systems. A series of articles on the house systems appeared during 1969 in *Kosmos*, a publication of International Society for Astrological Research. It is my impression that the so-called Birthplace House System, designed by Walter Koch, is the most logical and astronomically accurate, *Kosmos* (April, 1969), pp. 5–8.

33. Gay Luce, *Biological Rhythms in Psychiatry and Medicine*. NIMH: Mental Health Program Reports, No. 4, Washington, D.C., 1970.

34. Bailey, *Esoteric Astrology*, pp. 17, 19.

35. Gleadow, *The Origin of the Zodiac*.

36. Jeff Mayo, *The Astrologer's Astronomical Handbook* (London: Fowler, 1965).

37. Dane Rudhyar, *The Astrology of Personality* (Netherlands: Servire/Wassenaar, 1936), p. 194. "(this) is recommended on two grounds: 1) Polaris is probably the most brilliant star exactly on the circle described by the prolongation of the Earth's axis; 2) we believe that ideas always come to be accepted *about* the time when a crucial point in the working out of that to which the idea refers is occurring."

38. Bailey, *Esoteric Astrology*, p. 20.

39. *Ibid.*, p. 69.

40. Phyllis Dee Harrison, "Psychic Sensitive Points," *Kosmos* (December, 1968), p. 27.

41. *The Hermetical and Alchemical Writings of Paracelsus*, Vol. 2, trans. A. E. Waite (London: 1894; reprinted, New Hyde Park: University Books, 1968), p. 184.

ASTROLOGY II

The Planetary Perspective

*We do not try to discover something new,
but to recover that which is lost.*

G. I. GURDJIEFF

THE ORIGINAL MEANING OF ASTRO-logical symbolism in its application to individual evolution has evidently been lost. Present-day astrology, with few exceptions, concerns itself largely with the horoscope of personality, not the horoscope of individuality. Yet there are indications that this forgotten language will be deciphered again, reinterpreted in the light of modern astronomical knowledge, and tested by means of reliable methods of expanding awareness and perception.

Exoteric science continues to make observations of the interacting force fields of sun and planets, and of sidereal radiations, and to measure their effects on processes on earth. Esoteric science observes and studies the parallel processes *within*, as states and levels of consciousness. The premiss of the latter is that the planets and suns are not merely bodies in space; rather, they are intelligent beings who have the bodies that we see through our telescopes, and who are involved in purposeful, cyclic, evolutionary patterns, just as we are.

From any point of view, exoteric or esoteric, one cannot help but see evidence of conscious purpose and design in the rhythmic complexity, the harmony of cosmic movement, and the interweaving systems of energy transformation. We are somewhat in the position that a cell might be were it to become aware of the (to it) stupendous cyclic processes of metabolism flowing through the body on which it lives and dies. The physiological body is involved in energy transformations on a different scale than the cell; yet these processes profoundly affect the individual cell. Similarly, the body of the planet on which we live is involved in metabolic processes on a vastly different scale than ours, yet they clearly affect us. Our parent sun, or solar system, is in turn involved in still larger cycles, again as far removed in scale from it as we are from the sun.

Astrology is primarily concerned with cyclic processes on the next level of the solar system. Constellations and other sources of cosmic rays, the so-called fixed stars, are also studied, but to a lesser degree, because they are further removed in scale.

Thinking of the planets as intelligent beings on a larger scale, allows us to consider some of the mass effects of planetary field forces in an interesting way. For example, on the question of war, Gurdjieff stated that "war is the result of planetary influences. Somewhere up there two or three planets have approached too near each other; tension results. Have you noticed how, if a man passes quite close to you on a narrow pavement, you become all tense? The same tension takes place between planets. For them it lasts, perhaps, a second or two. But here, on the earth, people begin to slaughter one another, and they go on slaughtering maybe for several years." [1] It is not difficult to conceive of the cellular effects of psychic tension in an analogous way: psychosomatic disease is cellular warfare. Conversely, war is a disease of the planet, a kind of organic psychosis, recurring cyclically. But this does not mean it is an unavoidable pattern; disease-producing stress can be resisted by an organism that is basically healthy, whose organs and cells are resilient and functioning in a balanced cooperative manner. Planetary stress does not *have* to lead to war, if we can learn to transmute it. We must learn this transmutation first within ourselves. If we can learn to resolve "oppositions" and "squares" within, we have a chance of resolving them in our relationships with each other. Otherwise, clearly not.

The Greeks and other ancient peoples associated the planets with the gods. The physical planets were the bodies of the gods. If the planets have a consciousness, or psyche (called the "planetary Logos" in esoteric philosophy),

we can communicate, in consciousness, with the planets and perhaps with the stars. Among the ancient peoples, the gods ruled men; in astrology man "on the wheel" is ruled by the planets. These same gods helped the heroes—those who had chosen the path of consciousness and who struggled for individuality. Man "on the path" can learn to work *with* the planets.

Considering the solar system as a unit, we have seen that modern astronomy and esoteric astrology converge in the view that the basic energy flux from the sun is modulated and transformed in different ways by the planets. The Pythagorean school formulated this effect in terms of the theory of octaves, the "harmony of the spheres." Just as each note in an octave progression has a definite relationship to the tonic in terms of vibratory frequency, so each planet was presumed to stand in an analogous interval relationship to the solar tonic in terms of frequency of vibrations. Just as some combinations of tones sound harmonious, others discordant, so some combinations of planetary vibrations produce benign conditions on earth, others induce discord and conflict.

Another analogy has been made in terms of light and color. We can think of the planets as "so many prismatic lenses, each with a different refractive index, which enables it to reflect an individual color from the white light of the sun." [2] This is the basis for astrological attributions of different crystals and gems to the planets.

The solar system has roughly the form of a spinning elliptical disc, with the smaller, faster moving planets closer to the center, and the much larger, slower moving planets describing longer orbital periods. In general, the density of the planet decreases with distance from the sun, whereas the speed of axial rotation, the "vibratory rate" as it were, increases. The number of satellites supported by the planet also increases.

These physical factors are consistent with the esoteric teaching that the large outer planets (with the possible exception of Pluto) are more evolved members of the solar system. They are less dense, vibrating at a higher rate of frequency; they are also supporting more satellites

TABLE I: *Physical Characteristics of the Planets* [3]

Planet	Distance Relative to Earth	No. of Moons	Density Relative to Earth	Axial Rotation in Earth Days
Mercury	0.4	—	1.3	59.0
Venus	0.7	—	0.9	243.0
Earth	1.0	1	1.0	1.0
Mars	1.5	2	0.7	1.0
(Asteroids)	2.7		0.7	
Jupiter	5.2	12	0.2	0.4
Saturn	9.5	9	0.1	0.4
Uranus	19.2	5	0.2	0.4
Neptune	30.1	2	0.3	0.7
Pluto	39.5		?	6.4

themselves. They are perhaps closer to being suns.[4]

In this connection it is noteworthy that Jupiter, the largest planet (accounting for 71 percent of the total mass of the planets), with the largest number of moons, the second lowest density, and the fastest rate of axial rotation, has recently been found to be emitting very strong radio waves and to have a very strong magnetic field. Astronomers have made calculations which indicate that "Jupiter emits several times as much energy as it receives from the sun." [5] Again, these data are consistent with, though they do not of course prove, traditional astrology's assumption that Jupiter, after the sun, has the most beneficent effect of the planets.

Astrologically, Jupiter is associated with co-operation, fellowship, organizations, and collaborative groups on the interpersonal level; and with growth, expansion, magnanimity, ennoblement, and broadmindedness on the personal level. It is held to bring abundance when in favorable aspect; to further those qualities that enable one to magnetically attract material resources. Physiologically, it is traditionally associated with the liver, the chief organ of elimination and detoxification. Edgar Cayce also associated it with the pituitary, which organizes and balances the functions of the other endocrine glands.[6]

Traditionally, Jupiter and Saturn are thought of as polarizing expansion versus contraction; opportunity versus limitation; generosity versus caution; religious associations versus national states. According to Dane Rudhyar, Saturn represents the father-image in the psyche, the principle of authority as opposed to the mother-image represented by the moon.[7] In Edgar Cayce's readings, Saturn has a rather different role: it is said to rule change, especially sudden, drastic changes; material changes that test one's patience. This relates to the teaching that Saturn is the planet of lesson learning, of purgatory: "All insufficient matter is cast unto Saturn, to work out his own salvation . . . the entity or individual banishes itself . . . to Saturn go those who would renew or begin again." [8] In Alice Bailey's *Esoteric Astrology,* Saturn is described as "the planet which conditions primarily the point in evolution where choice definitely becomes possible, where rejection of opportunity or its acceptance can consciously be undertaken, and the shouldering of personal responsibility becomes a recognized fact in a planned and ordered life." [9]

This is one planet that would be seen very differently in the horoscope of the personality and the horoscope of the individuality. As one of the "Lords of Karma," Saturn represents limitations to the personality. But from the viewpoint of individuality, he represents opportunity for learning and choice and hence potential growth.

The symbolic relationship between Saturn and Jupiter in psychic life can perhaps be understood in the light of the myth relating to these two, known as Cronos and Zeus to the Greeks. Cronos (Saturn) killed and castrated his father Uranos, the sky god, who had banished him to Tartarus for being rebellious. Cronos then took over the throne, but it was prophesied that he in turn would be dethroned by one of his sons. To prevent this, Cronos devoured his children as they were born; but his wife Rhea, the earth goddess, was able to hide one son, Zeus. Zeus finally killed Cronos and became the chief of the gods. The goddess Metis became pregnant by Zeus, and an oracle prophesied that the child would depose him, as he had deposed Cronos, and as Cronos had deposed Uranos. Zeus thereupon incorporated Metis by swallowing her, and gave birth to Pallas Athena, the goddess of wisdom, who sprang fully armed from his head. [10] Thus Cronos-Saturn came to represent inescapable karmic retribution: he was killed by his son as he had killed his father. Zeus-Jupiter however avoided the retribution and remained chief of the gods. He resolved the karmic problem by merging the male and the female in one body: and the offspring of this alchemical union was—wisdom.

There is little or no agreement as to the physiological correlate of Saturn. Traditionally Saturn is associated with the skeletal structure, and with the spleen, though it has also been related to the gonads, and to the anterior pituitary. The complementarity with Jupiter is evident here again: the spleen, on the left side of the body, is involved in assimilative, anabolic processes; the liver, on the right, in eliminative, catabolic processes. One might say Saturn, on the level of the individual, promotes acceptance and assimilation of experiences past and present; whereas Jupiter promotes expansive, dynamic expression. The glyphs of these two planets show a cross and a crescent in complementary relationship: ♃ Jupiter and ♄ Saturn. It is said that Christ was born at a conjunction of Saturn and Jupiter in Pisces.

As is well known, it is only in the last two hundred years, at the dawning of the Aquarian Age, that the planets beyond Saturn were discovered. These have been linked by astrologers to transcendence and expanded awareness, to new beginnings and developments in knowledge and perception. Thus Sun to Saturn is one octave; then a new, higher frequency octave begins. The asteroid belt between Mars and Jupiter, believed by astronomers to be the debris of an exploded planet, is identified with the "planet that failed," spoken of in esoteric teachings. Thus we have the following progression:

Sun	do
Mercury	re
Venus	mi
Earth	fa
Mars	sol
(Asteroids)	la
Jupiter	si
Saturn	do
Uranus	re
Neptune	mi
Pluto	fa

In this perspective, Saturn completes one cycle of development from the sun and begins a new one. Uranus, Neptune, and Pluto are "higher octaves" respectively of Mercury, Venus, and Earth. It is not that this scheme is correct; rather it serves to organize some of the astrological attributes of the planets, as they have been described.

Mercury, traditionally, is the planet of mind, speech, communications, sense perception. Mercury-Hermes was the messenger of the gods. We have noted the observations collected by Nelson, which implicate the planet Mercury in the facilitation or disturbance of ionospheric radio communications. Certain other interesting facts about this planet have only recently come to light with new techniques of radar astronomy. Until recently it was thought that Mercury's closeness to the sun would "lock" its rotation so that it would always face the sun one way, as the moon does the earth. Now, however, it appears that Mercury "moves in its rather eccentric orbit in such a way that at perihelion—nearest approach to the sun—it faces the sun one way around this time and exactly the opposite way around the next. So it has two 'poles', east and west, which alternately face the sun at the time of nearest approach." [11] In other words, it has the properties of an electric current alternator. In addition to this polar alternation, Mercury also changes its direction relative to the earth, appearing to move retrograde about six times a year. It is also the fastest moving planet. Small wonder it is associated with winged Hermes, carrying messages with the speed of thought.

On the personality level, mind is the thinking, relating intellect. From the point of view of growth of individuality, mind is the catalyst, that which gives direction and determines the use to which energies will be put. Thus the ennobling influence of Jupiter, depending on how it is understood by the Mercury-mind, can become a factor for growth or a factor for personality self-aggrandizement. This recalls the alchemical conception of *mercurius duplex*, who can go to the highest or the lowest places. "Mercury is the expression of the dual aspect of the mind as it mediates between the higher and the lower. . . . This mediation [is] within the personality, analysing and distinguishing . . . and secondly, it carries messages between the soul and the brain and establishes right relations between higher self and lower self." [12]

Venus, astro-mythologically, signifies love, beauty, peace, harmony, magnetic attraction. The emotional nature, as compared to the Mercurial mental nature. Astronomically, we note that the planet Venus is closest to the earth, in distance and in density. And that its magnetic field has a measurable beneficent effect on magnetic perturbations on earth. Even more suggestive is the fact that Venus' axial rotation, unlike that of any other planet, is slower than its orbit around the sun and in the opposite direction. "Today's best figure [of rotation] of days is exactly the rate which makes Venus face the earth the same way around each time of the nearest approach of the two planets. . . . Venus recognizes the position of the earth." [13]

In esoteric astrology Venus has been called earth's alter ego or spiritual prototype. [14] Venus is said to be "negatively polarized" (retrograde rotation?) and this made "possible a mysterious absorption by the Earth of Venusian force." [15]

Thus, it is taught that there is a special link between the psyche of the earth and that of Venus, leading to a "planetary alliance." Classical astrology referred to Venus, when it rose before the sun, as Venus Lucifer ("light-bringer"); in the natal horoscope it indicated visionary aspiration. [16]

We see again the difference between the orthodox and the esoteric interpretation of Venus. For the former it is personal love relationship. For the latter it is the love of the Higher, Creator Self for its creation: the union and harmony of higher and lower natures.

Mars, the planet traditionally associated with biological and vital energy, sex, activity, struggle, assertion, adventure, sports, anger, war, was often paired with Venus: they were male and female, creative and receptive, expressive and attractive. The planetary glyphs ♂ and ♀ were adopted by biology to indicate male and female life forms. Their complementary nature in classical astrology is also shown by the fact that they were assigned the "rulership" of opposite pairs of signs on the zodiac wheel. Thus Mars rules Aries, the sign of springtime beginnings, bursting forth; its opposite is Libra, the first sign of autumn, a time of values, kinship, and harmony, ruled by Venus. The second sign of spring is Taurus, an earth sign ruled by Venus; and its opposite, Scorpio, the second sign of autumn, is a water sign ruled by Mars.

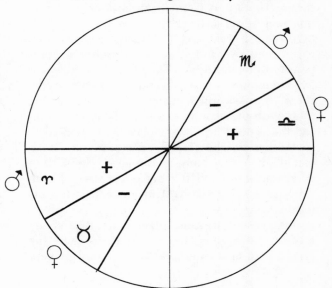

In esoteric astrology Mars is still related to activity, struggle, and sex, but the emphasis is different. It is the divine struggle of clashing opposites within, analogous to the role of the wrathful deities in Tibetan Buddhism, the forces of breakthrough and revelation. "The activity of Mars [is] potent to arouse the entire lower nature and bring about its final rebellion and the last stand, so to speak, of the personality against the soul." [17]

Mars supposedly rules and controls man's physical body, or vehicle of consciousness, while Venus and Mercury are related to the emotional and mental bodies respectively. Physiologically, there seems to be unanimous agreement (for once) that Mars is linked to the adrenal glands which, as is well known, function as physical activators and energizers. More generally, the effect of Mars is to vitalize the bloodstream and hence all parts of the body. Whether this vitalizing, energizing effect would produce creative inner struggle or destructive outer conflict and anger, would depend on the level of the individual—his response-ability.

The three trans-saturnian planets—*Uranus, Neptune*, and *Pluto*—have been associated with psychotic potential (breakdown) by some, and with psychic potential (breakthrough) by others. Again, the difference is whether the personality or the individuality is being considered. What is dissociative to the former can be revelatory to the latter. Great caution is necessary in interpreting these factors.

A psychiatrist, Harry F. Darling, has proposed a "co-conscious index," as a measure of "propensity to dissociation." The index is constructed by examining the strong aspects between the three "trans-saturnian malefics," and comparing them with the aspects made by them with Jupiter, the benefic. If all four planets are related to each other by major aspects, the pattern is "associated"; if one or more is unrelated, the pattern is "dissociated" and the personality is liable to experience severe stress if major malefic transits occur.[18]

But, these very same planets are related, by modern astrologers, to transcendence and the possibilities of higher consciousness and perception. *Uranus* is said to be the higher octave of Mercury; the Uranian consciousness is electric-intuitive. Neptune is said to be the higher octave of Venus; the Neptunian consciousness is oceanic-mystic.

Supporting the Mercury-Uranus association is the fact that Uranus' orbit exhibits a similar switching polarity, analogous to an electric current alternator: "The axis of Uranus lies almost flat upon the plane of its orbit. This means that . . . it turns its two poles in turn directly to the Sun and to the Earth." [19] While the other pole faces out into the galaxy. Edgar Cayce related Uranian influences with a tendency toward extremes—unusual abilities, especially in the area of scientific thinking and occult investigation, as well as extreme mood swings, from very high to very low.

The effect of Uranus is electrifying—it awakens personality to soul and Higher Self. It is associated with the Hierophant of the Tarot, who shows the hidden, occult way. "Uranus and Mercury in combination are dualities which the disciple learns to resolve and in the process of this resolution he shifts his focus out of the human kingdom into the fifth kingdom, the Hierarchy of souls." [20]

Neptune is associated with mysticism, which is more experiential-emotional-diffuse than the occult knowing associated with Uranus. On the personality level, Neptune rules imagination, dreams, films, music, interest in water and oceans. It is also said to be the planet of drugs, especially consciouness drugs. Esoterically, Neptune is related to higher emotional experiencing. "When Neptune is thus active . . . then emotion-desire have been transmuted into love-aspiration and are dedicated to and oriented to the soul; the entire emotional or sensitive nature is responsive to energies coming from 'the heart of the sun'." [21]

The role and influence of *Pluto* have, since its discovery in 1930, been the subject of much debate among astrologers, and it can only be said that it is far from clear. Most commonly, it is associated with regeneration, with consciousness development, and with the death and rebirth of psychic transformation. Pluto has also been related to secrecy and "depth" investigation, whether scientific (nuclear), psychic or political.

Compilations of esoteric teachings such as H. P. Blavatsky's *The Secret Doctrine* or Alice Bailey's *Esoteric Astrology* and other works, constantly emphasize that the cosmic and psychic nature and functions of these more recently discovered planets will only become clearer gradually, as our attitudes and perceptions change and we are able to observe and test their influences. In addition, other planets, now hidden, remain to be discovered. One of these is "Vulcan," which is supposed to be within Mercury's orbit and to represent the evolution of the soul-light throught the densest forms of matter. The relationship of planets to centers of force in the bodies of man is also changing in the new age as more of humanity embarks on the conscious path of evolutionary development. These assertions and predictions are not so easily dismissed as sheer speculation when we recall how uncannily close some of the most recent astronomical data and theories are to the concepts of the occult astrologers.

In regard to the role of the *moon* there is considerable variance between the classical astrological conception and the interpretation derived from esoteric philosophy. According to Rudhyar, the moon represents the mother-image, the function of adaptation and adjustment to life conditions, as opposed to the Saturnian father-image. Others have related the moon to physiological, instinctive levels of functioning. And this, as we have seen, has found some support in the data linking the fertility cycle in women to the phase of the moon. We are dealing here with the astrology of conception, not of birth.

Following the formulations of the Tantras, of Alchemy, and of Actualism, we may relate the sun to the dynamic, male aspect of the nature and the moon to the magnetic, female aspect. The sun relates dynamically to earth—earth receives radiation from the sun; and the moon relates magnetically to earth—drawing liquids on earth and in earth's creatures, receiving reflected light from earth. Experientially also, the moon exerts a magnetic, sometimes almost hypnotic effect on man's moods and perceptions; whereas we soak up the radiant power of the sun.

A different though not inconsistent perspective on the role of the moon is found in Gurdjieff's teachings. Here the notion that the moon is related to mother functions is reversed, as it were, and the moon is said to be "feeding on earth." In particular, the film of organic life on earth, which acts as a huge "accumulator" of energy from the sun, the planets, and the earth, provides food for the moon. According to this view, all movements, actions, and manifestations of animals, plants, and people, insofar as they are mechanical, are controlled by the moon.[22] Another way of stating this is to say the moon represents our evolutionary tail, and that the way of liberation is liberation from the dominance of these lunar, instinctive, residual programs and transfer to programing by inner direction from Higher Self. Compared to the ascendant and sun sign, the moon sign would represent the limitations and handicaps imposed by the *past,* whereas the sun sign indicates *present* level of development, and the rising sign *future* possibilities.

The transmutation of aspects

When an astrologer interprets the positions of planets in a natal horoscope he is aware that the meaning and influence of the planets are not fixed qualities. Not only do they vary according to whether personality or individuality is being considered, but the effect of the planet varies according to its sign, its house, and its aspects. (The latter refers to the angular relationship of the given planet with other planets, as seen from the earth.) Saturn in Leo is not the same as Saturn in Leo at right angles (square) to Jupiter in Libra. It gives a different perspective on the Saturnian influence, a different "aspect."

Johannes Kepler, in the passage quoted earlier on page 113, believed that the aspects of the planets, the angular relationships of their rays, could be determined by inner observation, since we have within us "the idea of the zodiac." In fact, Kepler considered aspects the most important part of astrology. In a letter to a friend, he wrote: "It is ten years now since I rejected the divisions into twelve equal parts, into houses; into dominations, trinities, and so forth. The only part I kept are the aspects, and I link astrology to the doctrine of harmonies." [23]

Numerology is also basic to the aspects: the meaning of an aspect relationship between two or more planets is given by the symbolic meaning of the number of divisions of the circle, which that aspect represents. The 90° aspect is called square, even though it is actually a right-angled triangle, because it divides the 360° circle into four; the sextile (60°) divides it into six; the trine (120°) into three; the quintile (72°) into five; and so on. And the meaning of these aspects is derived from the numerological meaning of the numbers.

Certain configurations of aspects have received special attention in astrology. There is, for example, the so-called Finger of God configuration, in which two planets each are in "quincunx" (150°) to a third planet. This third planet, the apex of the triangle, is supposed to indicate a specific karmic opportunity or evolutionary purpose in this lifetime. A kind of pointer to the next step on the "way". It is sometimes overlooked that basically all aspects can be reduced to triangles. In *Esoteric Astrology*, Alice Bailey represents planetary, sidereal, and psychic factors on different dimensions all interacting by way of different energy triangles. In the horoscope, any aspect between two planets is actually a triangle made up of those two planets and the earth. Thus, if two planets' rays meet at a 90° angle on the earth, they are "square"; if the angle is 120°, they are in "trine," and so on. The only exceptions are conjunctions and oppositions, which are alignments of planets with the earth.

The major configurations of aspects involving more than two planets are combinations of triangles. The T-Square is two right-angled triangles adjacent, so that a larger right-angled

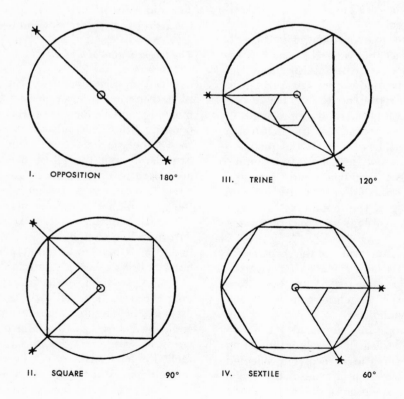

I. OPPOSITION   180°

III. TRINE   120°

II. SQUARE   90°

IV. SEXTILE   60°

triangle is formed. The Grand Trine is three equilateral triangles, with their apexes all meeting at the earth. The Grand Cross is four right-angled triangles, with their apexes meeting at the earth. It is said by some astrologers that the T-Square, supposedly a "malefic" configuration, can be "solved" by relating to the point (by planet, house, or sign) which is opposite the apex of the large triangle (point A). This would balance the configuration, make the triangle into a cross, and turn the trinity of planets into a quaternity, a more stable pattern. In Jung's writings there is much emphasis on the changing of a trinity into a quaternity as one of the key factors in the individuation process.

Actually, the same method may be applied to the simple aspects, which are all triangles (with Earth), as pointed out above. We are dealing here with a kind of *transmutation of aspects*— of planetary aspects and of corresponding personality aspects. Thus to resolve a "square" between two planets (which is actually a right-angled triangle with Earth), we form a cross by taking a point midway between them, and linking it to Earth. If there is a planet at or near this point, this planet becomes the balancing factor. For example, if a person has Venus on the "midpoint" [24] between Sun and Moon, then the triangle Sun-Moon-Earth is transmuted into a cross made by Sun-Moon and Earth-Venus. Psy-

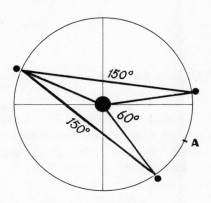

A. Finger-of-God.

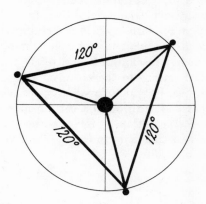

B. Grand Trine.

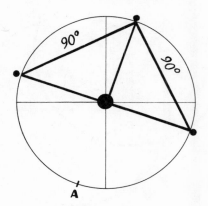

C. T-Square.

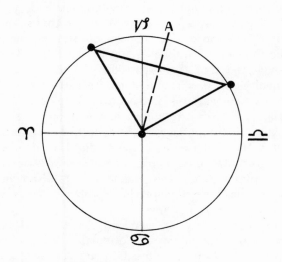

Square transmuted into cross; triangle into quaternity.

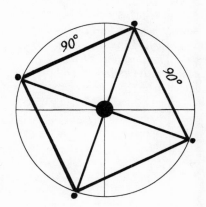

D. Grand Cross.

chologically, we could say that the dynamic, male aspect of the nature (Sun) and the magnetic, female aspect (Moon) are brought into balanced harmony by relating the love-nature (Venus) to the physical body (Earth).

If there is no planet on the midpoint, a balancing factor that has the necessary qualities can be created by the individual within himself. Since we are not dealing with the physical planets, but rather with conscious beings who are focussed in the planets, we can communicate with them in consciousness and relate the planet's kind of energy to the corresponding system in ourselves. The alchemist Agrippa wrote of this process: "For through a certain mental faculty our spirit can thus by imitation be made like some star, so that it is suddenly filled with the functions of a star." [25]

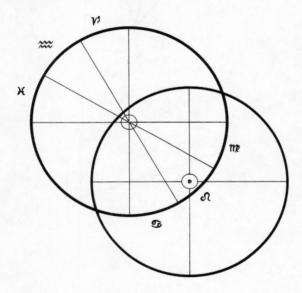

Geocentric and heliocentric perspectives: If the sun is in 15 Leo, seen from the earth, then the earth is in 15 Aquarius (exactly opposite), seen from the sun. The positions of the other planets will be different and must be determined from heliocentric ephemeris.

We can surmise that the new astrology will work with geometric maps of personality structure and its evolutionary transformations, showing the configurations made by the planets in their aspects—triangles, crosses, pentagons, star-patterns, etc. New kinds of spherical geometry, employing vectors, will replace the static two-dimensional models now current. The number and strength of aspects would indicate the general cohesiveness of personality structure. In particular, the degree of cohesiveness (aspect relatedness) between the inner, terrestrial planets (Mercury, Venus, Mars, Sun and Moon) and the outer giants, would indicate the degree to which the individual can assimilate unusual and intense experiences, outside the normal realm of conditioned awareness. It would be an index of his ability to "ground" or "earth" such experiences. Unaspected planets would indicate the individual has to focus particularly on bringing in the function represented by that planet, and relating it, with awareness, to other aspects of his nature.

Elements, crosses and signs

The geocentric, tropical zodiac as used in classical astrology may not be the framework the new astrology will choose to use. Perhaps a heliocentric system that corresponds more closely to the actual field structure of the interplanetary magnetic and gravitational fields will be found more appropriate. A system that shows both geocentric and heliocentric aspects might be deemed desirable; especially as it has been suggested that the expansion of consciousness involves, in part, a shift from an earth-centered to a sun-centered perspective. However, the classical geocentric zodiac has acquired a most extraordinary potency in the collective consciousness. Its influence on the mass mind is evidenced by its fantastic popularity in the face of strident opposition from the scientific establishment, which has little difficulty in imposing its point of view in most other areas.

If it is true, as has been said, that the zodiacal signs are thought forms, "originally constructed or anchored upon the mental plane . . . in Atlantean days," [26] then it will be necessary for us to understand and absorb the inner meaning of these thought forms before we can establish a valid new system. This is one of the functions of transition periods between ages: they are times in which we extract from the old maps their essential core and are then free to construct new ones for the period ahead.

Do we, for example, understand the meaning of the glyphs used by all astrologers to represent the signs? It must be presumed that they are not arbitrary but have a definite meaning in regards to the chief feature of the type. The meaning of the picture symbols is only slightly better understood. Much interesting material regarding the sun sign is given in Alice Bailey's transcriptions; unfortunately there is no space to go into this in any detail here.

However, certain general considerations regarding the zodiacal map may be of value. The

circle, representing the year, can be divided in a number of different ways, by two, three, four, six, etc. This leads us into numerology and harmonic analysis, the modern esoteric and exoteric descendants, respectively, of the Pythagorean theory of numbers.[27]

The division into two can give us, for example, the lower half (Aries through Virgo) concerned with intrapersonal relationships versus the upper half (Libra through Pisces) concerned with interpersonal relationships. Each sun sign type can learn a lot about the meaning of his sign by comparing it to the opposite sign, in the other half. If we adopt a heliocentric perspective, the sign opposite the sun sign will be the sign the earth is in, as seen from the sun. Here we are using the principle of interrelationships afforded by duality and complementarity to interpret the meaning of the signs.

The division of the zodiacal circle into three gives us the cardinal, fixed, and mutable crosses, which are related to the Law of Three found in all religious teachings. Any given sign can be interpreted in part through its relationship to one of the three fundamental forces, the plus-force (cardinal), the minus-force (fixed), and the neutral force (mutable).

The division into four relates the zodiac to the four elements of the alchemical tradition, to levels of consciousness. The division into six gives us the six positive and six negative signs which has been related to extraversion and introversion respectively. The twelve-fold division of course gives us the well-known twelve types; and finally we have the 360 degrees, each of which has been associated with a particular symbolic image, the so-called Sabian symbols.

In evaluating the personal meaning that any sign has in terms of inner growth and psychic transformation, the divisions into the four elements and the three crosses are perhaps most relevant. Recalling the discussion of the four elements in the chapter on alchemy, and anticipating somewhat the clarification that Actualism has brought to the concept of the higher bodies, or levels of consciousness, we may examine the following relationships:

Element	Body or Level	Linked to Physical Body via
Earth	Physical	—
Fire	Perceptual	Nervous Systems
Water	Emotional	Glandular Systems
Air	Mental	Brain Systems

Thus we would suggest that each sun sign type would tend to find his area of greatest sensitivity in the body and activity of the corresponding element or level of consciousness. This sensitivity could manifest creatively as a natural ease and freedom of movement on that level; or it could manifest as unbalanced hypersensitivity, if it is difficult to move from that level to others —the person is "hung" on that level. Integration presupposes equal facility and mobility on all levels. The sun sign element merely gives the present dominant direction, the preferred location of awareness.

The threefold division can be related to many of the esoteric maps previously considered. Here again, we can utilize the Actualist formulation of three modes of awareness: on every level of consciousness, awareness can be either in structure (fixed), or in function (cardinal), or in consciousness (mutable). The latter is the meditating principle. As awareness is expanded we perceive the interaction of consciousness and energy throughout the structures and functions of each level. Thus our point of awareness can be in physical structure or function or consciousness; or in the structures or functions or consciousness of the perceptual body; and so on for the other higher bodies.

Again, integration requires freedom to move freely and fluidly into and out of any of these modalities. One will usually not even know one has been primarily aware of one of the three modes until the beginning of change into the others is felt in awareness. As always, the most fixed hang-ups are the ones we don't notice—until at last they begin to loosen and we find that what we thought was normal, natural, or the way it is, is actually only one way among many.

This threefold principle is related to the astrological and other systems as follows:

Some Primitive Forms

Right   Round   Radiate

The three principles in natural and aesthetic form: right-dynamic, round-magnetic and radiate-energy.

Taoism	Creative (*yang*)	Receptive (*yin*)	*Tao*
Tantra	Siva	Sakti	Brahman
Gurdjieff	Affirming Force	Denying Force	Reconciling Force
Alchemy	Sulphur	Salt	Mercury
Astrology	Cardinal	Fixed	Mutable
Actualism	Function	Structure	Consciousness/Energy
Einstein	Radiation (*c*)	Matter (*m*)	Energy (*E*)
Electricity	positive (proton)	negative (electron)	neutral (neutron)
Mathematics	+	−	=

This list could be extended indefinitely: in one form or another this principle has appeared in every civilization, culture, and philosophic-scientific endeavor.

In its application to astrology, the combination of the three modes of awareness with the four levels of consciousness can give very valuable insight. It must be remembered though that these are probability patterns, not determinate sets. And of course they are modified by the positions and aspects of the other planets in a horoscope.

By way of example it is instructive to compare the psychology of Freud, Reich, and Jung in terms of the sun signs interpreted along these lines. Sigmund Freud was a Taurus, a sign associated in astrology with building and constructing foundations. It is a fixed earth sign. Thus, in terms of the inner life, we would expect an emphasis on the structural aspect of physical form. Freud had his most important insights in the area of body consciousness—the mechanisms by which energy is bound into structures (cathexes), displaced from one area of the body to another, and so on. He spent a great deal of time *constructing* formal patterns: the so-called psychoanalytic theory.

Wilhelm Reich, by contrast, was an Aries, the cardinal fire sign in which we would expect emphasis to be on the functional aspect of the perceptual-nervous system. Indeed, Reich was much more interested in energy flow and functioning than Freud; he called his work "bioener-getics" and his method "orgonotic functionalism." He considered one of his most important discoveries to be what he called the "plasmatic streaming" of the organism in a state of high charge. This is essentially a phenomenon of the perceptual-nervous system.

Carl Jung was a Leo, a fixed fire sign. We would expect him, from this point of view, to differ from Freud in being more at home in the perceptual than in the physical level. This is strikingly true, in that Jung was blatantly uninterested in the body. We would expect him to differ from Reich in being more aware of perceptual structures than of functions. This also is confirmed in that Jung's chief interest was symbols and images (which are perceptual structures), whereas Reich's was perceptual energy flow and functioning.

Comparing the three fire signs, we see they have in common an emphasis on communication, perception, power transmission. Aries expresses more the dynamic functioning aspects, Leo more the magnetic, charismatic power of the "born ruler," while Sagittarius, the sign of perceptual consciousness, is traditionally associated with intuition. Intuition, as commonly understood, is untrained perceptual sensitivity. With growth in understanding, intuition becomes true vision, as exemplified by Sagittarians William Blake, Beethoven, Paracelsus. The key word of this sign is: "I see the goal. I reach the goal and see another."

The three earth signs have in common a physi-

The Three Fire Signs: Aries (cardinal), Leo (fixed), and Sagittarius (mutable).

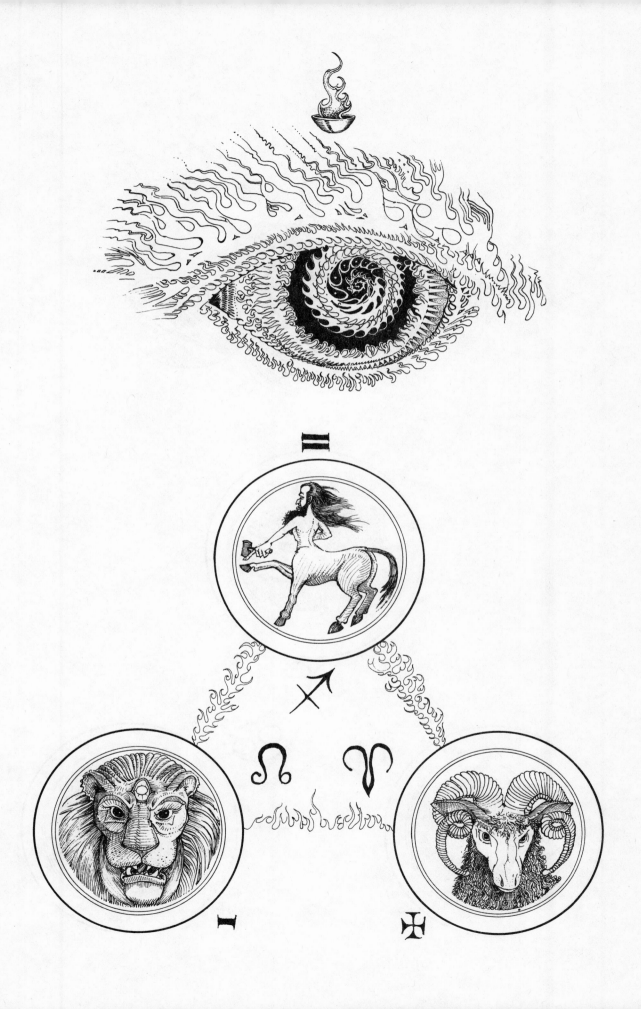

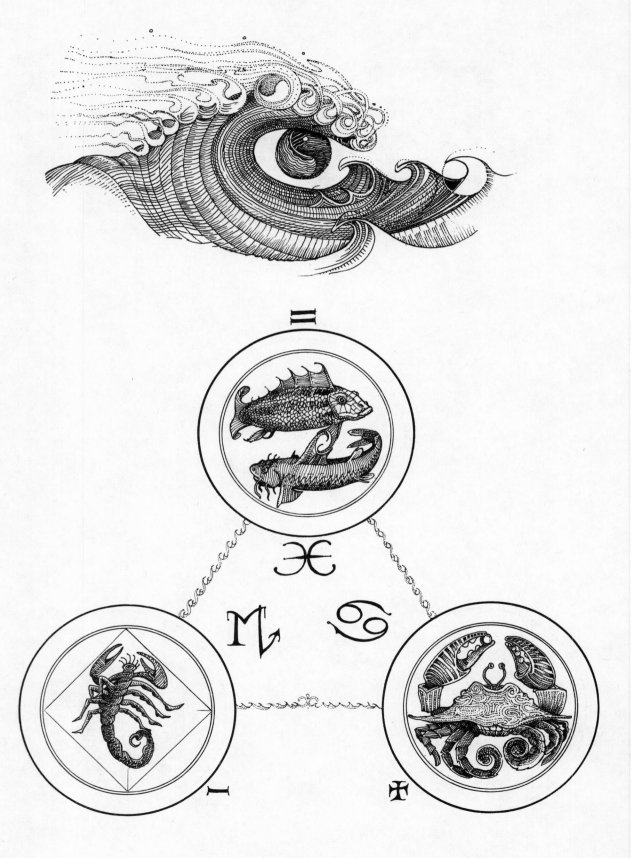

cal, time-space reality-based orientation. Capricorn, the cardinal sign, expresses the functional aspect in its concern with the lawful ordering of reality relationships, whether personal, social-political or scientific-natural. Taurus, as noted, is highly focussed in the basic earth structures; while Virgo, the mutable sign of earth consciousness, expresses the nourishing, cherishing care for material detail associated with the earth-mother mythology.

The three water signs have in common a primary awareness of and interest in the emotional quality of persons and situations. In Cancer (cardinal, functional) we find more the outflowing of feeling from the heart, a sense of warm enfoldment, a protective embracing; in Scorpio (fixed, structural) there is more of a dramatic feeling of polarities, of opposites in tension, of emotional depth and magnetic concealment; and in Pisces, the mutable sign of feeling consciousness, there is dual fluid sensitivity to both expressive and receptive flowing, diffusion and dissolution.

In the mental realm of air, Libra (cardinal, functional) expresses the beautifully balanced relating possible with detached mental functioning. Aquarius, the fixed, structural air sign, is the scientist-universalist whose garnered treasures of ideas are applied to the service of all. And Gemini is the mercurial, mental, mutable consciousness that flashes with brilliance and speed far and wide horizontally like the winds over the earth and oceans.

To apply these concepts to someone else, especially someone known only through their self-extensions, their creative products, not themselves, is of course of only tenuous validity and relevance. They do not in any way explain that artist's work: rather, they are points of view, perhaps more helpful in understanding the astrological symbols than in understanding the artist.

In the realm of musical expression, Beethoven (Sagittarius), Chopin (Pisces), and Mozart (Aquarius) are illustrative of some of the differences between fire, water, and air types. Bee-

thoven's highly-charged tonalities are predominantly electric-perceptual; Chopin's fluid melodic waves seem to resonate chiefly to the emotional level; whereas the luminous, almost geometrical lucidity of Mozart's harmonic patterns inspire higher-mind as the primary response level. Perhaps the qualities of earth-type music can be exemplified by the dense, almost textural structures of Brahms, who was a Taurus.

The symbol for Aquarius is a man showering stars onto the earth from a pitcher he is carrying. Mozart, Darwin, Galileo, Swedenborg are all examples of the Aquarian "down pouring" of mental inspiration from higher sources within, of tolerant objectivity based on knowledge of the unity of all, that are the key notes of the age we are entering. "And then the man who bears the pitcher will walk forth across an arc of heaven; . . . The wise will then lift up their heads and know that the redemption of the earth is near." [28]

The man on the path of conscious evolution, it has been suggested, consciously chooses (that is, Higher Self consciously chooses) to incarnate in a certain body, at a certain time and place, with a given personality pattern that will in time be modified by conditioning factors and experience. The personality is not aware of the soul plan, but it can become aware; at first externally, through the medium of maps of consciousness, such as astrology, if skillfully and wisely interpreted. In the next stage, he is aided in his growing awareness, still externally, by a teacher. Finally, he is able to attend to the teacher within. He shifts his attention from the outer to the inner zodiac. He knows the "planets" within —that is, that factor within him that stands in relationship to the consciousness of a given planet. In successive incarnations he enters the signs with more and more awareness, at progressively higher rates of frequency. "When the conditioning planetary forces, the expanding energies of the sun sign and the driving energy of the rising sign are all being controlled and directed by the illumined spiritual man, you will

The Three Water Signs: Cancer (cardinal), Scorpio (fixed), and Pisces (mutable).

then have a soul upon the very verge of liberation." [29]

When he is able to fuse the energies of all the signs, express all the qualities, not just the ones of his sign, he will begin to live as an integrated being. The zodiac then becomes not just a circle of twelve types but an upwardly expanding synthesizing spiral of evolution.

EXPERIENTIAL EXPERIMENTS

The more it is possible to base understanding of astrological factors on actual observations, rather than on interpretations obtained from reading, the more concrete and effective this understanding becomes. It takes a little time to learn the three symbolic alphabets of astrology, as it would any language.

It is good to start out by having your horoscope cast by a competent astrologer. Even though at first, and perhaps for a long time, the map thus obtained will mean very little. As you then gradually learn the meaning of various factors, they can be checked out by references to your own horoscope. In this way you learn about astrology and about yourself, at the same time.

To avoid being overly influenced by the inevitable subjective interpretations of one astrologer, it is even worthwhile to have the horoscope cast and read by several. I have had mine read by four different astrologers; since each one emphasized somewhat different facets— some made sense to me while some did not—I began to get a feeling for the possibilities of different perspectives on the same configurations of planets. I might add here that my first reading was a kind of revelation in that it enabled me to see certain character traits, for which I had tended to blame myself, as planetary tendencies given at birth. These then became factors I could work with or through rather than faults I had to overcome.

Since the horoscope is a complicated, highly condensed abstract map, it is useful to begin by listing some of the aspects and factors separately. Thus, you can make a list of conjunctions, oppositions, squares, trines, etc. It is also helpful to make geometric diagrams of the aspect triangles, as described above. What I am suggesting here is a kind of "unpeeling" of the many layers of the horoscope so that they can be understood separately and then synthesized. The art of arriving at a total synthetic picture of a horoscope requires a high degree of intuitive perception, and presupposes that the various elements in the chart are first understood separately. At a certain point, there may be a kind of gestalt perceptual click, as the whole suddenly becomes clear.

As mentioned previously, it is particularly important to pay attention to planets that have no, or only minor, aspect relationships to other planets; they would indicate factors in the personality systems which are particularly difficult to integrate. Successful integration here would be especially fruitful.

To obtain a sense for the meaning of the different sun sign types, it is useful to make a list for yourself of all the people you know of each sign. When I first did this I began to notice similarities and differences among my friends and acquaintances that I had not observed previously. You may also add to these lists public personages that you feel you know in some way. Astrologers are fond of doing the horoscopes of politicians, statesmen, and other famous people; but in terms of the psychological meaning, artists, writers, or musicians, because their inner world is accessible through their creations, would probably be more helpful. Great artists are often those who have particularly vividly expressed their type essence.

The symbolic animals of the zodiac signs can be worked with analogously to Tarot images. Let the image work in you, observe your own emotional reactions and mental associations to it. What in me is like a bull, or a ram, or a dolphin-goat, or an archer-centaur, or two fish swimming in opposite directions? And in what way? How do I feel about this animal? Do I have that feeling about something in me? How does the animal move? What in me moves that way? Try actually moving like the corresponding animal in order to get a feel for it in body consciousness.

Groups of persons of each sign can meet and discuss and compare their reactions and feelings; and they will observe how the same sign can manifest in different ways and on different levels.

You can add up the planets in each element, in your natal horoscope, and compare the relative predominance of each corresponding level of consciousness. Thus, if you have no planets in a water sign this does not of course mean that you have no emotions, but it may indicate that you would have some difficulty relating your emotional experiencings to other levels of consciousness; or in relating emotionally to others.

The following list of nature symbols and the characteristic attitude of each sign type might be found helpful:

Sign	Nature Symbol	Attitude
I. EARTH-PHYSICAL		
Capricorn	Rocks, Mountains	I use
Taurus	Plains, Fields	I have
Virgo	Caves, Valleys	I analyze
II. FIRE-PERCEPTUAL		
Aries	Volcano	I am
Leo	Sun	I will
Sagittarius	Lightning	I see
III. WATER-EMOTIONAL		
Cancer	Sea	I feel
Scorpio	Deep Pool	I desire
Pisces	River	I believe
IV. AIR-MENTAL		
Libra	Rainbow	I balance
Aquarius	High Clouds	I know
Gemini	Wind	I think

NOTES AND REFERENCES

1. P. D. Ouspensky, *In Search of the Miraculous* (New York: Harcourt, Brace & World, 1949), p. 24.

2. Rodney Collin, *The Theory of Celestial Influence* (London: Stuart, 1954), p. 46.

3. Data from Jeff Mayo, *The Astrologer's Astronomical Handbook* (London: Fowler, 1965); "Planets," *Van Nostrand's Scientific Encyclopedia* 4th ed. (Princeton: Van Nostrand Co., 1968); and Thomas Gold, "The New Planetary Astronomy," and other articles in *Technology Review* (October/November, 1969): 44. The last-mentioned source summarizes recent radar-astronomy measurements, which have led to revised rotation and density figures for Mercury and Venus. Figures for the asteroids are included because many astronomers believe them to be the debris of an exploded planet.

4. "Planets are but the form or reflections of solar influences. But they too may in some way aspire to be suns, and with Jupiter and Saturn we see their transformation already far advanced. The planet, organizing the earth or matter available to it in imitation of its sun, becomes sun to its own satellites and system." Rodney Collin, *Theory of Celestial Influence*, p. 56.

5. John S. Lewis, "The Chemistry of the Largest Planet," *Technology Review* (October/November, 1969).

6. Margaret Gammon, *Astrology and the Edgar Cayce Readings* (Virginia Beach, Va.: A.R.E. Press, 1968).

7. Dane Rudhyar, *An Astrological Study of Psychological Complexes and Emotional Problems* (Netherlands: Servire/Wassenaar, 1966).

8. Gammon, *Astrology and Edgar Cayce*, p. 35.

9. Alice Bailey, *Esoteric Astrology* (New York: Lucis Trust, 1951), p. 20.

10. Robert Graves, *The Greek Myths* (Baltimore: Penguin Books, 1955), pp. 37–47.

11. Gold, "New Planetary Astronomy," *Technology Review*, 44.

12. Bailey, *Esoteric Astrology*, p. 353.

13. Gold, "New Planetary Astronomy," *Technology Review*, 44. Cf. references given under note 17 of previous chapter.

14. Bailey, *Esoteric Astrology*, p. 683.

15. *Ibid.*, p. 674.

16. Rudhyar, *Astrological Study*, p. 132.

17. Bailey, *Esoteric Astrology*, p. 211.

18. Harry F. Darling, *Organum Quaternii* (Lakemont, Georgia: CSA Press, 1968).

19. Collin, *Theory of Celestial Influence*, p. 300.

20. Bailey, *Esoteric Astrology*, p. 438.

21. *Ibid.*, p. 21.

22. Ouspensky, *In Search of the Miraculous*, p. 85. The physical facts of the earth-moon system are supportive of an interpretation along these lines. The total mass of all the planets in the solar system is but 1/800th of the sun's own mass. But the mass of the moon is 1/80th that of the earth. "The Earth seems to be carrying ten times more weight, size for size, than does the Sun. . . . The Earth is like a man swinging a two-pound weight at the end of a 30-foot cord. . . . From one point of view . . . the Earth is the most hard-pressed planet in the Solar System. Conditions upon it are *less free* than elsewhere." Collin, *Theory of Celestial Influence*, p. 110.

23. Quoted in Michel Gauquelin, *The Cosmic Clocks* (New York: Regnery, 1967), p. 47.

24. "Midpoints" play a major role in the German school of *cosmobiology*, founded by Reinhold Ebertin, and are being used by increasing numbers of astrologers. Ebertin, R. *Combination of Stellar Influences* (New York: Astrology Center, 1969). In this system, neither the traditional signs of the Zodiac, nor the houses, are used. Instead, midpoints (or half-sums) between planets, and between angular points such as ascendant and midheaven, are computed, and used as the basis for predictions and prognosis. If no planet occupies a midpoint, the configuration is said to be latent, until activated by a transit. Thus, for example, the sun/moon midpoint in this system denotes male-female relationships; if "contacted" by Venus, love-marriage is indicated; if Mars makes the contact, sex is indicated; if Jupiter, birth; if Saturn, separation; if Uranus, sudden events.

25. Quoted in Carl Jung, *Alchemical Studies*, vol. 13, *Collected Works* (New York: Pantheon Books, Bollingen Series XX, 1967), p. 181.

26. Bailey, *Esoteric Astrology*, p. 69.

27. The astrologer John Addey has applied harmonic analysis to the understanding of the zodiac, "The Basis of Astrology," *Astrological Journal*, Summer/Autumn, 1964; see also *Kosmos*, August, 1969. "Astrological symbolism is based upon the harmonics of symbolic circles of relationships." He argues that there is no reason to restrict ourselves to the usual harmonics when analysing astrological relationships. His data showed, for example, that in the birth patterns of physicians and clergymen, analysis in terms of the fifth and seventh harmonics and multiples thereof gave very striking results. "When we consider the relationships of two planets to each other, we say they are in aspect when they reach any one of a dozen or so angular relationships, neatly spaced round the 360 degrees. But we should really get much more out of it if we could begin to think of them as always in some potentially significant relationship, *a relationship which derives its significance from the number by which it was necessary to divide the circle in order to describe the relationship*" (my italics).

28. Levi, *The Aquarian Gospel of Jesus the Christ* (Los Angeles: De Vorss & Co., 1969), p. 10.

29. Bailey, *Esoteric Astrology*, p. 52.

ACTUALISM

The Actual Design of Man as a Cosmic Being

. . . where God-children eternally play
out the infinite variables of the
Cosmic Learning Game.

RUSSELL PAUL SCHOFIELD

WE HAVE SEEN HOW THROUGHOUT history, in different parts of the world, certain fundamental teachings, often called esoteric, appear again and again in different forms and metaphors. Although the basic goal and essence of these teachings would seem to be the same, yet there are great differences in formulation; emphasis is placed differently, according to the needs and conditions of the time and the society where the teaching arises.

Actualism is a teaching that enables the student to experience the evolutionary processes and purposes of man. It is a teaching formulated for the twentieth-century Western mind. It teaches and enables one to experience the fact that man has divine potentials, and that it is the goal of evolutionary growth and development to actualize these potentials and objectify them in creative expression. Most importantly, it teaches a method, *Agni Yoga,* by which this may be experienced and validated by the individual. *Agni* means "fire," *yoga* means "union"; so the method is "union by fire."

The teachings and techniques of *Agni Yoga* were developed by Russell Paul Schofield over a period of twenty-five years and have been extensively tested. He worked with several clairvoyants and sensitives in making comparative observations and experiments on different states and levels of consciousness. One would rise in consciousness while the other remained to record; then roles would be reversed. In comparing observations they constantly noticed differences due to the fact that thought and speech processes are programmed differently in each individual, so that systematic deviations and distortions entered into the information. Renewed experimentation and verification was necessary to reduce or eliminate these deviations. The observations and formulations thus obtained were related to and synthesized with modern scientific conceptions, as well as with corresponding ancient teachings. By reading the akashic record it was possible to determine the original content of many of the ancient teachings, before it was deviated and distorted by commentators and translators who did not have first-hand knowledge of the methods.

The methods of *Agni Yoga* were known in India thousands of years ago, at a time when the caste system was, as originally designed, a system of division of responsibility and social function rather than the hereditary power and status division, which it later became. In those times the priests would sift sensitives from all strata of the population and bring them into the yoga schools for training.

Similar practices existed until comparatively recent times among the Tibetan Buddhists, who, partly because of their geographical isolation, were able to preserve the methods and teachings in less deviated form. Western observers have documented instances of the *lāmas* clairvoyantly perceiving the birth of high-level sensitives, known as *tulkus,* in far-off villages and then sending a search party to find the child and bring him to the monastery. The method of *dumo,* "inner fire," was central to the Tibetan teachings.

Around the turn of the century a Tibetan teacher entered into telepathic communication with several Western sensitives, who became his disciples. Over a period of many years these students, among whom were Madame Blavatsky, Alice Bailey, Maurice Nicoll, and others, made extensive transcriptions of his teachings. Here also much distortion of meaning entered into the process of translation from thoughts received to verbal formulation. The Tibetan knew of this distortion, mentioned it and lamented it, but was unable to prevent it.

Traces of the methods of Fire Yoga can be found among the Chinese, in *The Secret of the Golden Flower*; among the Hawaiian Kahunas and other Polynesian cultures; in ancient South American civilizations and some North American Indian tribes; in ancient African and Middle Eastern civilizations, especially those of Egypt and Persia; and, of course, among the medieval alchemists and related groups.

That Jesus taught with light and healed with fire will be evident to anyone who reads the lines of the uncanonical gospels or between the lines of the orthodox gospels. And he taught also that "What I do all men can do. I come to show the possibilities of man." But, as has happened so many times in the past, his teachings were distorted so that men emphasized the worship of *him* as a divine being, rather than the practice of his teaching, which was—for each man to recognize that he is himself a divine being, to seek the kingdom of heaven within, and to bring it forth into manifestation.

This is why it is necessary for the actual design of man as God-child to be taught anew in every age and country; and to be taught with the methods that make the recognition of man's inherent divinity possible, so that it becomes a living, actual experience, instead of something only known *about.*

"As in all valid approaches to life and living, Yoga as taught in the School of Actualism, must be verified by the student. This might be termed the theorematic approach. The student accepts a theorem formulated as a technique, which he experiences; first, with the teacher; next, without the outer aid of the teacher; and finally, in practical application in the activities of daily living, as well as in practice apart from outer activity.

"He learns to carry the light of his own inner fire into home, business, profession, social life, sports, etc., gradually bringing a growing creative expression into every activity in which he is engaged. He finds his own interior sources of strength, wisdom, good will and love, as he experiences the fact of his own immortal individuality, the creator of the personality systems." [1]

In *Agni Yoga* the living fire is used to bring light into darkened areas of consciousness; and the consuming fire aspect is used to burn out obstructions to the free flow of energy from inner sources. Thus the actual design of personality systems is illuminated and the distortions and obstructions produced by conditioning are eliminated.

Here is one way in which *Agni Yoga* differs from virtually every other contemporary method of psychological change: the latter are based on the assumption that it is enough to bring something into awareness, to "make the unconscious conscious" as psychoanalysis puts it. Encounter groups are based on the same premise: that to express the hitherto unexpressed leads to liberation. Experience has shown, however, that this is far from the case. To activate conditioned images and emotional mechanisms operating below awareness is the smaller part of the process of transformation; the greater part is to eliminate the images and mechanisms obstructing and deviating energy flow through the various structures and functions of the personality systems.

It is not generally recognized that experiences leave psychic residues, just as the ingestion of food leaves physical waste matter. And just as insufficient assimilation or elimination of physical food can clog up the biochemical-physiological energy exchange processes vital to health, so unassimilated experiences can becloud perception and awareness. What psychiatry calls a complex is essentially an undigested perceptual, emotional, or mental experience; one that "couldn't be stomached." It is rejected by the individual and thus separated off from awareness, though still active on other levels of consciousness; a barrier of fear prevents recognition. We do not see our own blind spots though they may be blatant to others.

In *Agni Yoga* these separated, undigested, psychic energy-packets, or images, are handled with light-fire—that is with high-frequency energy. Analogously to the processing of food, what is of value in them is extracted and assimilated; what is not is eliminated, burned out. By practicing this method we find that the structures and functions of the body and the various levels of consciousness both above and below the physical are programmed with numerous false-to-fact images and mechanisms which distort, deviate, and obstruct the actual functioning of the structures, and limit our perception and awareness to an infinitesimal fraction of what it could potentially be.

"As these personality systems are gradually lighted from within, the creative expression of Actual Self grows in freedom from false-to-fact designs, that have come to overlay the actual design of man, deviating his interrelations with nature and his fellow mankind."

An example may make this clearer. Among the most destructive image distortions are those existing between parents and children. Joan Grant, in her autobiography *Far Memory*, relates how distressed and frustrated she felt as a child when grown-ups treated her as a "little child." We overlook that children, as immortal Actual Selves, are just as big as we are. By treating them as "little" merely because they are temporarily inhabiting a smaller form, we gradually induce them to accept identification with a small body—an identification that often long outlasts the time when the body has grown. The adult, because of this conditioned misplacement of identity may then feel small, weak, inferior, or stupid in ways that are quite at variance with the facts.

While working with *Agni Yoga* methods to establish inner communication with my three-year-old son, who was living in another city, I finally recognized the instant that our Actual Selves made contact. Inadvertently, I had been thinking of him as "my little boy"; and his first response to me was clear and emphatic: "Don't you 'little boy' me." By this, his Immortal Self made me aware how our relationship had been falsely based on outer appearance. Later, when I was with him physically, I found that if he was crying in a way that would tend to evoke the poor-little-boy image, and instead of going along with that image I remembered the recognition of his giant Actual Self, he would quickly stop crying.

This and other experiences taught me how subtle and pervasive the images are that deviate our relationships with each other. It is impossible to relate to another in a way that expresses the actual unity that we have as God-children until and unless these deviations are recognized and cleared out within one's own levels of consciousness. While many have observed these obstructing images and described them, and even recognized them in themselves, to be actually free of them is quite another proposition. It is not enough to wish they were not there, or decide mentally that one is not going to react to them. Unless the imprinted and conditioned programs are eliminated by consuming fire on each level of consciousness, they will continue to operate in personality behavior outside the sphere of awareness.

In ancient Indian philosophy the illusory play of images was referred to as *māyā*, the veil. The consuming fire was symbolized in the *Dance of Siva:* Siva is shown surrounded by a ring of flames, crushing an ugly dwarf under his feet. The dwarf represents the images which "dwarf" our consciousness. When they are consumed through the transforming power of inner fire, man can become the God that he actually is.

Later interpretations of Indian mythology misrepresent the role of Siva as an external cosmic destructive force. But the actual structures are not destroyed by the *Dance of Siva*—only the false-to-fact images superimposed on the structures are stripped away, so that the Being of light within can shine forth. Jesus said, according to the Gospel of Thomas, "within a man of light there is light, and he lights the whole world." Far from destroying or denying structure, as ascetic and martyr images would have it, the high-frequency energies actually support and vitalize the structures and functions of the different levels of consciousness: they become lighted instead of obscured, lightened instead of heavy, awakened instead of asleep, free instead of bound.

> "Each lamplighter
> Creates and recreates
> His creature body
> Till all frequencies
> Of Light
> Flow creatively
> In every touch of

> 'I am that I am'
> The Presence within
> Each human form." [2]

Russell Schofield has used the metaphor of a deep-sea diver who has all the connections for food, air, and communications to the upper, lighter world above the surface, but who has somehow forgotten how to use them; they have become tangled up and useless so that he is trapped in this dense domain, instead of being able to move up or down freely and at will. So man, according to actual design, has the capability of moving up or down in vibratory rate of consciousness; but he has lost the connections to the higher frequency realms and hence feels trapped and immobilized by the conditions and events of the external world, the so-called reality.

The myth of the fall of man refers to this situation: once we lived close to God, the God within; now, false-to-fact designs have cut off our awareness so that we feel alone in the world, fighting for survival, victimized by "the slings and arrows of outrageous fortune." Man carries within him the archetype of his actual freedom, however deeply it may be buried under layers upon layers of genetically transmitted and culturally acquired imprints that take form as images.

It is another distortion to say, as the legend is now interpreted, that we were expelled from the garden, and that it was as a punishment. This is a guilt-blame mechanism which keeps us all the more securely trapped. The fact is that we were given free will by the immortal Actual Self to leave the higher Paradise levels of consciousness; and we chose to enter into space-time incarnation in order to carry out a particular evolutionary purpose. We were given this free choice and we still have it. Each personality can choose whether to follow the inner direction of Actual Self, or whether to continue on a stimulus-response bond basis following only external goals. This free choice is a necessary aspect of the "cosmic learning game."

Of course, the will of mankind has long since ceased to be free. Freedom of choice has be-

Dance of Siva.

come completely conditioned and hypnotized by images that have been created by mankind and passed down the generations, and now these images and false-to-fact designs victimize and enslave the personality. Like somnambulists we stagger around with our eyes closed to actual light, following the dreams and fantasies which have become our "reality." Yet at each step of the way, as the will is gradually freed from the slavery of conditioning, it has the choice of accepting the freedom and using it for evolutionary growth or sinking back into the lulling sleep of image-dominated existence.

Not only does each personality have free will, but each personality system, each organ, each cell even has free will. In conditions of impotence or frigidity for example, the sexual organs are asserting their free will, refusing to cooperate with the behavior proposed by another system with which they are not in agreement. In contemporary depth psychology such phenomena are taken as indicating the existence of "unconscious" factors. From an Actualist point of view however, the notion of the "unconscious" is a mind-created barrier to self-knowledge. Rather Actualism would say that with the expansion of awareness and extension of perception we are awakened to the consciousness existing heretofore outside of awareness: therefore we can experience energy flow and forces at lower and higher levels of consciousness.

Similarly, what Jung called the "collective unconscious," though collective, is far from being unconscious: rather it is the total collection of mass-mind images and designs with which we are constantly programmed at all levels of consciousness, both above and below those of which we are aware. As such programmed response takes place in a personality, in groups, in nations, the mass-mind thought forms gain in power, and are thus able to program our consciousness even more powerfully, according to the manner in which stimulus-response bonds are established. Prejudices, ideologies, religious dogmas, patriotic emotions, as well as the more ephemeral waves of fashion, glamour, etc., are all examples of mass-mind conditioning.

The relationship between individual consciousness and mass-mind is a two-way symbiosis: one feeds on the other. Newspapers, magazines, radio, television are the means, the media, by which this connection is reinforced and maintained. Thus a good sampling of mass-mind image factors can be obtained by scanning the media and noting the recurrent themes. They correspond in detail to the major imprints and images governing human interactions in the spheres of daily living.

This symbiotic relationship is a major determinant of the impact of the media. For example, the degree of violence portrayed on television is a reflection of conditioned tendencies toward violence existing in the mass-mind as well as at some levels in individual consciousness. Yet the media do more than merely mirror these conditioned tendencies and image-factors: they selectively dramatize and even idealize violence and destructiveness which is then accepted by millions of individuals and thus further reinforces the power of the mass-mind to motivate more and more individuals accordingly.

Thus again and again, in the name of dramatic effect and realism, more and more power is given to false-to-fact designs and images of self and others that obstruct and pervert man's awareness of his interrelations with others, as well as the interrelations within his own personality systems. The media, functioning as the nervous system of the social body, communicate and amplify these imaged distortions of man's actual nature wherever they arise. However, as these are gradually eliminated from within more and more individuals the motivating power of the mass-mind factors in the thought-field (or "noosphere") of the planet and their dominance of the media will diminish and gradually disappear.

"The long, slow
Heavy ages
Of man's inhumanity
To man,
Are ending
As heart-mind union
Sealed by Soul fusion
Is externalized . . ."

Destructive behavior and thinking are due to *inversions* of the flow of higher energies as they enter into image-deviated personality systems. The inversions are possible because these systems have been given free will.

"The false-to-fact designs that deviate outer expression at every level of consciousness are due to numerous causes that have arisen out of the free will, that each creator gives to his personality systems. Free will is required for lesson-learning along the earth evolutionary path. The calculated risk is that free will may be inverted to counter-will. Inversion of the great good will, which is higher will, produces irritability, ill-will, anger, rage-fight and exploitation.

"In social relationships inverted higher will manifests as the abuse of power, the exploitation of those who have not developed, and do not yet have the use of their own inner power. History past and present illustrates these tendencies in human relations, whether under the so-called divine right of kings or emperors and their aristocracies, or under elected officials and their bureaucracies."

On the individual level, inverted higher will manifests itself as the punitive Freudian superego, the rage and ill-will channeled by sets of images, usually derived from early parental influences, toward the structures and functions of the body and personality that don't meet the perfectionist demands of this superego.

Besides higher will, the energy of love and the energy of wisdom are also inverted by false-to-fact designs and images. "Love, the great power to constructively organize, harmonize and unify, is inverted to dislike, intolerance and even to the complete inversion expressed as hate-kill; herein lies the formidable power to disorganize, disharmonize, disunify, and finally to destroy."

On the individual level, inversions of the love energy between human level of consciousness, body level of consciousness, and organ level of consciousness lead to pain and ultimately disease as the structures and functions are subjected to dislike and hatred instead of the organizing power of love. Inversions of love between human, perceptual, emotional, and mental levels of consciousness are experienced as disorganiz-

ing psychic conflicts, ambivalent emotions, confusion, and self-hatred; projected outward, they obstruct relations with others, even ones undertaken with the best of intentions.

"The energy of wisdom inverts to fear and flight in separation from Actual Self. This basic fear becomes projected outward and generalized in the desire to separate from this or that person or people in general or certain kinds of people. This is the distance-creating, detached, viewpoint of the intellectual."

The inversion of wisdom to fear-separation is symbolized in the myth of the fall from Eden. Having eaten of the fruit of the Tree of the Knowledge of Good and Evil, Adam and Eve allowed the wisdom to invert to a sense of separateness. Separated from the Creator-God within ("the Lord in the Garden"), they experienced a fall from unity, from the Eden consciousness of only the good. Blaming the serpent, the power of generation, is a rationalization imposed after the fact on the basic energy inversion.

"The subtle factor in all inverted will, love, wisdom and other deviations from actual design, is the capacity of the 'desire-mind', the image-dominated intellect, to find a rationale that supports the irrationality of counter-will as rage-fight, of counter-love as hate-kill, and the foolishness of counter-wisdom as fear-flight."

Most often, it is only these rationalizations of which we are aware, not the subtle inversions, which underlie them. So we find ourselves saying or thinking "he shouldn't have done that," or "why don't they cut their hair," or "that was a mean thing to say," etc., not realizing that these are surface rationalizations of our own underlying emotional response which has already occurred. "I can't stand that (thing, behavior, person)" is a statement of inversion: the person literally cannot stand upright in wisdom or love in the face of that situation. He is then "hung up" by his images; like the Hanged Man of the Tarot, his light has become inverted.

Martin Luther called reason a "whore" when he recognized this rationalizing tendency of the mind dominated by image-inversions. Esoteric psychology refers to it as "desire-mind." She will "lie" with any images—the idealized (called good), the hated (called bad) and the worth-less (called blah), and any combinations of them. Every criminal has a rationalization for his act ("he deserved to die, anyway"). The most impeccable logic is often found among lunatics: a psychiatrist friend recalls asking a female inmate why she was repeatedly bending down to the ground in a jerky motion and picking up worms. The answer came, with regal dignity— "I'm the queen of the birds."

Until and unless the random, image-triggered, stimulus-response associated "fluctuations of mind-stuff" give way to the inner direction of Actual Self, our minds will continue to land us, in consciousness and in body, in the strangest places. According to the second law of energy, as formulated in Actualism, "Energy follows thought." So we react, mentally, emotionally, perceptually, physically, and with our organs and cells, as we follow the polymorphous, perverse, promiscuous wanderings of desire-mind intellect.

The situation here is not unlike a bus in which different passengers are constantly competing and scheming to take over control of the driver's seat, and when they do, they take the whole bus and all the other passengers on their trip. For example, someone makes a contemptuous remark to us: this is the cue for a hated or worthless image to take over the driver's position. Egos at every level of consciousness go on the trip of rage or rejection, directed at the other and/ or at self. The heart beats violently, the cells shiver in fear, the other is perceived as mean or stupid, etc.; and whatever trip the bus was on before is, of course, completely disrupted while all systems go on this detour.

Alternatively, the sight of a well-shaped breast may be the cue for an idealized lover image to take control of the whole organization, and send it spinning off on a wild, careening, imaged sex-ual-romantic adventure, with desire-mind schem-ing how to convert this image to reality, and reacting with emotional (and organic and cellu-lar) frustration at exterior and interior barriers. Needless to say, the situation becomes almost hopelessly complex and dangerous when we con-sider that others are also acting and reacting as uncoordinated, uncentered collections of chaotic

images and egos. We are not only in a labyrinth, but in a labyrinth that is constantly changing its pattern and coordinates.

The way out of this metamorphous labyrinth is formulated in Actualism's first law of energy, which states that "Thought directs energy." By thinking, then letting, then observing, we can di-rect light-energy and focus it wherever needed, so that, more and more, we can operate from center, within, instead of reacting to external im-age stimulation.

"We gradually learn, as we take these steps, to channel, direct, focus, concentrate energy flow into and throughout our own energy sys-tems, then to exterior energy systems. This starts the awakening process—awakening the created energy systems to the creator within them—the teacher-knower within, the physician within, etc.—all of the many aspects of the creator."

The process of bringing light-fire into the obscured and obstructed energy systems of the body and personality is of necessity a gradual, step-by-step procedure in which one learns to channel and direct the high-frequency energy with increasing capacity. Acceptance of the light on one level of consciousness is often accom-panied by resistance on another. Gradually, each level, each energy system awakens to the pres-ence of Actual Self within and then becomes capable of shifting from image-dominated func-tioning to functioning by inner direction.

In the literature of spiritual and mystical phi-losophy there is a misleading concept of sudden illumination, as if we change in a flash from functioning as a merely mortal, human person-ality to functioning as an immortal God-child. Seekers are conditioned to expect sudden *satori* or mystical revelation, not realizing that in the reported instances of such sudden illuminations extensive preparation and training preceded the breakthrough. This myth gained in popularity with the advent of psychedelics. On several oc-casions I have embarked on a trip with a kind of "make or break" attitude, determined to reach Buddhahood, fasting for days beforehand and taking a double dose, to make sure; only to find that unless the capacity is increased, the systems are not capable of accepting or sustaining the increased high-frequency energy charge temporarily induced by the drug.

Which is not to say breakthroughs do not occur. The process is like the melting of ice on a river. The gradual increase of heat, what the alchemists called "gentle cooking," loosens the rigidified, frozen crystallizations of energy. They melt slowly, though sometimes major chunks may suddenly break off, greatly increasing the flow of energy.

The method of *Agni Yoga,* as taught in Actualism, may be compared with most other forms of yoga as laser light compares with ordinary light. Ordinary light, and the usual technique of psychic focussing, diminishes rapidly in intensity as it fans out from the point of concentration. Laser light, which is single frequency rather than mixed, can be focussed with great intensity on a very small point. The inner fire, of different frequencies according to purpose and need, can be similarly sharply focussed on a specific block to energy flow on any given level of consciousness. False-to-fact images and designs can be dislodged from structures with a laserlike beam of energy. This is the esoteric significance of the lightning bolt of Zeus-Jupiter, or of Thor in Nordic mythology. The Immortal One throws off the images that have taken possession of the structures and functions of the personality systems.

"Hurling
Brilliant javelins
Of Love
And Light
Into
The deepest
Dark place,
To lift
The splintered parts
Of lonely ones —"

The Tarot card called The Lightning-Struck Tower depicts the laser light of Jupiter Fulminans striking the structure and throwing off the false images of self which fall like dead men from the tower. The story of Jesus driving the money lenders out of the temple has a similar symbolic import: the body, the temple of the Creator-God, has become a market place for usury and barter, for the external-materially oriented interests of personality egos, until the Christ-light drives them out. These images are like tenants we once let into our house, who now refuse to leave. They assert, falsely, that they are we: in other words we have given them identity.

I remember, not long after beginning the study of this form of yoga, a dream in which a city was overhung with dark, billowing, noxious clouds. In the sky was a large, powerful, eye-shaped disc of golden light shining through the dark clouds. People in the streets below were scurrying in fear of the light. Only much later did I comprehend the meaning of this dream: the scurrying people are the images in which we have placed identity which cannot stay in the light of the knowing "I".

With light-fire the imprints and programs, which are not according to actual design are stripped away and eliminated. But this is not a rejection or separative procedure: in fact, whatever is found unacceptable to self first has to be accepted, in order, second, to be transmuted or eliminated with light. To reject or separate oneself from the images merely gives them increased power and recognition. This is why defense mechanisms, which start as a protective maneuver, so often end up destructive in effect. Suppression, repression, projection, denial, etc., increase the energy of the separated component that is being suppressed, repressed, etc.

In Actualism, we begin by accepting whatever is found. Since we proceed in a step-by-step manner we find only that which we have the power to handle. At the same time, we abstract identity more and more from the false images in which it has been bound, and shift it to Actual Self. Where the personality may feel it can't handle the factors against which defenses have been built up, such as intense rage or fear, the Immortal Self can handle them, namely with the transforming power of light-fire.

It is a widespread misconception among both Western and Eastern sensitives, seekers on the evolutionary path, that spiritual work involves giving up pleasure and joy, and denying the body through fasts and special diets, as well as abstinence and continence. This has been part of the mass-mind programming inculcated by both occidental and oriental asceticism for centuries. Christ himself was quite explicit on this point: "It is not what you put in your mouth that defiles you, it is what comes out." This may be extended: it is not *what* we eat, or experience, that causes us to become bound in illusory image entrapments; it is the *manner* in which experiences (and food) are assimilated and transformed, and the quality of what we express outwardly, in our microcosmos and in relations to others. "By their fruits ye shall know them"— the fruits they bring forth, not those they take in.

Actualism distinguishes three kinds of food, three modalities of input into the human energy systems. Third-order food is the physical matter, in solid, liquid, and gaseous form, that we eat, drink, and breathe. Its quality and purity is important, but overruled by the quality and purity of second-order food, which is the psychological attitudes, thought, feelings, and perceptions (both our own and those of others) we let pass into and flow through our systems. This, in turn, is secondary to the prime-order food—the life-light energies we channel. In other words, any experience, and any food, can be assimilated and either digested or eliminated, if it is accepted with light-fire.

So, far from requiring a deprivation of pleasure or joy, the process of removing obstructions to energy flow on the different levels of consciousness actually brings about greater and greater joy as communication within the microcosmos and communication with the external environments and other persons becomes increasingly free. Actualism's third law of energy states that "Obstructions to energy flow cause discomfort, if mild, or pain and dis-ease, if strong."

As obstructions are washed out, increasing inner unity allows increasing degrees of unity with others. Communication between personalities horizontally then gives way more and more to communion—the experienced vertical unity of immortal God-children working in peaceful joy together to organize, harmonize, and unify at all levels of manifestation.

"Having given free will to his prodigal-creation, the creator now has the infinite and eternal joy of finding the creation returning to the creator of its own free will, not to be destroyed nor punished, as overlaid false-to-fact designs portray, but to be lifted up into creative expression of a joyous order and magnitude all too seldom known on this planet—that which is the heritage and birth-right of all upon this planet."

Basic to the understanding of the human organism as a microcosmic energy-transforming system is the perception and awareness of polarity. We have seen how in Chinese Taoism, *yang,* the creative, the male, heaven, flows downward; and *yin,* the receptive, the female, earth, flows upward. In the Hindu *Tantras* we have the energy currents *idā* and *pingalā,* or Siva and Sakti, on the right and left side of the body respectively. In alchemy also, Sol, the King, on the right, and Luna, the Queen, on the left, together accomplish the transmutation of substance in the hermetic vessel.

In Actualism it is taught that the body and its organizing field, or rather all the bodies and their fields at different levels of consciousness, are polarized dynamic-male on the right and magnetic-female on the left. The right is our active hand, controlled by the left cerebral hemisphere. Recent neurological work by Penfield and Sperry has confirmed that the two halves of the brain mediate two quite distinguishable types of consciousness, which under certain conditions can become separated or dissociated.[3]

The notion that man has an organizing field is also not unknown to exoteric science. In the 1930s Burr and Northrop at Yale, and later, Becker and associates at Syracuse, did pioneering research demonstrating the existence of fields in plants, animals, and men, and their importance in processes of growth and vitality.[4] More recently Karagulla has assembled large numbers of observations on the interpenetrating fields of the human being that can be seen and described by sensitives and clairvoyants.[5]

In addition to the right-left polarization, man's organizing field is also polarized dynamic-front and magnetic-back. We move forward and outward into the world, and take on loads and burdens on our backs. This is the basis for such colloquial expressions as "get off my back," or "pain in the neck," or "chip on his shoulder." The early anatomists acted with intuitive accuracy in naming the topmost vertebra, which supports the head, the Atlas. Like the old Titan of that name, we carry the world on our shoulders, the imaged world our minds have created and given the weight of reality.

Dynamic, male energy flows downward and outward, expressing through function. Magnetic, female energy flows inward and upward, expressing through structure. "Downward" and "upward" refer here to differences in vibratory rate, not spatial directions. In the *I Ching* this is spoken of as the downward flowing of *yang* energy, from heaven (within); and the upward movement of *yin* energy, from earth (without). Structure is magnetic to function, accepts and receives function moving in and through it; function is supported by, "backed up" by, structure.

> "Man
> Moving outward -
> Man
> Moving inward -
> Receiving,
> Giving,
> Giving-receiving—
> Till all creation
> Creatively expresses
> The noble
> Image and Likeness
> Of the giving-receiving
> Father-Mother-Creator-God."

The process of inner unification involves, among other aspects, the balancing and harmonizing of dynamic and magnetic energies between structure and function, right and left, front and back, higher and lower, within the microcosmos and on each level of consciousness. Only as these polarities are balanced and harmonized within, at least to some extent, is it possible to relate to others in a fully satisfying way.

Since everyone, man or woman, has both aspects, a relationship predominantly based on a linkage of only one polarity (most usually the man's dynamic and the woman's magnetic) can only be short-lived because sooner or later the unexpressed halves of the two natures will feel discontent and frustration. Since our conditioning is always toward externals, the person will then seek another external person to whom he or she is able to relate in a more satisfying way. Since the reason for the one-sided relationship is nonacceptance of one or another side of one's own nature, the attempt to find a fully satisfying interrelation, imbalanced in this way, is bound to fail again.

Until and unless the two sides are balanced within the nature, the image obstructions will constantly be projected outward onto the other and block the renewed attempts to relate to another. Relating by the false images as to what a man is or what a woman is will inevitably lead to an inversion of love as soon as the chosen external man or woman fails to live up to the idealized expectations and images we have projected into the relationship. This is why Gurdjieff stated that "emotional love always turns into its opposite." If two people are both balanced and equally expressing their dynamic and magnetic nature, they can relate and communicate on a free exchange-communication, a reciprocal giving and receiving genuinely fulfilling to both sides.

If one person is balanced and the other not, the former can switch polarity according to the need of the situation. A therapist, or teacher, for example, has to be able to switch polarity with patient or student, in order to permit the relationship to develop in a satisfactory way. It is not at all recognized in contemporary schools of psychiatry or psychotherapy that the therapist, who goes magnetic to the patient, in listening to and trying to understand and empathize with his problems is actually acting as a psychic garbage collector. Unless he has some way of clearing his system of the loads he takes on, the therapist's physical instrument and personality systems will become loaded down with uncommonly heavy, discomforting and destructive images. This may very well be the reason for the abnormally high suicide rate among psychiatrists, which is four to six times the rate for comparable age groups.

Furthermore, simply allowing the patient to

"unload" on the therapist does not help the former any more than the latter if the patient does not learn how to free himself from his own loads, or how to avoid taking them on again. This is the difference referred to in the old Zen saying: "He who gives a man a loaf of bread feeds him for a day. He who teaches him how to fish feeds him for a lifetime."

Freud discovered that patients project images derived from past relationships onto the therapist, and named this the "transference." The transference and projection phenomenon however is not restricted to therapeutic relationships, but occurs in all relationships to a greater or lesser degree.

What is commonly called "falling in love" is a sudden polarization on the chemical-biological level, accompanied by mutually matching idealized images. The very use of the term "falling" (rather than "rising into love") indicates that the evolutionary species-preservation force is involved here; truly, the lovers say: "This thing is bigger than both of us." Idealized images of self are projected out onto the other—which is why lovers look endlessly into each other's eyes and request to be loved "as I love you."

After a time, idealized images give way to hated images as the external partner is unable to meet the criteria set up. Mutual adoration, which was self-adoration, then gives way to mutual recrimination, which is self-recrimination. Sometimes one or the other or both will attempt to make themselves over in the image of the other, a misguided attempt doomed to failure since an idealized image can never be satisfied, either by oneself or far less by another. Which is not to say that relationships that are in some ways satisfying cannot be established, or even last for considerable time, as long as the images and polarities continue to match.

Lovers have the ability to wound each other and to be vulnerable because they have given each other the weapons. This vulnerability, often idealized as "openness," is actually the result of mutual projection. We reject in ourselves what we find painfully unacceptable, and project it outward onto the other. Thus we give to the other the ability to be a constant irritant and reminder of that painful aspect of ourselves. Since the

other is operating under similar mechanisms, we have the uncanny, unaware, matching of self-defeating images. The masochistic woman attracts the sadistic male; the impotent man attracts the castrating woman. And these are only extremes of ubiquitous patterns. Non-physical "crimes of passion" are committed every day.

Idealized images are projected as much as unacceptable images. When these shatter the person feels betrayed, as if "part of myself" had been taken away; and it has, but only because that part of myself, that image of self, was given to the other in the first place.

Who has not had the experience of looking at the shattered fragments of a love relationship, like a child looking with supreme surprise at the empty place in his hands where a pretty bubble was just before? And who has not reacted with hurt and anger and blame as the beautiful picture one tried to grasp shattered on the rock of fact? And do you remember that moment of feeling ridiculous when you both realized that the illusion you were both chasing had caught you both in its web?

The Greeks celebrated this human frailty in the story of Ares and Aphrodite. Ares, the god of war, lay with Aphrodite, the goddess of love and beauty. But her husband, the lame smith of the gods, Hephaistos, found them in bed, and in an instant fashioned a golden, gossamer-thin, but very strong net, which he cast over them. He then invited the remaining Immortals who came and laughed uproariously at the couple, as they lay trapped in the bed of imaged desire.

We speak of being "involved" with another and do not realize just how specific this involvement is. If our own magnetic and dynamic polarities are not balanced and centered with respect to each other, we are constantly looking toward an external person to complete us, make us feel whole. The ties thus established will often remain long after the relationship has ceased on the outer plane. This gives rise to the well-known feeling that there are "ghosts" from past relationships in a present one.

One time, while working with a certain *Agni Yoga* technique, I became aware of how my dynamic was still involved in the magnetic of someone who had been my mate quite a long time ago. As I merged with the Immortal of that one, this fragment was released and returned to fill my own magnetic. As I did the same with every other I had ever related to, tremendous surges of energy returned into my own systems and fields. Analogous processes take place on the magnetic aspect, which tends to become filled with external dynamics of those we have loved under the influence of possessive images. When freed of images, magnetic and dynamic polar aspects relate to those of another in perfect giving-receiving reciprocal exchange, accepting and letting flow and returning and fulfilling, without holding or obstructing.

> "With
> inner freedom
> from the snare
> of image-induced
> illusion, delusion
> and obsession, —
> two or more
> can merge
> and flow
> into
> the
> Eternal Sea
> of
> Love's
> Infinity,
> with
> myriad millions
> expressing
> Love and Life
> in ceaseless
> and joyously
> changing
> expressions
> of
> rhythm
> color
> and tone."

The ubiquitous mechanism of projection can well be compared to the projection of images in a film. (Just as the computer is a good analogy for one aspect of cerebral functioning, so film is a good analogy for image-dominated perceptual processes. Our media are extensions of our senses, as McLuhan has pointed out.) We have a "projection beam," in our head, that passes through a set of images programmed into our "projector," and thus casts replicas of these images, large as life, onto the screen of external reality. We sit in the movie house of our minds, like the prisoners in Plato's cave, suffering and rejoicing with the phantasms on the screen, forgetting that we ourselves have within us both the light-source and the superimposed images.

And if we don't like those repetitive, closed-loop melodramas, with those familiar actors and actresses always "playing themselves," we have the potential ability to replace the film of images with another, more productive and with a happier ending. This is essentially what hypnosis, behavior therapy, and most psychotherapy attempts to do. Or better yet, we can remove the film of images that veil clear perceiving, so that instead of beaming only through preselected programs, we let the radiant light shine on what actually is. This is the goal of the *yoga* of light, as taught in Actualism.

The beam is not only a projection beam, but simultaneously a radar tracking beam. It keeps the eyes tracking and seeing what we most fear (in the case of hated images) and most desire (in the case of idealized images). The puritan (and the lecher) see rampant sex; the timid man (and the bully) see violence everywhere. It was this projection and tracking beam that Jesus referred to when he counselled his disciples to remove the beam in their own eyes before attempting to discern the mote in another's.

As we abstract identity from images, we take more and more of the power out of them. It is because we have identity in them that we react as though they were fact, even though the facts are quite contrary. Desdemona's complete innocence did not diminish Othello's jealousy one bit; because he was responding to preprogrammed images, not fact. In most situations, where there is a kernel of truth in the false image, it is that much harder to recognize that our emotional reaction is still to the imaged, not the actual, situation.

As the power is taken out of the images, more and more the competitiveness within our nature, and with others outside, is replaced with co-operation based on the experienced fact of unity. The heart, the gut, and the brain are in fact united, though superimposed designs would have it otherwise—leading to conflict, discomfort, tension, confusion, worry, etc. When they are able to experience their unity they can function each according to its special unique way. Similarly, the experience of unity with others, which can only follow the experience of unity within ourselves, leads to a synthesizing merging which does not, contrary to popular images, obliterate or submerge the individual, but rather permits us to express our actual indivisible nature, freed from the need to compete, win approval, feel superior (or inferior), etc.

Unity-mergence has two effects: first, what Buckminster Fuller and others have referred to as *synergy*—the power of the whole which exceeds the summated power of the parts (as the strength of an alloy exceeds the sum of the strengths of the component metals); and second, what might be called *potentiation*, or empowering—the power of each individual component is augmented by the power of the unified whole (as the power of a representative or ambassador is augmented by the power of the group to which he belongs).

These principles have direct relevance to the work of inner transformation that is the essence of *yoga*. As conflicting images and false designs are burned away, the increasing experiencing of unity allows for greater and greater *synergistic* channeling of energy. It also allows each part—hand, or eye, or brain, or heart, or voice, or member of a group—to express this unity with *potentiated* creative energy, in full awareness of its uniqueness and appreciation of every other's uniqueness. This is no abstract theory but an experimentally verifiable fact. The difference between the hand of a mediocre painter and the hand of a Leonardo lies in the internal relationships that have been established, the degree of creative fusion the hand expresses.

Psychophysical synergy and potentiation, understood and practiced, make obsolete a whole host of debilitating images that assert the superiority of one aspect of the nature over another, and teachings that encourage one at the expense of another. We do not need to condemn feelings for being illogical; or assert that "gut reactions" are more real than thoughtful ones; or argue whether intuition is better than reason; or spontaneous response better than planning. Each has its place and function.

Under the divide-and-rule philosophy brought about by separative images we find the tragicomic scene of rational men and women going to encounter groups to learn to recognize feelings or to sensory awareness groups to become acquainted with bodily sensations. Or we have devotional-emotional cults both Eastern and Western that seek to become lost in rapturous feelings, or unquestioning faith, or ecstatic experiences. Or we have the cyberneticists, autohypnotists, scientologists, general semanticists, and others who attempt to "clear" thinking, or to eliminate confusion, by disconnecting the thinking processes from the emotional processes.

The separative and obstructive nature of images and preprogrammed designs is extremely evident in experiences induced by psychedelic drugs. In these experiences one's awareness and perception of actual structure and function is amplified and false-to-fact, superimposed images are also amplified. An example of the former is that a person may frequently perceive that he has a field-structure that extends for several feet beyond the boundaries of his physical body. An example of the latter is that a person may, in looking at another's face, literally see the images of that person (both his own and the other's) peeling off like so many masks. Psychedelic substances are nonselective awareness amplifiers. To actually see the multiform plastic shapes in which personality-egos cloak themselves gives valuable pre-views of a state of image-free perception. However, one needs the tools of light-fire to consume the images, otherwise the experience will be temporary and limited to the drug state.

Gurdjieff referred to these imaged delusions as "egoplastikoori," and his strategy consisted in awakening the observing "I," so that by becoming aware of these false, automatically programmed images a person could re-member himself, *i.e.*, become re-united to his Actual Self. Since Gurdjieff was working primarily with second-order factors (ideas, feelings, and perceptions generated by him in his unique, provocative *Sūfi*-style), the method was very much dependent on his own presence to provide the impetus to awaken the observer within.

The observer function is a basic necessity in yogic work. In *Agni Yoga* a person learns by observing the effects of light-energies of different qualities, at first on the physical level of consciousness, and gradually on the higher and lower frequency levels also.

To attain inner wholeness it is necessary to accept all structures and functions at every level of consciousness and to abstract identity from those image-factors that cause the illusory feeling or perception of separation, superiority, or worthlessness. From communication we move to cooperation and finally to communion as the various structures and functions of each level of consciousness come to experience the unity they have in the immortal presence of the Actual Self which created them.

"Upon reaching the goal of wholeness within, one is capable of knowing and carrying out the purpose for which he entered in as a God-Child upon the creative venture of the Father-Mother-Creator-God of this macrocosmos."

The rarity of this condition of wholeness and fulfillment of evolutionary purpose, and the consequent maleficent effects upon the human condition on this planet under image government, can be seen by noting the life span of creatures. In general, life span appears to be about seven times the number of years to maturity. Thus, animals that take two years to mature, live to about fourteen, and so on. According to this generalization the human being should naturally live to about 140–150 years. In ancient times such an age, and much greater ones, were not uncommon, to judge by the legends of the patriarchs. Even in our time, certain Himalayan tribes, living under exceptionally favorable circumstances, will not infrequently have persons who reach the

age of 125. But the general life span of man is about one-half what it could be; and, except in childhood, we do not have even the vitality of our friends in the animal kingdom.

The relationship between the animal and human levels of consciousness within man is indeed much obstructed with false images of separateness and superiority on the part of the human, and corresponding resistance and hatred on the part of the animal, leading to extremes of repression and compensating idealization. The ecological disaster brewing on the planet, the total lack of communication between our species and the species of animals and plants whose life cycles we ignorantly and ruthlessly destroy, only outwardly mirrors the chaotic relationship that exists within.

Modern neurological researches have confirmed what esoteric philosophy has long taught: that man has not one brain, but three, superimposed one upon the other, following the sequence of phylogenetic evolution. The reptile brain, located in the brain stem, extending upward from the spinal cord; the mammal brain, located above and behind the brain stem; and the primate/human brain, folding around, above, and to the front of the other two.[6] Our reptilian and mammalian brains mediate our animal heritage. Coded into the consciousness of our organs and cells (via DNA and RNA molecular configurations) is the evolutionary history of our species. Between conception and birth we recapitulate this billion-year-old evolutionary "tail," telescoped into a flash of nine months.

Consciousness at the animal or creature-body level, mammalian and reptilian, and at the organ and the cell levels, can be experienced in *yoga*, or in alterations of consciousness induced by psychedelic drugs or otherwise. With the *yoga* of light-fire it is also possible to bring light into these levels and to increase the communication between them. It is lack of communication, inversion of wisdom, that causes the human to fear our (and others') animal passions or to disapprove of sensuality. Conversely, it causes the animal to mistrust the dictates of human reason, and to resent the imposition of the conditioning we call civilization. Freud, in true Taurean

Urobouros. *"This surely is a great miracle—that in a venomous dragon there should be the great medicine."*

fashion, lamented this situation in his book *Civilization and its Discontents.* This is also the origin of the idealized image of "divine discontent"; and the worthless image of "the naked ape."

It is not the denial, but the transmutation, based on acceptance and communication and synergy, of the evolutionary tail, which leads to the inner wholeness for which we are actually designed. In hermetic philosophy and alchemy, this fusion of energies was often symbolized by the *urobouros* serpent swallowing its own tail.

The human and animal levels of consciousness are close, but not identical; like a matrix to a mould. The subtle and elusive interblending involved here was symbolized by a very ancient, unknown, pre-Egyptian civilization in the mysterious figure of the Sphinx: the feline body with human head and inscrutable gaze. With the awakening energy of light-fire this immobilized creature will experience the divinity within, will crawl, then walk, and finally fly.

According to the teaching of Actualism, it is the human or matrix body that is referred to in esoteric philosophy as the "etheric double," and that separates from the creature body in most recorded instances of out-of-the-body travel, and so-called astral projection. In cases of sudden or violent death, when the personality is unaware that it has died, this human body may stay earth-bound for some time, and become visible under certain conditions as a "ghost."

The riddle which the Sphinx posed to all travelers was: "What has four legs in the beginning, two in the middle, and three at the end?" Exoterically this riddle was reputedly solved by

Oedipus when he stated that it referred to man as an infant, man in maturity, and man with a supporting stick in old age. The actual meaning however can be taken to point to man's four-footed mammalian body consciousness, his two-legged human body consciousness, and his androgynous, bipolar bodies with central vertical axis.

This is a sequential unfolding of evolutionary process that is played out in the history of our species on the planet (phylogenesis), and in the embryonic history of each individual (onto-genesis); and finally, in the expanding awareness brought about by the *yogic* work of transforma-tion by fire.

> "The widening
> Boundaries
> Of evolutionary process
> Are guide lines
> Holding firm
> God-Child progress
> From point of light
> To brightening star
> To Radiant Sun of Manifestation."

The integration of the human level of con-sciousness, the human body, with the lower frequency levels—the animal, organ, and cell—is one aspect of the work of inner unification. Another is increased communication, coopera-tion, and communion with the higher-frequency levels or lesser density bodies: the perceptual (sometimes called "lower astral"), the emotional (sometimes called "astral"), and the mental. These are literally subtler bodies that can be experienced as interpenetrating and extending beyond and coaxial with the physical time-space body.

In our normal condition these bodies are all so heavily imprinted and programmed with images and false-to-fact designs that they are effectively immobilized. At night, when the creature body sleeps, the others are slightly more active—which activity, translated by the symbolic machinery of the brain-mind, we register as dreams. The chan-neling of energies into these systems induces them to gradually awaken to the fact of the pres-ence of the Immortal One within so that they can begin to move and creatively express the nature and purposes of Actual Self on the evolutionary path.

In oriental art, the awakened many bodies of man as a cosmic, divine being were symbolized in the statues of deities with many arms and many heads, one on top of the other. This is a three-dimensional image of a multidimensional fact: the heads are actually higher in frequency rate rather than in space. By aligning and balancing the bodies with respect to the com-mon central vertical axis we decrease the resistance and increase the capacity of the struc-tures and functions to channel energy. Man is a two-way transformer of energy: lower fre-quency energies, imprinted with our personal, collective, and evolutionary past, are transmuted and raised in frequency; higher frequency, cosmic energies are stepped down in frequency and brought from their inner source into objec-tive manifestation and creative expression in the outer world.

The centers along the vertical axis, known in India as *cakras*, are focal points for the processes of accumulation and distribution of energies on the various levels of consciousness. Contrary to popular misinterpretations of *yogic* teachings, these centers are not opened by the teacher or any external agency. More like flowers, they open from within, when the veils and crusts of images obstructing them have been removed, so that, like flowers, they can receive light from above and nourishment from below. The literature is full of warnings against attempting to open the *cakras* prematurely. If opened without prior purification and balancing they tend to freeze on a particular frequency band. They would then be like a radio we can't turn off; which may ac-count for some of the "voices" of the psychotic.

In our normal condition, the centers are crowded and encrusted with myriad images and false-to-fact designs that reduce their potentially powerful functioning to a bare minimum. Adepts of ancient times who encoded their teachings in symbols, legends, and fairy tales, invented the story of Snow White and the Seven Dwarfs to express this situation. Snow White is the human form, most beautiful in nature but trapped in a poisoned sleep by the machinations of the Wicked Queen, who is hung up in external images of beauty ("Mirror, mirror on the wall, who's the fairest of them all?"). So Snow White has to live in a house (body) with Seven Dwarfs, the seven dwarfed centers of the body. Finally, she is awakened from her poisoned sleep by the kiss of the Prince, the immortal Actual Self.

"Personality-Self
Sealed
Within the sepulcher
Of "Self"-denial,
Becomes separated
From
The gift of Beauty,
Until "I" Presence
Breaks the seal,
Flooding the form
With vibrant beauty
And looks with joy
Upon the world
Of the Beloved . . ."

As long as our personality systems are conditioned to react to externals, according to stimulus-response principles of conditioning, instead of being able to respond to inner direction, fixed attitudes, feelings, and perceptions will continue to crystallize at the different levels of consciousness, obstructing the free flow of energy. The task of cleaning the structures seems impossibly overwhelming. It was this situation that the Greek sages described in the story of the fifth labor of Hercules. Hercules was an initiate whose twelve labors represent twelve basic steps on the path. His fifth assignment was to clean the stables of the ten thousand horses of King Augeas. As soon as one part was cleaned another would be dirtied. It was impossible to do in a piecemeal fashion. The solution was to rechannel two rivers through the stables, thus keeping them constantly cleaned. By channeling the energy sources potential in everyone so that they are constantly pouring through all structures and functions, we can maintain an unobstructed instrument, as images coming from ourselves or from others are consumed in the burning-ground fires.

Objective consciousness is possible only when one has learned not to remain in any fixed positions, either physical, perceptual, emotional, or mental. The Buddha, when asked what opinion he held on the afterlife, said he *held* no opinions; since to hold means to place identity in temporary, evanescent energy packets in the form of images or concepts. Whereas the actual essence-fact, the philosophers stone, can only be experienced and known, internally or externally, when all "holding forces" (*samskāras* in Hindu psychology, *cathexes* in Freudian) are removed and one can "stand firmly on a moving point" of totally fluid attitude and perspective, mentally, emotionally, perceptually, and behaviorally.

These statements are not presented as the truth; no claim is made to their acceptance. They are theorems, indications, and can only be verified and validated, by anyone who chooses to do so, in the actual practice that yields the perception, the knowing and the knowing that one knows.

The practice of the method leading to validation through experience is the primary safeguard against inversion and deviation of the teaching. All teachings that have appeared in the past concerning man's inherent divine potential and evolutionary possibilities have suffered deviation because followers have worshipped the external teacher-personality instead of finding the kingdom of heaven within. It is much harder to break through the resistances to inner unification than it is to achieve a semblance of peace and harmony by becoming a follower of a teacher. The same holds true for man-woman relationships: it is relatively easy to relate one's magnetic or dynamic nature to an external dynamic or magnetic, on one level or another. Paradoxically, much greater resistance is encountered when one attempts to fuse them within.

"To those who would worship the personality of a teacher, rather than the truths taught by the teacher, it must be said that such worship brings about the counter-love of the Christ love, the counter-wisdom of the Buddha wisdom, the counter-will of the good will of all great ones who come as way showers. The blind worship of these as personalities has set in motion 'holy wars,' crusades, tortures, oppression, martyrdom, etc., in the name of the personality of the teacher, in direct opposition to the truths which they taught, inverting the light which they implanted in the earth of this planet. . . .

"To avoid this dilemma in the new age, now dawning, the responsibility will fall not on the personality systems of one person, but rather upon a group formation of highly trained and well prepared personality-systems; each of whom has achieved a high degree of wholeness. Having reached such a degree of wholeness within, free of superimposed designs that are false to actual design, this group can function under the greatest good will of higher will; the great power of love to organize, harmonize and unify microcosmically as it does macrocosmically; the brilliant illumination of the wisdom light; the effulgent radiance of the full spectrum of energies playing throughout each living temple—each new creature—each illumined creation—and extending outward to all members of each Kingdom of Life on planet Earth."

EXPERIENTIAL EXPERIMENTS

Agni Yoga, as taught in the School of Actualism, is not the adoption of physical postures as in *Hatha Yoga*, but rather the adoption of perceptual, emotional, mental attitudes and positions that facilitate the flowing of energy once the connection to the inner source has been established. The body is placed in such a way as to permit maximally free flow throughout all structures: sit on a chair, relaxed but with back straight, legs uncrossed and comfortably apart, feet flat on the ground for "earthing," hands on legs.

The energy work is begun by thinking of a point of white light (white being the synthesis of all frequencies of light), located six inches above the center of the head. Since the law is: "Thought directs energy," it is only necessary to think of it, let it be, and observe it. Those with strong optical visualizing ability may see it, others may sense it or feel it.

Having made the contact by thinking, letting, and observing, think of the point of light as opening up and pouring down, giving the entire body and field an internal shower of white light energy that purifies and lightens. Again, thinking, letting, and observing are sufficient.

Doing this preliminary exercise for just a few minutes each day can already have a very pronounced effect on your sense of well-being and ability to relate to internal or external situations.

Following the third law, which states that "Obstructions to energy flow cause discomfort, if mild, or pain and dis-ease, if strong," we can focus the white light energy downpour in those areas of the body where discomfort, blockage, or pain is experienced, letting these structures awaken to the presence of light. Bringing light into the structures often makes us aware of discomfort or pain where there had not been any before. This is exactly analogous to the pain experienced when your leg, asleep because cut off from circulation, wakes up again as the circulation is restored. Here we are dealing with what Taoists called "the circulation of the light."

Another very useful exercise is to sit in the position described above but to place the hands so that the right palm is on the solar plexus, the left palm on the heart region, while the white light is pouring down. The dynamic flowing through the right hand allows the solar plexus to tune in to its own higher energy sources instead of vibrating sympathetically to external feeling states, as it tends to do especially strongly in sensitives. The magnetic energy flowing through the left hand induces organizing and harmonizing of magnetic and dynamic in the heart-center of personal relationships. The combined effect of this *mudrā* is a calming and soothing of emotional or interpersonal turbulence or anxiety.

THE FOUR LAWS OF ENERGY ACCORDING TO ACTUALISM

1. Thought directs energy.
2. Energy follows thought.
3. Obstructions to energy flow cause discomfort, if mild, or pain and dis-ease, if strong.
4. Energy is concentrated where thought is focussed.

NOTES AND REFERENCES

1. Unless otherwise noted the prose passages in quotation marks are all from Russell Paul Schofield, "Transmutational Mergence as Taught in the School of Actualism," and are reprinted by permission. Russell Schofield, is a teacher, writer, poet, and founder of the School of Actualism. The subject of this chapter will be treated in more detail in a forthcoming collaborative book on Actualism—"The Actual Design of Cosmic Man." This will present the actual, inner meaning of myths, legends, sacred symbols, and writings in which have been delineated the steps along the evolutionary path to individuality and wholeness.

2. All verse quoted in this chapter is from Russell Paul Schofield, *Imprint Unmistakeable,* © Russell Schofield (privately printed, Los Angeles, 1969), reprinted by permission.

3. Wilder Penfield, "Consciousness, Memory, and Man's Conditioned Reflexes," *On the Biology of Learning,* ed. K. H. Pribram (New York: Harcourt, Brace & World, 1969); and Michael Gazzaniga, "The Split Brain in Man," *Scientific American,* 27 (1967): 24–29.

4. See *Main Currents of Modern Thought* (September/October, 1962), a whole issue devoted to biological field processes. Also see, R. O. Becker et al., "The Direct Current Control System," *New York State Journal of Medicine* (April 15, 1962); G. Stromberg, "The Autonomous Field," *Journal of the Franklin Institute,* 239 (1945): 27–40; G. P. Barnard and J. H. Stephenson, "Fresh Evidence for a Biophysical Field," *Main Currents of Modern Thought,* 24, no. 5 (1968).

5. Shafica Karagulla, *Breakthrough into Creativity* (Los Angeles: DeVorss Press, 1969).

6. R. S. Buckley, "The Brain," *Minnesota Medicine,* 50 (November, 1967).